Personal Effectiveness

A Guide to Action

Professor Diana Winstanley was Director of Postgraduate Programmes at Kingston Business School. She held a PhD from Southampton University in recruitment and HRM, and was a fellow of the CIPD. Her previous publications include *Case Studies in Personnel* (1992), *Managing in the NHS: A study of senior executives* (1995), *Management Development: Strategy and Practice* (1998) and *Ethical Issues in Contemporary Human Resource Management* (2000).

The CIPD would like to thank the following members of the CIPD Publishing Editorial Board for their help and advice:

The Chartered Institute of Personnel and Development is the leading publisher of books and reports for personnel and training professionals, students, and all those concerned with the effective management and development of people at work. For details of all our titles, please contact the publishing department:
Tel: 020 8612 6200
E-mail: publish@cipd.co.uk
The catalogue of all CIPD titles can be viewed on the CIPD website:
www.cipd.co.uk/bookstore

Personal Effectiveness

A Guide to Action

Diana Winstanley

Chartered Institute of Personnel and Development

Published by the Chartered Institute of Personnel and Development, 151 The Broadway, London, SW19 1JQ

First published 2005

Reprinted 2007 twice

Design by Fakenham Photosetting, Fakenham, Norfolk

Typeset by Fakenham Photosetting, Fakenham, Norfolk

Printed in Great Britain by Cromwell Press, Trowbridge, Wiltshire

British Library Cataloguing in Publication Data

A catalogue of this manual is available from the British Library

ISBN 1 84398 002 9
ISBN-13 978 1 84398 002 5

Chartered Institute of Personnel and Development,
151 The Broadway, London, SW19 1JQ
Tel: 020 8612 6200
E-mail: cipd@cipd.co.uk   Website: www.cipd.co.uk
Incorporated by Royal Charter.   Registered Charity No. 1079797

Contents

List of definitions

Lists of figures and tables

Lists of examples and exercises

Examples

Exercises

List of scenarios

Acknowledgments

I am deeply grateful to all the support and help I have had from my former colleagues at Tanaka Business School over the years: John Sheldrake for his humour, Andrew Sturdy for his warmth and constructiveness, Yiannis Gabriel for his wise insights and care, Anne Benjamin for her friendship, Mike Brocklehurst for his cameraderie, Dot Griffiths for her support. Also to Jean Woodall whose work with me over the years has motivated me to start and finish many projects – not just this one.

I very much appreciate the help of Ruth Lake and Sarah Brown at the publishers for being so patient with me and being helpful at critical stages of this work. I would also like to thank also the reviewers who provided some very constructive comments to which I hope I have done justice.

Finally huge thanks go to my friends and family for putting up with me through this process and Graeme for being foolish enough to accompany me up Kilimanjaro on completion of this book.

Note on Front cover photograph

A picture of Mount Kilimanjaro (5895m high, the highest mountain in Africa and the highest freestanding mountain in the world). Picture taken by the author from the Machame Route in August 2004. Although I swore at the time never to climb another mountain– it is the best and worst of experiences – everyone should try it!

Introduction

Personal effectiveness is about producing desired behaviours and outcomes whether at home or work. It is having the capability to achieve personal objectives – 'the can do', and the will to put this into action – 'the will to do.' This book covers a number of key areas of personal effectiveness and guides you through the necessary mindsets, skills, behaviour and capabilities in each area, providing practical examples to illustrate these in real life situations as well as practice exercises for you to develop your personal effectiveness in action.

Although these personal capabilities are relevant to everyone, and transferable skills apply in a number of different work and study contexts, this book is designed specifically to meet the personal development needs of:

- business study students on postgraduate, masters, doctoral and professional development programmes
- some undergraduate students who may also find this information useful to accompany their study
- professionals and managers wishing to improve on their personal effectiveness at work.

There are a number of very good study skills texts (for example Cameron 2002, Cottrell 2003). Although this book covers study and coursework skills (particularly in Chapter 1 on learning and Chapter 6 on presentation skills) it is intended to cover the wider area of personal effectiveness in general, and is designed for a business practitioner audience as well as students. The benefits of improved personal effectiveness for the individual are improved confidence and competence, but these benefits also translate into advantages for the organisation. Having managers with improved personal effectiveness has an impact on the organisation and ultimately the business bottom line as well, as managers exhibit greater motivation (which affects themselves and those working with them) and improved performance.

The chapters of this book correspond to parts of the National Occupational Standards (NOS) for management and leadership, devised by the Chartered Management Institute. The Institute can be found at http://www.managers.org.uk/institute and the standards at http://www.management-standards.org.uk/June 2004.

To see how the chapters of this book connect to these standards see Table 0.1.

Tutors and course deliverers on taught postgraduate and professional programmes may also find it helpful to link the material of this course into their professional syllabi and the requirements of the Quality Assurance Agency for Higher Education (QAA) for masters and doctoral study – see http://www.qaa.ac.uk/crntwork/progfilehe/guidelines/progfile2001.htm

Increasingly all postgraduate and doctoral programmes are expected to provide students with a full grounding in transferable research and personal skills. This is backed up by the research councils who fund many of the doctoral programmes and stipulate a variety of personal effectiveness skills to be covered, and who also earmark nearly £1,000 per year per student for this purpose.

Table 0.1 *Chapter content relevant to the National Occupational Standards for Management and Leadership*

Chapter	NOSML
1. Learning	A2: Manage your own resources (identifying your learning styles and development plans)
2. Time management	A1: Manage your own resources (time management, planning, setting objectives) A2: Manage your own resources and professional development (time management, objective setting, prioritising)
3. Creativity	C1: Encourage innovation in your team C2: Encourage innovation in your area of responsibility C3: Encourage innovation in your organisation (ideas generation, encouragement and creativity)
4. Group dynamics and team working	B5: Provide leadership for your team (communicate purpose, encouragement and support)
5. Communication and interviewing skills	A3: Develop your personal networks D1: Develop productive working relationships with colleagues (effective communication) D2: Develop productive working relationships with colleagues and stakeholders (effective communication and consultation)
6. Presentation skills	A3: Develop your personal networks (presenting information) B7: Provide leadership for your organisation (presenting information, developing commitment and enthusiasm)
7. Assertiveness	A3: Develop your personal networks (communication when conflicting goals) B6: Provide leadership in your area of responsibility (communicating assertively)
8. Negotiation skills	A3: Develop your personal networks (dealing with conflict situations and where interests differ)
9. Dealing with difficult people and difficult situations	D1: Develop productive working relationships with colleagues (sorting out conflicts) D2: Develop productive working relationships with colleagues and stakeholders.
10. Managing personal and organisational change	A2: Manage your own resources and professional development (recognise the need for change and act accordingly) C4: Lead change C5: Plan change C6: Implement change

For those tutors and students attached to The Chartered Institute for Personnel and Development (the publishers of this book) professional development courses will find that this book can be used to support personal development and also Continuing Professional Development (CPD) –see http://www.cipd.co.uk/mandq/develop/cpd.

Alternatively link the content to modules within the CIPD standards for the Leadership and Management Programme. For example:

- Preparation for return to study induction modules, support for working on assignments and assessed work – Chapter 1 (learning) and Chapter 6 (presentation skills) are particularly relevant.
- The module 'Managing and Leading People' may utilise Chapter 1 (learning), Chapter 4 (group, which links to leadership issues), Chapter 9 (dealing with difficult people and difficult situations – the parts on stress and bullying).
- The module 'Managing Resources' may utilise Chapter 2 (time management), Chapter 3 (creativity), Chapter 4 (groups, which links into team working), Chapter 5 (communication and interviewing skills), Chapter 7 (assertiveness), Chapter 8 (negotiation skills), Chapter 10 (managing personal and organisational change).

Many universities run 'People and Organisation' courses as part of BA, BSc, MBA or MSc programmes in business, management or human resource management, and this book could be used to support these. Increasingly many of these courses are now providing skills-based modules in 'core management skills' to support the programmes and this book is particularly appropriate in helping to develop these skills.

So why has there been so much activity around raising the profile of personal skills, which used to be the poor relation of the more academic courses and areas of learning? One reason is that it is not enough just to accumulate knowledge, and the competence movement pushed for this knowledge to be in evidence in practice. Against a background of research over the last 20 years to suggest that managers lack key skills and training, there has been the realisation that management and personal skills are not optional add-ons at the periphery, but are vital for managerial success and career development, as well as the effectiveness of their organisations.

This book is therefore not designed only to be read and then left on a dusty shelf, but is intended to be enjoyed and used 'in action'. It uses theory and research, but only where it is useful to aid practice. It intends to be a lively read, accessible and encouraging. I very much hope you enjoy reading it and using it at work, in study, and maybe elsewhere.

The book is arranged into three areas: the first three chapters all relate to individual personal capability areas – individual approaches to learning, time management and ideas generation. The next chapter moves onto the individual within a team and team-based skills. The following five chapters (5–9) all relate to interpersonal skills and communication, and the final chapter (10) is intended to integrate all the ideas and theories into exploring personal and organisational approaches to change and putting change into action – one of the intended outcomes of this book.

Every chapter has:

- an introduction to the topic

- learning objectives
- illustrative examples of skills in practice
- a range of activities and exercises to enable you to practise the skills and also apply the knowledge to your own life
- supportive and further reading
- website material to give further feedback on exercises and to provide more detailed diagnostic instruments to help you appraise your own skills, approaches and mindsets. The website also has further illustrative case studies, sample exam questions, self-evaluation tests and tutor material, including feedback notes and Power point slides.

A good place to begin would be to look up the website now and attempt the Personal Effectiveness Diagnostic tool, which should help you identify your main learning needs and which chapters will be of particular utility.

REFERENCES

CAMERON, S. (2002) *The Business Students' Handbook: Learning skills for study and employment.* 2nd ed. Harlow: Pearson, FT/Prentice Hall.

COTTRELL, S. (2003) *The Study Skills Handbook.* Basingstoke, Hants: Palgrave Study Guides.

FURTHER INFORMATION

Chartered Institute of Personnel and Development: http://www.cipd.co.uk
CIPD;
151 The Broadway
London
SW19 1JQ
Tel: +44 (0) 20 8612 6200

Chartered Management Institute: http://www.managers.org.uk/institute
Corby:
Management House,
Cottingham Road,
Corby,
Northamptonshire,
NN17 1TT
Tel: 44 (0) 1536 204 222
Fax: 44 (0) 1536 201 651
enquiries@managers.org.uk

London:
3rd Floor,
2 Savoy Court,
Strand,
London,
WCRR 0EZ
Tel: 44 (0) 20 7497 0580
Fax: 44 (0) 20 7497 0463
enquiries@managers.org.uk

List of chapters

Learning

AIMS AND LEARNING OUTCOMES

This chapter is intended to help you reflect on your own learning, and become a more effective learner.

When you have completed this chapter you will be able to:

- **Reflect on barriers and difficulties you may have in learning, and find ways to deal with these.**

- **Have awareness of your own assumptions about learning and your views on how you learn.**

- **Explain the difference between cognitive, behavioural and humanistic ideas on how we learn.**

- **Identify your preferred learning orientations**

- **Utilise tools to enable you to learn from experience and become a lifelong learner.**

INTRODUCTION

Learning is something we do all the time, whether consciously or unconsciously. Think of an average day – listening to the radio, reading the paper on the train, talking to people at work, walking to the local shop, watching a movie – these are all opportunities for learning, thinking, reflecting. As we are bombarded with information – the weather, e-mails, conversation – we are processing it, sorting it, allowing it to impact our thinking, allowing our thinking to develop. Just because we do it all the time, doesn't mean it is either simple or easy. In fact, in this chapter we will explore just how complicated and difficult it can sometimes be.

We often conceive of learning as the acquisition of knowledge or a skill, but it is much more than that. It is not just an activity we perform with our minds; we use our senses, emotions and behaviour too. Through learning we gain much more than knowledge; we gain understanding, wisdom, new perspectives, new ways of thinking, feeling, doing and being.

DEFINITION OF LEARNING

Learning is the acquisition of knowledge or skill that enables us to realise something new, or be able to do something we haven't done before. Learning is to do with thought and sense making – it is an active process of making meaning out of material we come up against (whether through formal development and training, or through informal and incidental experience). Learning is also transferring knowledge into action – it is about developing competence and being able to put the knowledge into practice.

Think of one illustration of learning in your own life: for example learning to drive a car. This requires mastery of a skill, but also learning what it feels like to drive a car, the sense of freedom, exhilaration, independence, maybe even fear and trepidation. Skills do not develop in a vacuum, they are embodied, and in this chapter we will get the chance to explore some ways in which our feelings and thoughts get in the way of our learning, and also how they can enrich it. We will explore some of the learning blocks and barriers and discuss ways these can be overcome.

This chapter will draw your attention to how you learn in order to enable you to find ways to maximise your own learning and develop your capacity to learn. It will invite you to stand back from focusing on the content of what you are learning and engage more with the process of how you learn. Addressing your own learning issues should enable you to find ways to take more responsibility for your own learning and to discover ways of gaining more satisfaction from formal learning situations such as courses and training, and to find more opportunities to learn from a wider range of life experiences.

LEARNING SHOCK

Before taking a look at those informal, incidental opportunities to learn, let's begin by examining what happens when facing up to a new, formal learning situation: beginning a new course or training scheme.

For an adult returning to study for a masters degree for example, learning may contain a number of fears. Although they may have a number of years' work experience, their previous study for school, degree, or diploma may feel like a long time ago. They may feel some trepidation at the thought of re-entering the realm of education, and returning to study. There are some barriers and obstacles in the learning process that are particularly pertinent for those who have been in work or out of the education system for some time. These can be exacerbated by moving to study in a foreign culture, or by deciding to juggle work and learning through embarking on a part-time course.

One way of describing this is by seeing it as 'learning shock'. Research conducted by myself along with Yiannis Gabriel and Dorothy Griffiths (see Gabriel, Griffiths and Winstanley 2003, 2004) at Imperial College has coined this phenomenon and sees it as akin to the 'culture shock' exhibited by some entering a new or unfamiliar country or culture (for example see Adler 1981). Culture shock combines powerful feelings of loss associated with leaving all that is familiar, with the helplessness and disorientation of a bewildering array of new customs and norms, meanings and cues. Learning shock similarly refers to the experiences of profound frustration, confusion and anxiety experienced by some when exposed to unfamiliar learning and teaching methods, bombarded by unexpected and disorientating cues, confused over expectations and debilitated by performance anxiety and self-doubt. Although in its acute form it can be paralysing, many experience it to a lesser extent, particularly at the start of a new course of study or training.

So what are the features of learning shock?

The first cluster of features relates to entering a new environment, and feeling disorientated, different, and maybe even an outsider:

Little fish in a big pool

Imagine someone who has spent a number of years in work moving up through an organisation or across several organisations until they have achieved some power and prestige, maybe even holding a high position within the organisation. They have earned respect and a good reputation. They may have had a number of people willing to help with the more routine duties, leaving them to get on with the more important decisions and work. It can then be a shock to return to academic study and suddenly find that they are no longer a 'big fish in a little pool', but have suddenly become a 'little fish in a big pool'. No longer 'savvy' with 'how things are done round here', and consulted about how to do things. Even worse, being in a position of confusion and powerlessness, but witnessing other students exhibiting much more confidence and ease in the learning process. This can be very unsettling, and can knock confidence and self-esteem. The ego may also be bruised by having to do much of the basic work – how long ago was it since they took detailed notes? They may have had an administrator to take notes. When did they last get asked to produce a PowerPoint presentation? They may have had an assistant to produce the slides.

An impostor

Noticing that everyone else on a new course or in training appears to be coping well and enjoying their studies, can make someone feel worse about the fact that they are struggling with the change. Feelings of self-worth are further eroded as they try to put on a good front and appear as confident and happy as other students. This can lead to feeling like 'an impostor' or a fraud. They may start to question whether they deserve to be on the course at all. The fact that employers, family or even a bank have given or lent money for the course or training may make the feelings of failure even worse, as their confidence in the student appears to be based on an act of deception.

Another part of 'learning shock' does link more explicitly to 'culture shock', and the shock of learning within another culture:

Language and culture shock

For some people leaving a familiar culture, the homesickness and strangeness of new lands can be overwhelming. In studying abroad they may be faced with the culture shock of finding that ways of doing things are very different. They may begin to feel clumsy, inadequate and slow as they try to master a language and customs that others on the course take for granted. Speaking in a language that is not their first language does present a disadvantage, because no sooner have they mastered their thoughts in order to make an interjection in the discussion, than the conversation has moved on. They may feel they stand out as being different from those around them. This can be exacerbated by isolation if studying abroad away from family and friends. The opportunity to talk to people who are close friends and family can often put bad learning experiences into perspective, but if this opportunity is absent, the loneliness and time spent alone can magnify the unease and distress.

The third set of features relate to fantasies and disappointment:

Disillusionment and disorientation

Before starting a new course it is common to feel excited and start anticipating what it will be like. Inevitably there will have been some mismatch between these expectations and the experience in practice. It may be a pleasant surprise, but there are bound to be some areas of disillusionment, disappointment or disorientation. The study groups may be larger than expected with little time for personal interaction with the tutor. The instructional style may be confusing: for instance a new student may have expected to sit down and listen, and with shock suddenly find they are expected to conduct a role-play. Alternatively they may have hoped to contribute their experience in an interactive small group, and instead find they are being lectured to by someone who has far less experience in the area than they do.

A re-evaluation of success

Another learner may come to question her own abilities – perhaps she was kidding herself all those times when she thought she was a successful manager, perhaps actually she is incompetent but hadn't realised it until now! It can lead to a re-evaluation of the previous ease and skill, perhaps believing it to have been a sham. It can be shattering to a person's identity to question what has for long been taken for granted.

Over time we can pick up a number of bad habits in the way work is conducted, and it can be a shock to find that these need to be unlearned. In trying to do things differently there may be a period when it feels unnatural, and incompetent, again a knock to the ego. In learning we may go through a process of (see O'Connor and Seymour 1990: 27):

- unconscious incompetence (where we don't know we are incompetent)
- conscious incompetence (where through the course we realise there are areas where we are not competent, and it is at this stage we begin to have self doubts)
- conscious competence (where over time we begin to practise new behaviours and skills, maybe slowly and laboriously)
- unconscious competence (where the learning we have developed becomes embedded and becomes second nature)

Let's go back to the example of driving a car. Initially I may not even have thought about driving, not tried it or sat behind the wheel, so I don't see myself as incompetent. That only really registers once I am faced with the reality of learning. As I take driving lessons I become very conscious of how I should be driving, maybe driving pedantically and with great concentration. Once I have passed my driving test and driven for several months, I probably don't even think about my skills of driving – I just do it automatically. You may experience a new course or training in this way, as initially you are re-evaluating your skills and may feel incompetent, but this is a natural part of the learning process and over time it is likely that this will diminish.

If you experience any of these 'learning shocks' it is helpful to seek out the support and help of friends and family, other peers who may be experiencing similar problems, and those responsible for providing pastoral support in your study such as personal tutors, and maybe even professionals such as counsellors and therapists.

Not all barriers to learning are identifiable and experienced at the individual level; some are more systemic, arising out of the organisational and environmental contexts and the tension between study and other aspects of life such as home or work life. Common barriers here include:

Study – work – home tensions – the juggler

It is tempting to suggest to someone considering a new course or period of study – forget your work life, your relationships, your doing-up-your-new -house – cut off everything and just study. But we are human, we don't work that way, and for most people there will be competing claims for time. Particularly tricky is balancing work and part-time study, or balancing a new baby, young children and study. I can remember one student who sat in an examination room, with her mother holding her newborn baby in the next room, in case it wanted feeding during the exam. How on earth did she manage to get that far in the course, and go on to pass with flying colours? Of course this is an extreme example, but life doesn't go on hold whilst we take time out to study. If you are embarking on a new course or training, it is worth reflecting on what competing claims you have on your time, and how you are going to deal with them. Have you a space to work in at home, will you get periods of uninterrupted time to study, can you make time for the course where you will not be disturbed by children, partners, pets?

A lack of interplay between learning and work

Learning is enhanced where there is an opportunity to practise the learning, and where there is interplay between thinking and doing. If you are currently in work and studying part-time, you need to give thought to ways in which your learning can be taken back into practice in the workplace – Exercise 1.1 below should help you with this.

A lack of a supportive environment for study

Many work cultures require long hours working, and where your work does not actively support you by allowing time off to study or train, or providing you with the necessary resources, you may find your learning is hampered. It is important that you have invested the time making arrangements with those in a position to provide you with a supportive environment for your study.

EXERCISE 1.1 FOR THOSE STARTING A NEW COURSE OF TRAINING, OR RETURNING TO STUDY

What fears do you have about starting the course or training or returning to study? Jot these down – you could also put them in a personal learning journal (mentioned below, see p23).

Are any of the points raised above likely to be relevant to you?

What support are you going to put in place to help you deal with these fears?

Relook at these fears and ask yourself:

- Are these fears a natural response to the situation?
- Are other people on the course/training programme likely to be experiencing these fears?

OVERCOMING BARRIERS TO LEARNING

The previous section has raised the possibility of 'learning shock' and barriers to learning that face someone starting a new course or returning to study. In this section we look in more depth at some of the barriers to learning that derive from how we feel about ourselves and our ability, capacity and capability to learn. These can impede us in both formal and informal learning situations.

Neuro-linguistic programming

Neuro-linguistic programming (NLP) developed in the 1970s out of the ideas of John Grinder and Richard Bandler. To find out more about NLP see O'Connor and Seymour 1990. NLP examines how we structure our experience and organise what we see, hear or feel, and how we simplify the world and filter it to be able to make sense of it through our beliefs, our language and our senses. It is particularly appropriate for helping people to overcome barriers to learning. NLP suggests that our senses and perceptions are what create our fears or excitement about facing learning. If we approach learning looking for an expansion in our knowledge we will find that, whereas if we approach it looking for problems, then problems are what we find. For example, if we believe we will fail and this will be disastrous then when we have difficulties we will feel useless. Whereas on the contrary, if we see failure as feedback from which we learn, we will see it as a part of our development. Therefore we need to approach learning with a view of our outcomes, and a positive expression of what these might be. We need to find ways to harness our beliefs to support us in learning, not impede us. Another theory that suggests that training our beliefs to support us is central to creating a positive attitude to learning is that of social cognitive theory and its ideas about self-efficacy.

Self-efficacy

Many of the ideas about self-efficacy come from research into social cognitive theory, and a key authority in this area is Bandura (see Bandura 1977a, 1977b, 1986). Bandura suggests that self-efficacy relates to 'beliefs in one's capabilities to mobilise the motivation, cognitive resources and courses of action needed to meet given situational demands'. Self-efficacy in learning is belief in our ability to learn and produce the desired effect.

People with high levels of self-efficacy are willing to put more effort into learning, and develop better coping and persistence skills when challenged by obstacles that may impair their performance and ability to learn. On the other hand people with low self-efficacy are more likely to express doubts on their capabilities to learn, and also be more susceptible to stress and burnout in the process. It therefore seems important to build up our self-efficacy to learn, as otherwise this could severely hamper our progress.

So how is self-efficacy built and destroyed? To some extent our self-efficacy is part of our make-up, a result of our genetic composition and also our formative experiences. However, it is in our control to enhance or extinguish it through our actions and choices as we go about our learning. The list below gives some ways in which you could enhance your own feelings of self-efficacy when faced with a new learning situation.

Table 1.1 *Ways of enhancing self-efficacy*

(developed from the work of Bandura 1977a and b, 1986)

Performance accomplishment Having high self-efficacy increases our ability to learn and our superior performance at learning then feeds back into increasing our self-efficacy. Therefore there is a virtuous circle where the better we perform the higher our self-efficacy and then the increased capacity we have to learn. You therefore need to find tasks in your learning where you perform well, and build up your confidence through gradually attempting more and more difficult tasks. If you throw yourself straight away into activities that are very difficult and challenging to you, you may be building up a feeling of failure.
Opportunities to develop and acquire new skills The opportunity to practise in a safe and supportive environment is vital to self-efficacy. Therefore make sure you have got opportunities to practise new skills in ways that are not risky, but build up capability.
Vicarious experience Observation of role models performing a task and seeing how they do it and perform can be a way of building up confidence and self-efficacy. Make sure you make use of your interaction at work and on courses to observe and learn from good role models.
Verbal persuasion Supportive coaching and encouragement can be helpful. The belief of others in you, such as your boss at work, or your tutor on a course, is important. You need to build up a trusting relationship with your peers mentors and coaches – and if you haven't got a coach or mentor, get one (this is discussed further below).
Psychological well-being Getting enough sleep, exercise and good nutrition all builds up our capacity for resilience, and if we are in good physical and physiological shape we are more likely to feel confident. Tiredness is a particular problem, where long hours of studying can lead to demoralisation and lack of focus and energy.
Emotional well-being People who have a high level of emotional arousal when faced with difficult and challenging tasks may find this gets in their way and leads to feelings of greater incompetence and lack of self-efficacy. For example if you get very anxious and worked up about an assignment, then you may lose sight of what you are trying to achieve. It is better to be more task focused, so if you find yourself getting too emotional when studying, take a step back, take a break and reflect on what is happening. Calm yourself down and reassure yourself before reapplying yourself.

Now try Exercise 1.2 to examine your own levels of self-efficacy with relation to a specific learning opportunity. You could also turn to Chapter 10 where Exercise 10.4 provides a rating exercise on self-efficacy with relation to making changes – this could equally apply to learning.

EXERCISE 1.2   SELF-EFFICACY

On a scale of 0–10 (0 being low and 10 being high) rate your current feeling of self-efficacy in relation to one learning opportunity or situation that faces you. You may want to separate out different aspects of the situation as you may feel you have high self-efficacy in some areas and low self-efficacy in others.

Now review the list of ways in which self-efficacy can be enhanced and work out some ways in which you can put this into practice over the next month, particularly in those areas where your self-efficacy is low.

Review your level of self-efficacy in a month's time, and then keep checking on it regularly over your course – you may want to build this into your personal journal (see p23).

Thinking faults and self talk

The way we think, or the 'self-talk' that goes on in our heads, can also impede our learning. Aeron Beck's pioneering research in the early 1970s and since, on depression and other emotional disorders, identified 'thinking errors', cognitive distortions and self-defeating thought processes as important in shutting down people's capacity to learn, flourish and grow. Some of our thinking errors and distortions rise up when we are faced with a difficult project or task, and lead to demoralisation. These you should watch out for and try to counter with more realistic appraisals of the situation. They are particularly likely to surface when you are in difficulties, and are starting to lose confidence in yourself. Apart from thinking distortions, the way we talk to ourselves in our heads can make us feel worse or better about ourselves and our learning.

Table 1.2   *Common thinking faults*

1. Catastrophising and anticipatory anxiety	You anticipate the worst that can happen: *'It will all go horribly wrong'*. The way we anticipate events and run them through in our head in 'what if' scenarios doesn't help either: *'What if I blow it?'*. By the time the event happens you are a wreck, although usually the anticipation is worse than the actuality.
2. All or nothing and over-generalising	You see a situation in only two categories instead of on a continuum. For example *'If I'm not a total success at my course, I'm a total failure'*. Or if one tutor has given you negative feedback on an assignment you assume the whole of your work is rubbish. Similarly, over-generalising, – this is using 'never', 'always' and 'ever' statements. For example: *'I'll never get this work done in time'.' 'I'm always in a muddle'.*
3. Magnifying the negative and discounting the positive	When you evaluate yourself, another person, or a situation, you exaggerate or magnify the negative. For example: *'Getting mediocre feedback on my report proves how inadequate I am'* or *'That trainer criticised my approach, he really hates me'.* You may undue attention to one negative detail instead of seeing the whole picture. For example: *'Because I got one low rating on my evaluation, it means I'm doing a lousy job'.*

Table 1.2 *continued*

	You also reject the positive experiences or qualities by insisting they don't count. For example: *I did that project well, but that doesn't mean I'm competent, I just got lucky'*.
4. Categorical imperatives – should and must statements	You have a precise and fixed idea of how you or others should behave and you over estimate how bad it is that these expectations are not met. For example: *'I shouldn't have made so many mistakes', 'it is terrible that I couldn't do those calculations, I should be able to do them.'*
5. Can't so shan't	Without even trying you assume you cannot do something, and therefore you won't even try. *'That exercise looks so difficult I can't do it. I'll leave it until later.'* You even talk yourself out of doing something by saying things to yourself like *'I'm rubbish' 'I'm no good.'*
6. Be perfect rather than good enough	You are a perfectionist and cannot tolerate mistakes, to the extent that your work doesn't just have to be 'good enough', you think it must be 'perfect'. For example *'I have to get it 100 per cent right, even if it means I have to stay up all night, and be too tired for work tomorrow'*. This is explained in more detail in Chapter 9.
7. Personalisation and internalising blame	Everything is all your own fault! You believe others are behaving negatively because of you, without considering more plausible explanations for their behaviour. For example: *'That guy in my group keeps getting angry all the time, it must be my fault, I must be provoking him'*.
8. Externalisation and blaming others	It's not my responsibility! *'The trainer is awful, it is all his fault I can't learn'*. Blaming others for everything is a way of avoiding taking any responsibility for your own learning.
9. Emotive reasoning	You assume that your negative emotions reflect the way things are. For example: *'I feel so angry, this proves I must be being treated really unfairly'* or *'I feel so scared of flying to that conference, it must be dangerous to fly'*.
10. Mind reading and clairvoyance	You believe you know what others are thinking, failing to consider other more likely possibilities. For example: *'The way my tutor looks at me I know he thinks what a silly person I am'* or *'She always goes past me without saying hello, so I know she thinks I'm not worth talking to'*. You also believe you can predict the future and do so negatively, without considering other possible outcomes. For example: *'I'll be so upset if I don't get an A, I won't be able to function at all'* or *'I won't be able to say anything that makes sense when I give that presentation, it will all be a disaster'*.

Note on source: there are a number of other variants of these 'thinking faults', for example see Neenan and Dryden's list of 'distorted thinking' (2002: 5), but the original source for 'thinking errors' and cognitive distortions was the work of Aaron Beck from the University of Pennsylvania, for example see Beck 1976, 1980.

HOW DO I LEARN? HOW DO WE LEARN?

There are different theories and approaches to how we learn. Here are some ideas from cognitive, behavioural and humanistic approaches.

Cognitive approaches

Cognitive approaches focus on the thinking processes involved in learning. The psychologist Piaget (Piaget 1963) researched the learning of children and found that they were like little scientists, constructing their world through interaction with experience. They make sense of the world through a prior schema and templates. For example a child may have developed the category for 'horse', but then she sees a 'zebra', but she has no template for it so sees it as a type of horse. Thus she assimilates new information to fit into the existing categories. She then has to 'accommodate' and develop the schema to make sense of new information, so may set up a new category called a 'zebra' which is like a horse but different. The child also 'adapts' developing her schema to make sense of 'zebras' 'dogs' and 'horses', and so may set up a new category called 'animals'. She stretches her concepts and powers of understanding through similarity and difference.

The same can be true of adult learning. Initially we may try and adapt new ideas to fit in with existing templates, but when eventually 'the round peg doesn't fit the square hole' we may begin to accommodate and adapt our schema. Learning, therefore, can have a significant impact on us – it can change the whole way we see the world and make sense of it.

Another way of understanding our processes of developing and expanding our templates, as well as destroying and changing them, is in using Chris Argyris's (see Argyris 1994) Single and Double Loop Learning.

> Single loop learning is learning within our current frameworks, norms and conventions.

> Double loop learning is where we have to change our current operating assumptions, norms and values.

An example may be in marketing – you may be a manager in an organisation retailing books, and realise you need to learn through customer feedback. Over time you gradually change your range of books, the way they are marketed, two-for-the-price-of-one offers, the highlighting of particular sections such as personal development, and so on. This may all occur within the existing framework of how you go about your business. There may come a time when you need double loop learning, to challenge your existing assumptions and norms: for example by deciding to move your business to the Internet, and interact with your customers in a very different way.

To learn is taking the risk of going outside our comfort zone. We may have to stretch our comfort zone like an elastic band, but stretch it too far and it will snap. To stretch it successfully we need a supportive holding environment, and there are some ideas for developing this later in the chapter.

Festinger's cognitive dissonance theory

Another way in which cognitive approaches may relate to your learning is in applying Festinger's cognitive dissonance theory (Festinger 1957). Cognitive dissonance theory suggests that when we gather new information, if it doesn't fit our current perceptions of problems or the world, or there is a gap where our current thinking doesn't have the concepts or constructs to deal with the new information, then a tension is created in us. Marketers are familiar with post-decisional dissonance: for example Sheila might be tempted to buy a new jacket, but this she can ill afford. This creates a dissonance for her – she cannot afford new clothes but has just bought an expensive jacket. She may reduce this dissonance by arguing to herself that she really needs the jacket for work, it will improve her presentation and confidence and so really is a worthwhile expenditure and not a drain on her resources.

Take for example Peter in the scenario below.

EXAMPLE 1.1   COGNITIVE DISSONANCE

Peter believes in a healthy lifestyle.

Peter smokes.

Peter knows that smoking can cause all sorts of health problems and even death.

Clearly there is dissonance in Peter's situation. He can try and ignore the dissonance, which can become very uncomfortable. Or he can take action to stop the smoking, deciding that his health is important after all. Alternatively he may decide that the pleasure of smoking outweighs his interest in health and perhaps lower his aspirations to be a healthy individual, or redefine 'health' to reduce the dissonance.

Cognitive dissonance can be a motivator to learn, for example where our existing frameworks cannot solve a problem or help us deal with a new situation. This is particularly the situation with problem-based learning.

EXAMPLE 1.2   COGNITIVE DISSONANCE AND THE MOTIVE TO LEARN

One example of this is in relation to case studies. You may be presented by a case study that has a problem to be solved or a decision to be made, but you don't have the knowledge to know how to go about solving this problem or making this decision. You may then be motivated to learn to bridge this gap and address the case study.

Behavioural approaches

Behavioural approaches to learning tend to focus more on ways in which desired or appropriate behaviour can be encouraged or discouraged. For example Skinner (1953, 1974) linked learning with external goals. Positive reinforcement encourages behaviour to be repeated, so in the case of a course, achieving praise on an assignment and an A grade will encourage the student to continue to receive good feedback. However, negative reinforcement may also be used, where for example continued lack of attendance on scheduled course dates may lead to penalties and negative feedback, and even punishment. The idea is that people want to avoid the negative feedback and achieve the positive feedback, and so become conditioned to behave in the desirable ways. Learning therefore occurs through conditioning. This doesn't just apply to learning, it is widely used in management practices, for example many appraisal and performance related reward systems are based on the assumptions of conditioning theory – a positive performance rating may be linked to a bonus or performance related pay, whereas a poor performance rating may identify someone who needs to improve, and may even warrant the invocation of disciplinary procedures.

Humanistic approaches

Humanistic approaches to learning are based on the work of writers such as Abraham Maslow (1943), Frederick Herzberg (1959) and Carl Rogers (Rogers and Freiberg 1994). People are seen as self-actualising beings who strive to become more fully what they are capable of. Given the chance, everyone is positive and social and will move towards self-actualisation and growth. Rogers gives the analogy of the potato – that if you provide the plant with the right conditions, sunlight and warmth, it will grow its shoots towards the light, and even in the dark the shoots try and grow, though pale and spindly.

Learning is a way of being, and we learn through experience where we are given autonomy and respect, empathy and positive regard. Rogers outlines this approach in his book *Freedom to learn* (Rogers and Freiberg 1994), and some courses are designed around Rogerian principles, where people set their own goals and even learning contracts, work out their own syllabus and how to get the information they need, and set up systems for self-evaluation. The emphasis is self-directed learning aimed to build up personal responsibility, autonomy and power. It also forms the basis of much small group learning, and links to other practices such as learning sets. As Rogers suggested, 'we must not be tourists in the classroom, we must be citizens' (Rogers and Freiberg 1994: 9).

It is worth reflecting on how you can be a citizen in courses you attend, participating and feeling a sense of ownership over your own learning, rather than passively allowing the tutors to direct you through your learning, absorbing a few highlights as you superficially peruse the artefacts of knowledge.

LEARNING STYLES AND ORIENTATIONS
Thinking, doing observing, theorising and Kolb's learning cycle

Learning is an iterative process between reflection and acquiring knowledge on the one hand, and putting it into practice on the other. It lies at the juncture between thinking and doing. It is unlikely that you will learn from simply sitting in a lecture, or by just attempting a new task. Knowledge and action are both important.

However, it is likely you have a preference for a particular style of learning, whether you are taking an educational or training course, or engaging in informal work-based learning. There are individual differences in our take-up and experience of learning. Kolb's learning cycle (Kolb 1984) identifies four styles of learning. We all have preferences for each part of this cycle, but we need to develop learning from every part of the cycle:

> *Concrete experience* – we are *activists* who like doing.

Reflective observation – we reflect on our experiences and observe what happens, we learn through reflection and reviewing, we are *reflectors*.

Abstract conceptualisation – we like to build theories and constructs to learn, we are *theorists*.

Active experimentation – once we have a theory, we learn from testing it. We are *pragmatists* who enjoy planning and testing and experimenting.

Each learning style favours different types of activities. Someone who is an 'activist' on a course will enjoy more practical activities, such as writing a business plan. In training they will enjoy practising new skills, so rather than learning about the theory of interviewing, they will prefer to conduct a mock interview, putting the guidance into practice in a real or hypothetical situation. They will also enjoy action learning, where knowledge and feedback from learning is put into practice in an ongoing way. A 'reflector' will enjoy reflecting on learning from a case study, or at work may appreciate opportunities to reflect on their experiences. A 'theorist' may enjoy writing an essay that critiques and develops theory, whereas an experimenter or 'pragmatist' may appreciate the chance to test out new ideas in practice – for example a project involving two different interventions in an organisation to see which works better. Another way to utilise the learning styles is to try practising and developing learning in the areas that are not those of automatic preference.

Imperial learning orientations

Kolb's learning styles tell us some information about the way we may prefer to learn, and about the different types of learning activities in which we may engage. However, we can go wider and explore our 'learning orientations.' These have been developed using Imperial Business School (now the Tanaka Business School) MBA graduates, where research by the author with the Imperial team (Winstanley et al 2003) has found that there are a number of ways in which students on a formal course differ in their expectations and behaviour. The research utilised interviews with students at the beginning, during, and at the end of, their course, and a few years after their studies. It identified four primary learning orientations, each having an active and passive form (see Table 1.3).

The first learning orientation is 'the implementer'. This relates to the application of learning to practise, either in current roles and jobs or future ones. The active form of 'implementer' is the 'experimenter' – someone who actively finds ways in which to practise skills from a management course in the workplace. At the other extreme is the 'concealer' who has no interest in using the learning in the workplace, and may even go further to conceal their newfound skills or position on a course for a variety of reasons. They may fear the envy of others or that in some way their position on an MBA or masters programme may be resented

Table 1.3 *The learning orientations*

Learning orientations	Active form	Passive form
Implementer	Experimenter	Concealer
Lover of learning	Seeker	Sponge
Badge collector	Earner	Purchaser
Affirmer	Validator	Observer

within the organisation. Others merely prefer to keep their world of learning and their world of work separate.

The second learning orientation is the 'lover of learning'. These students have high intrinsic motivation in learning, they love learning for its own sake. The active pole here is the 'seeker' who actively seeks to develop learning, seeking out new learning opportunities and enjoying the opportunity to reflect on new ideas. At the passive end is the 'sponge'. The sponge sees learning as a process of absorption, the soaking up of knowledge from 'experts' or tutors as a way of learning. A sponge-like approach can be promoted in some learning cultures, for example didactic learning situations where the learner is the 'audience' to learning. Cultures that encourage respect for a tutor, and finds question asking and interruptions to be rude and disrespectful may also invite an orientation that leans towards the one-way absorption of knowledge.

The third learning orientation is the 'badge collector' – someone who is focussed on the qualification per se and sees the 'sign' value as the most important aspect of the learning experience. The value of the qualification may be for a variety of reasons – for prestige, status or career. The active form is the 'earner', someone who wants the qualification but still accepts they have to earn the letters after their name and prove themselves on the course. 'Purchasers', on the other hand, act more like consumers, assuming they have paid their money, purchased the course like a consumer good, and expect it to be delivered on a plate. This may involve a fair amount of 'satisficing' behaviour – doing the minimum to get by.

The fourth learning orientation relates to identity and we classified this as the 'affirmer'. The active type, the 'validator' wants to confirm their own identity or assess their own behaviour or performance in relation to others. They continually benchmark themselves against others to see whether they match up. To do this they network continually, seeking out opportunities to find out about others on the course and their experiences. At the other extreme is the 'observer' who is more of an outsider on the course, a social isolate who may not feel a sense of belonging as part of the course community, preferring to stay on the outside, separate to other participants.

If you are entering a course it would be interesting to reflect on your expectations and anticipated behaviour and see how this would relate to these learning orientations. It seems likely that your experience of the course, the satisfaction you get from it and your performance will all be impacted by these orientations. What do you think would be the likely implication of adopting the learning orientation/s you lean towards in terms of satisfaction and performance, as well as learning style? You could attempt the self-diagnostic questionnaire provided on the website to identify your own learning orientations.

METAPHORS FOR LEARNING

The metaphors we use to understand our experience and the learning process tell us a great deal about how we view our learning. Exercise 1.3 is intended to help surface your metaphors of your learning experience.

EXERCISE 1.3   METAPHORS FOR LEARNING

Find a place where you can relax and take a few minutes to reflect on one experience of learning you have had in the last year. What metaphor comes to mind to describe your experience? Write a paragraph elaborating on this metaphor, outlining ways in which the metaphor fits your experience.

Our metaphors for learning tell us about our primary frames of reference and our orientation to learning, as well as our motivation to learn. Some metaphors for learning resemble *entertainment*. A passive approach to learning, based around 'learning as entertainment' could be for example the metaphor of 'watching TV'. Others connect to the core value and motivation of *challenge*. This challenge could be seen as a test of endurance, for example the metaphor of 'an assault or survival course'. Another framework could be of *growth*, and metaphors here could be naturalistic ones like 'being a plant blossoming or a tree coming into leaf'. Other forms of metaphor focus on *transitions* and movement – for example the metaphor of a journey or voyage of discovery. Examine your metaphor and identify what it tells you about your motivation and attitude to learning. Do you think this attitude is appropriate and of benefit to you? Will it enable you to get the most out of your learning? Does it suggest an active or passive approach to learning?

PERRY'S WORK ON LEARNING AND LEVELS OF INTELLECTUAL SOPHISTICATION

In the 1950s and 1969s Perry interviewed students at Harvard (all were male) over the duration of their courses using open recorded interviews on the topic of their approaches to and experiences of learning (Perry 1999 and 1981). He found that all students have learning strategies, their basic assumptions about what is expected from learning, and how they may learn. Also all tutors have implicit in their teaching, models of how they believe students learn. You are likely to have underlying assumptions about how you are going to learn when you start a new course, and these will have a huge impact on the way you go about your studies. Exercise 1.4 should help to bring some of these assumptions to your consciousness.

EXERCISE 1.4   APPROACHES TO LEARNING AND THE NATURE OF 'TRUTH' AND KNOWLEDGE

Look at the following statements and work out which one you feel most relates to your view either in relation to a course you are on or one you have taken in the past:

Some differences of opinion are legitimate but temporary.

I have to make my own decisions in an uncertain world – there is no one to tell me I'm right.

When tutors do not ask for the right answer, they ask for the right way of thinking.

Tutors know, and we must learn the right answers from them.

When tutors do not know the right answer, all opinions are valid.

I need to make commitments to key values and priorities in my learning and balance them. I have to fight for my values, but be open-minded and question them, and be ready to learn from others. I will have to keep retracing my learning journey making choices and question them over and over again.

There are true and false theories and experts; we must learn to reach the right answer by independent thought.

Truth is relative – meaning depends on context, theories are metaphors for reality.

From Perry's research he developed a scheme of increasing levels of intellectual sophistication, as over time and increased exposure to learning students develop from a position of a simplistic dualism, through to relativism through to personal responsibility. Perry's work on 'levels of intellectual sophistication' suggests the following:

Dualism

1. Tutors know and we must learn the right answers.
2. There are true and false theories and experts, we must learn to reach the right answer by independent thought.
3. Some differences of opinion are legitimate but temporary.

In the first three stages there is a dualism, where there is a separation out of good versus bad, right versus wrong. Right answers exist somewhere for every problem, and tutors know them, our task as a learner is to memorise these right answers by hard work. As we move through this dualism we have to deal with certain uncertainties – what about different opinions and disagreements between tutors and authorities? We move from position 1 to 2, but then we find that even good tutors admit they don't know all the answers yet. In position 3 we comfort ourselves by the thought that they may not know fully the answers now, but they are working towards 'the truth'.

For example, take a hypothetical module on the study of leadership. You may begin (at level 1) thinking that tutors know what the attributes of a good leader are and you need to learn this information from them. Then in a lecture on leadership, you discover there are different theories of leadership: trait, style, behavioural, contingency, situational, transactional, transformational, etc. You may then decide that through thought you can work out which theory and theorist is right (level 2). You realise that the theorists on leadership have different opinions, but may believe that with further research, for example a comparison of successful and ineffective leaders, the right answers can be found, it is just our lack of empirical data that stops us from being sure which theory is correct (level 3).

Relativism

4. a) When tutors do not know the right answer, all opinions are equally valid.
   b) When tutors do not ask for the right answer, they ask for the right way of thinking.
5. Truth is relative, meaning depends on context, theories are metaphors of reality.

The next development is to move to a position of multiplicity and relativism. Multiplicity means that a diversity of opinion and values is recognised as legitimate in areas where right answers are not yet known. Opinions are atomistic without pattern, and no judgments can be made so 'everyone has the right to their own opinion, no one can be called wrong'. Relativism suggests that there is a diversity of opinion, values and judgment derived from coherent sources but we can see some patterns for analysis and comparison. Some opinions may be found worthless, and in other areas there are matters about which reasonable people will reasonably disagree. Knowledge is qualitative depending on contexts. Development therefore moves from 'anything goes' (at position 4a) to an appreciation that there must be some basis for marking and grades, and opinions can be supported with facts and reasons, so we have to justify how we come by our viewpoint (at 4b). Ultimately this requires us to understand the rules within each context. For example what constitutes knowledge and learning in the writing of an executive summary may be different to that of a thesis. We have to think actively about our thinking as well as the context (at position 5).

To return to our example of leadership, the plethora of different theories on leadership may lead you to reject the basic dualism of right and wrong altogether, and instead move to a position of all the theories perhaps having something to contribute – there is no way to decide which is best, it is all relative (level 4a). Or you may say that there may not be a right answer about what constitutes good leadership, but if in my presentation I provide a logical structure for evaluating the theories, and show a high level of critical analysis and reasoning skills, then whatever my conclusion, I will be demonstrating that I am learning and producing good pieces of work. I therefore need to find out the rules that each tutor adopts on what constitutes good work (level 4b). You may also discover that in one course leadership is seen as a practical skill that needs to be developed, whereas another takes a more critical approach to leadership and is more interested in critiquing the relationship between power, control and leadership. You start to discover that what counts as legitimate learning varies from course to course and according to context – what is useful in the classroom may be less relevant when you are practising leading a team within a business organisation, (level 5). The theories are people's stories and metaphors of reality – not reality itself.

Commitment

6. I have to make my own decisions in an uncertain world – there is no one to tell me I'm right.

7.–9. Increasing levels of commitment to the truth.

> I need to make commitments to key values and priorities in my learning and balance them. I have to fight for my values, but be open-minded and question them, and be ready to learn from others. I will have to keep retracing my learning journey making choices and questioning them over and over again.

I need to make commitments to key values and priorities in my learning and balance them. I have to fight for my values, but be open-minded and question them, and be ready to learn from others. I will have to keep retracing my learning journey, making choices and questioning them over and over again.

If everything becomes relative then we ask ourselves what is the basis of making the right choice in our learning. Choice and evaluation lead us to make decisions, and these we make based on our own judgment, bearing in mind our values and priorities, which we constantly need to re-examine and question. The journey is never ending.

Going back to our example of learning about leadership, there may come a point where instead of focusing on the context, others and their rules to make decisions about the validity of knowledge, you realise the need to make your own decision. You may decide that from reviewing the theories and observing the practice of leadership, you develop your own criteria for evaluation (level 6). Through developing self-knowledge and study, you can, through your own thought processes, develop your own ideas on what constitutes good leadership, and become increasingly committed to this. For example the author has developed an interest in the ethics and values of leadership, and has developed a commitment to 'ethical leadership.' (levels 7–9).

This progression of thinking and learning is all very worrying; it opens up so many avenues of doubt. It is not uncommon to experience some of the following at various stages of learning:

Confusion – what exactly are you expected to learn and how are you expected to learn?

Alienation and resentment – you expected to be given the information you needed to learn, but you are finding that it is not as clear and simple as that. What exactly are you investing time, money and resources for?

Retreat – your existing ways of learning don't seem to be working, so you feel like retreating from learning – either doing the bare minimum or even withdrawing from the course.

Avoidance – because it has all become so complex, you revert to very straightforward modes of learning, focusing on clear-cut facts and information that can be absorbed and about which there are right and wrong answers.

It may help you in your learning to know that these experiences of anxiety and confusion are all natural parts of the learning process, and are likely to occur particularly at those points where you are relinquishing one frame of reference for your learning and are developing more sophisticated approaches to learning or are in some way adapting your learning style and process to new information – an essential part of learning itself. However, Perry's theory is also open to refutation and doubt. For example, perhaps it is culturally specific – an Anglo American view of the world. Perhaps other cultures would not agree on this hierarchy. Many of Perry's respondents were male – and Belenky has suggested that women have other ways of knowing (Belenky et al 1997).

Surface, deep and strategic learning

Another way to encapsulate different approaches to learning is to separate out surface, deep and strategic approaches to learning (for example see Entwistle 1987, Marton and Saljo 1984). Surface learning is more likely to be in evidence in Perry's levels 1–3, whereas deep and strategic learning are more likely in the later stages.

Surface learning directs information towards learning the text and content of the literature or lecture itself, and is in evidence in the approach identified under A in Exercise 1.5. Deep learning directs attention towards the underlying meaning of the text or lecture and is found in the approach identified under B. Strategic learning focuses on the needs of the learner and is found under section C.

The approach that you take is likely to be influenced not just by your own personal preferences and style, but by past experiences you have had and your assessment of what seems to have worked, and by the assessment system used in your studies. Surface learning is quite a passive, albeit exhausting, approach, and does focus on expediently passing exams and assessments through 'parrot' style learning, but it is likely that over a period of time the learning will be forgotten and become obsolete. Its style is akin to 'sponge' in Table 1.3. Deep learning on the other had invites you to reflect actively and proactively on the meaning and value of the learning and so has a greater impact on your own thought processes and therefore tends to be more likely to be remembered and used in later life. Its style is akin to the 'seeker' in Table 1.3. Strategic learning as with surface learning takes an expedient approach, but more responsibility is taken on by the learner to manage your own learning. It is a highly effective process when under time constraints as it invites prioritisation of your time. However, its expedient process may mean that some deep meaning and the opportunity to reflect on issues from different points of view get lost if it is not also combined with deep learning approaches.

EXERCISE 1.5   SURFACE, DEEP OR STRATEGIC LEARNING?

Identify one topic that you have studied. This could have been study through lectures or through independent and guided reading or both. Reflect on your approach to learning in this session and ask yourself which of the following categories is most prevalent in your approach to learning.

A.

   I focus on detailed information in the text/in the lecture.

   I focus on completing the task requirements and treat this as an external given.

   I focus on sections of the text/lecture in sequence, and on discrete elements rather than integration.

   I concentrate on memorising the information needed for assessments.

   I take copious notes of all the information I can.

   In revising and consolidating, my learning I am focusing on being able to reproduce the information I have absorbed.

   I do not bother to reflect on the purpose of the work given and the strategies I employ to do it

B.

   I focus on the overall meaning of the text/lecture, and try to understand it.

   I attempt to search for the author's/lecturer's intentions and what his/her main message is.

   I vigorously interact with the content.

   I try to identify the main parts of the argument and supporting facts, and examine the logic of the argument.

   I relate the new ideas to my previous knowledge.

   I relate the new concepts to my everyday experience.

   I relate the content to the conclusions.

C.

   I focus my attention on getting the best possible grades I can, and also on what I want to get out of the text/lecture.

   I reflect on consciously developing my own agenda and bringing into awareness my needs.

   I make sure that I take away the information I need in a form that I can access.

   I organise my time and distribute effort to greatest effect, and I prioritise my work, making decisions about what to attend to and what to ignore, I recognise I cannot do everything.

   I ensure I have the materials and conditions suitable for studying where appropriate.

   I am alert to clues about marking schemes, and use previous exam papers to predict questions.

MAXIMISING LEARNING FROM EXERCISES, ROLE PLAYS AND CASE STUDIES

Of course to get the most out of learning, it is not just a question of having an appropriate learning orientation, and following your own personal journey and quest for 'truth'. There are some very basic skills that are going to help you learn. It will help if you can develop some familiarity with different methods of learning, and an understanding of what behaviour and techniques are appropriate for each. For example, in a lecture we may need to absorb quickly and digest large quantities of information, gleaning the intention of the lecturer, focusing on the main points we need to learn and summarising these in useful notes. However, most courses require more active learning skills.

Exercises

With all exercises you are given, you need to work out what is the purpose of the exercise – is it to acquire or practise skills, to reflect more deeply on an issue, to think about a problem in a different way, to reinforce a point made in a lecture, or even just to have fun, and interact with a group of people. In an induction programme it is interesting to see people getting carried away in competing in a business game, only to find at the end that the purpose of the game was to facilitate group interaction and to enable people to reflect on their group roles. Read the instructions careful, and if you are not sure about the purpose of an exercise, or what you are supposed to learn from it, check your understanding with the lecturer.

Case studies

Case studies are written around a problem or situation facing an individual, group or company; they can vary from half a page to over 50 pages. There are a variety of different types of case study and reasons for using them. They may be to:

    demonstrate good practice

    illustrate a way of conducting business or tackling an issue

    develop analytical and problem solving skills

    enable the student to appreciate how the theory applies to the practice

    follow through the implications of decision-making into its effects – such as a business decision to enter a new market, or a medical decision to change a medication for an asthma sufferer.

If the case study is used as a problem solving exercise, generally you will be invited to:

    identify the problem if there is one and understand the situation

    analyse issues

    generate and evaluate possible solutions

    present, implement and communicate solutions or recommendations.

One widely known user of case studies always began his case study sessions with the questions 'What is going on in this case?' 'What is this case about?' and would shoot this question at the person who looked the most vacant, bored or distracted. If you are provided the case in advance this usually means you are expected to have read and digested it before the session. It is humiliating if, in answer to the above questions, you fumble around with your papers looking embarrassed and wishing you were anywhere but sat at the back of that lecture theatre. Once you have got to grips with what is going on in the case, as with all problem-focused exercises, don't jump to conclusions before you have fully identified the problems and possible alternative courses of action and their implications.

Role-plays

Role-plays are particularly good for enabling you to practise skills; they provide a safe arena in which you can develop skills before you are competent enough to practise in a real situation. For this to work, they require you to immerse yourself into the role, which may even require you to adopt another personæ. Some people cringe at the thought of acting something out, but by holding back from a role-play, for example by sniggering, shuffling and entering the role in a half-hearted way, you are cheating yourself of the opportunity to gather perspectives on a situation that are much more difficult to see from outside. On the other hand, some drama queens take to the role like a duck to water, but the problem is they lose sight of the purpose of the role-play in pursuit of that 'Oscar'. Role-plays are there for the purpose of practising and developing your skills and giving you insight into a situation, and if you enter it with a willing and open-minded attitude it is interesting to note how, by enacting a role, you get much greater insight than by just examining it from the outside. It is quite likely that in a session comprised of lecturers and a role-play, the role-play will have much greater impact on your understanding of a situation, to the extent that you may remember much more afterwards. As well as practising new skills it also enables you to stand in the shoes of someone else, see a situation from their perspective and develop 'empathy'. This might be particularly useful in a coaching situation where you have a problem with somebody and cannot understand their point of view; acting out a role from their perspective will give you greater insight into how your own behaviour needs to be adapted to improve the communication. Some senior executive coaches insist their senior manager role play a problematic situation they are facing, sometimes taking their own role and sometimes taking the role of the other person. In some counselling situations, some counsellors invite the client to role play an interaction they may have with someone; sometimes in the use of 'Gestalt' approaches this can be called 'two chair work'.

LEARNING FROM EXPERIENCE: INFORMAL AND SELF-DIRECTED LEARNING

So far we have focused on more formal learning opportunities, and in particular participation in courses and learning programmes. However, there are many other ways in which we learn.

A didact is a self-taught person. In Jean-Paul Sartre's book Nausea the didact taught himself by working his way through the public library, starting at A and working through authors to Z. Much learning takes place outside of formal courses, and may be incidental and self-generated.

We also learn from experience: observation, reading, newspapers, conversations, stories, and experiences. One way of maximising learning is not to limit it to the realms of 'formal' experiences from lectures, seminars, assignments, group work, etc, but instead to seek out experiences that will provide learning opportunities. Learning from experience requires immersion in experience and also reflection (this returns us to the stages of the learning cycle mentioned above). Schon's (1983) work on 'the reflective practitioner' highlights the importance of reflection in action, reflecting experience and making meaning out of our practice. One way of promoting this is to use a learning journal – to jot down ideas and reflections that occur to you through your work life. It will contain your reflections on what and how you have learnt, including thoughts, feelings, actions, insights, reflections, ideas, problems, learning. The journal could also be used to record learning objectives and the extent to which these are being achieved, or are changing. You could also make note of action you could be taking to enhance your learning and that of others.

Some workplaces formalise these through personal development plans that are created through discussion with a supervisor at work, and may even have training opportunities and learning interventions attached. Others will even go so far as to set up learning contracts, but this is usually in association with formal learning.

Observation is also an important part of learning. Dawson et al's (1995: 218) research on 'Senior Management Competence in the NHS' found that managers ranked positive role models as the most important influence on their learning. Second came negative role models! Third came informal coaching and mentoring.

Mentoring

Mentoring as a concept has developed out of the notion of 'apprenticeship' moving beyond a master/apprentice relationship to one of mentor/mentee. Mentors are influential people who support and help you to achieve your goals, reach your career aspirations and learn from your experience. Mentoring can be set up as a formal or informal relationship. Ideally a mentor would have no other influence on your work, they would be objective and independent, but at the same time have a wealth of experience to draw on within your area of work. As well as expertise in, or at least familiarity with, your area, they need coaching, developmental and therapeutic skills. Although mentoring can be set up as a formal relationship through work systems, many people like to choose their own mentor – for example finding a retired boss or previous colleague or even college lecturer. The nature of the relationship is also important, it is a trusting one where you feel you can bring your development plans, your difficulties and problems, to discuss them fully and frankly. Typically people meet their mentors once every couple of weeks or a month in a confidential meeting for an hour. This relationship can be particularly helpful in sifting through work experiences to examine how effective someone's personal competences are, how they relate to their tasks, their goals, and their colleagues. Mentors may go beyond discussion to rehearse dealing with difficult situations, such as standing up to a bullying colleague, or negotiating a change of role at work. A good introduction to mentoring is David Clutterbuck's book *Everyone Needs a Mentor* (Clutterbuck 2001).

Learning sets

Not everyone wants to utilise a one-to-one relationship of this type, and another way to learn from experience is through learning sets, a form of learning derived from the work of Reg Revans (1982). Some people form a learning set from working on a course together and continue to after the course is over, generally meeting once a month to talk about work-related issues and problems and engage in inter-organisational learning. Some learning sets are developed within one work organisation or area and the participants come together to share experiences, difficulties or maybe even focus on learning from one project or activity. In some sets there is an agreed focus topic, in others the participants take turns to raise the issues on which they want feedback and discussion. A professional facilitator to help surface issues, support active participation and maximise learning is used by some learning sets. Others manage without, and operate more as a self- support group. Learning sets capture the social process of learning: learning through interaction with others. Another way to make use of social interaction is through communities of practice.

Communities of practice

At the outset of this chapter it was stated that learning is more than the acquisition of knowledge. Lave and Wenger (1991) and Wenger (1998) highlight these broader processes of social participation, identity development and belonging, where learning is not just an individual process, but is situated in social contexts. A community of practice (Wenger 1998: 4) focuses on 'learning as social participation' and 'being active participants in the practices of social communities and constructing identities with relation to these communities'. A community of practice is a social configuration in which we participate, and at any one time we belong to a number of communities of practice: for example our family, our workplace community, our professional community and our educational community. For individuals, 'learning is an issue of engaging in and contributing to the practices of (our) communities' (Wenger 1998: 7) and for communities 'learning is an issue of refining practice and ensuring new generations of members'. Lave and Wenger (1991) also discuss the concept of 'legitimate peripheral participation', which broadens the traditional connotation of the concept of apprenticeship from a master/student or mentor/mentee relationship to one of changing participation and identity transformation in a community of practice. Legitimacy is about treating newcomers as potential members of a community: for example being useful, being sponsored, or in some way being given a sense of belonging. Peripherality is similar to full participation in these communities, but without facing the risk and exposure of full practice, for example through supervision, assistance, guidance and support. The learning is about community because it is about belonging to a social group with shared skills, perspectives or goals, and about practice because of the close connection between learning and doing, and because it is the act of doing that really brings one fully into contact with an experience or a way of being.

The community of practice view of learning is complex, and inevitably it has become watered down in everyday connotation to denote the ways in which we learn from our experience of engaging with peers in a variety of contexts to develop and promote learning.

Continuing professional development

One particular learning community is a professional group. Most professional groupings now require continuing professional learning and development to maintain membership of a profession. Increasingly professionals and managers are being encouraged to take on more responsibility for engaging in learning, an activity which is seen as important and also as a lifelong process. It is worthwhile considering what continuing professional development you are involved in and reflect on whether your own learning could be developed further.

SUMMARY

This chapter has covered a whole panorama of learning perspectives and approaches. It began by exploring formal learning opportunities and identified the blocks and barriers that can impede learning. It then provided an overview of theoretical approaches to learning and discussed the very different ways in which the learning process can be modelled and distilled. Finally it turned to learning outside of formal courses and training and looked at learning opportunities through experience, in the workplace and in communities of practice, and also ways in which these can be maximised, such as through mentoring, learning sets, personal development plans and personal learning journals. Ultimately the only sense that can be made of all this for you is by you. It would be worth taking a few minutes to tackle Exercise 1.6 to give yourself ownership of learning from this chapter, and identify some actions that would be helpful to you.

EXERCISE 1.6   HOW DO I LEARN?

Look back through this chapter and answer the following questions:

1. Can you think of an example when you have used single loop learning and one where you have used double loop learning? Can you think of a situation facing you where double loop learning may be the most appropriate?

2. In what ways in your recent work life have you received positive reinforcement and negative reinforcement? Do you think these achieved their desired objectives?

3. In what ways can you develop yourself to become more of a 'citizen' rather than a 'tourist' in your learning?

4. Identify at least two ways in which you have recently utilised informal learning.

5. Which stage of Kolb's learning cycle do you think you prefer? Examine how you can develop your learning to have capability in each of the stages of the cycle.

6. Relook at the Imperial Learning Orientations – when you have taken a course do you think you have adopted any of these orientations, and if so what impact has it had on your experience of the course, your satisfaction and your performance?

7. Learning can be enhanced through the use of a personal learning journal, personal development plans, learning sets, having a mentor, or even just making more effort to be a reflective practitioner and learn from experience and learn within communities of practice. Identify one way in which you can improve your own learning using these ideas or any that have been presented in this chapter.

REFERENCES AND FURTHER READING

ADLER, N. (1981) Re-entry: Managing cross-cultural transitions. *Group and Organizational Studies.* 6, 341–356.

ARGYRIS, C. (1994) *On Organizational Learning.* Oxford: Blackwell.

BANDURA, A. (1977a) *Social Learning Theory.* Englewood Cliffs, New Jersey: Prentice Hall

BANDURA, A. (1977b) Self efficacy: Towards a unifying theory of behavioural change. *Psychological Review.* 84, (2), 191–215.

BANDURA, A. (1986) *Social Foundations of Thought and Action: A social cognitive theory.* Englewood Cliffs, New Jersey: Prentice Hall.

BECK, A. T. (1976) *Cognitive Therapy and the Emotional Disorders.* New York: International University Press.

BECK, A.T. (1980) *Feeling Good: The new mood therapy.* New York: Signet and Avon Books.

BELENKY, M., CLINCHY, B., GOLDBERGER, N. and TARULE, J. (1986/1997) *Women's Ways of Knowing: the development of self, voice and mind.* New York: Basic Books.

CAMERON, S. (2002) *The Business Students Handbook: learning skills for study and employment.* 2nd ed. Harlow, Essex: Pearson, FT/Prentice Hall.

CLUTTERBUCK, D. (2001) *Everyone Needs a Mentor.* 3rd edition. London: CIPD.

O'CONNOR, J. and SEYMOUR, J. (1990) *Introducing Neuro-Linguistic Programming: the new psychology of personal excellence.* London: Mandala, Harper Collins.

COTTRELL, S. (2003) *The Study Skills Handbook.* Hants: Palgrave Study Guides.

DAWSON, S., WINSTANLEY, D., MOLE, V. and SHERVAL, J. (1995) *Managing in the NHS: a study of senior executives.* London: HMSO.

ENTWISTLE, N. A Model of the Teaching-Learning Process. Chapter 2 in RICHARDSON, J. EYSENCK, M. and WARREN-PIPER, D. (eds) (1987) *Student Learning.* Milton Keynes: SRHE and Open University.

FESTINGER, L. (1957) *A Theory of Cognitive Dissonance:* Stanford: Stanford University Press.

GABRIEL, Y., GRIFFITHS, D and WINSTANLEY, D. (2003) *Learning Shock: The incidence of traumatic experience amongst returning postgraduate management students.* Report of Research funded by Imperial College Teaching Research Grants Scheme. London: Tanaka Business School.

GABRIEL, Y. GRIFFITHS, D. and WINSTANLEY, D. (2004) *Learning Shock: The trauma of return to formal learning.* Paper presented at European Group for Organizational Studies (EGOS) conference, Ljubljana, Slovenia, 1–3 July 2004.

HERZBERG, F., MAUSNER, B. and SNYDERMAN, B. (1959) *The Motivation to Work.* 2nd ed. Hants: Chapman and Hall.

KOLB, D. (1984) *Experiential Learning.* Hemel Hempstead, Herts: Prentice-Hall.

LAVE, J. and WENGER, E. (1991) *Situated Learning: Legitimate peripheral participation.* Cambridge: Cambridge University Press.

MARTON, F. and SALJO, R. (1984) Approaches to Learning. Chapter 3 in MARTON, F., HOUNSELL, D., and ENTWISTLE, N (eds) *The Experience of Learning.* Edinburgh: Scottish Academic Press.

MASLOW, A. (1943) A Theory of Human Motivation. *Psychological Review,* 50, (4), 370–396.

NEENAN, M. and DRYDEN, W. (2002) *Life Coaching: A cognitive-behavioural approach.* Hove: Brunner-Routledge.

PERRY, W. (1981) Cognitive and Ethical Growth: The Making of Meaning. Chapter 3 in CHICKERING, A.W. (ed) *The Modern American College.* London: Jossey-Bass.

PERRY, W. (1999) *Forms of Ethical and Intellectual Development in the College Years: a scheme.* San Francisco: Jossey Bass.

PIAGET, J. (1963) *The Origins of Intelligence in Children.* Cornwall: Norton.

REVANS, R. (1982) *The Origins and Growth of Action Learning.* Kent: Chartwell Bratt.

ROGERS, C. and FREIBERG, H. (1994) *Freedom to Learn.* 3rd ed. New York: Macmillan College Publishing Company.

SCHON, D. (1983) *The Reflective Practitioner: How professionals think in action.* New York: Basic Books.

SKINNER, B. (1953) *Science and Human Behaviour.* Hants: Macmillan, and (1974) *About Behaviourism. London:* Jonathon Cape.

WENGER, E. (1998) *Communities of Practice: Learning, meaning and identity.* Cambridge: Cambridge University Press.

WINSTANLEY, D. GABRIEL, Y. and LITTLEJOHNS, M. (2003) *From Learning to Practice.* Report of research funded by Imperial College Teaching Research Grants Scheme, Imperial College, London: Tanaka Business School.

Time management

AIMS AND LEARNING OUTCOMES

The aim of this chapter is to make you more effective at work and study through better management of your time. There are two main points to understand in this chapter: one is that time management is a choice, over which we do have control, and the other is that it is a habit, which requires practice to learn.

As a result of reading this chapter you will be able to:

- **identify your own time management problems and time bandits**

- **appreciate common problems of balancing priorities, and keeping to objectives**

- **identify a realistic approach to improving your own time management**

- **develop a more disciplined approach to your work**

- **prioritise well, and be more effective at work**

- **create good habits in time management, by putting thought into action.**

INTRODUCTION

This chapter will begin with a definition of time management, and will then discuss common time management problems, and invite you to identify your own issues. It then moves on to examine possible solutions and the guiding principles of time management. To check your understanding there will be a number of scenarios and exercises to practise time management skills, followed by a personal contract aimed at improving your own approach to time management.

WHAT IS TIME MANAGEMENT?

Time management involves making the best use of time, and getting more done in the time available. It means not wasting time on irrelevant things, instead focusing on important parts of the job. Ultimately this means working calmly and effectively, avoiding the panic and anxiety of the last-minute rush.

In the western world, time is treated as a valuable resource which people spend. Most managers claim that they do not have enough time. Often this is blamed on the organisation and colleagues for making too many demands. However, we all have at least some control over how we spend our time. We can and do make choices. Recognising this is the first step on the path to effective time management.

DEFINITION OF TIME MANAGEMENT

Time management means taking more control over how we spend our time and making sensible decisions about the way we use it.

If good time management is about taking control, it involves finding those areas where you do have control, and also finding those where you think you don't, but really you do. For example you may have far too many things to do and this makes you feel helpless, but maybe you have the option of renegotiating some parts of your work, or even delegating some activities. There may still be some areas where you don't have control – for example if a key part of the job is to be available at a certain time to provide advice to others, you cannot just decide to be absent. Or you may have a coursework assignment to submit – some deadlines are not renegotiable. In these areas it is more sensible not to waste time railing against these commitments; instead concentrate on finding those areas you *do* have the power to change, and make the changes that will help you to become more effective.

Exercises 2.1 and 2.2 should start to help you identify those problem areas and areas where you would like to make changes.

PREPARATION FOR CHANGE

Before reading further in this chapter it is helpful for you to have an idea of how effective you are as a time manager. Reflecting on your own time bandits and traps will make this chapter more useful and relevant to you.

Begin by brainstorming three barriers that you think prevent you from being effective at work, or at study, as indicated in Exercise 2.1. Now go on to Exercise 2.2 and rate your effectiveness using the list provided. This list has been developed by distilling some of the common problems that have been identified by several hundred staff and students in workshops held over the last five years at Imperial College. Further exercises and self-evaluation checks are provided on the website.

The accuracy of this tool depends on you being honest with yourself, so make sure you rate yourself according to how you actually behave, not how you would like to be. Once you have done Exercise 2.2 you can return to Exercise 2.1 and see if the barriers you first identified relate to those issues you have rated 3 in Exercise 2.2, and if necessary add to, or amend, your answers to Exercise 2.1.

EXERCISE 2.1   BARRIERS TO BEING EFFECTIVE
What are the three main barriers you have that prevent you being effective?

EXERCISE 2.2 DIAGNOSING YOUR TIME MANAGEMENT PROBLEMS

Go through the list of time management problems below and rate each one with relation to its frequency as a problem for you and also its severity using the following ratings: 0 = this problem does not relate to me 1 = this problem partly relates to me, relates some of the time 2 = this is a regular problem for me 3 = this is a major problem for me, it severely hampers my effectiveness	**Note: assess your behaviour as it is not as you would like it to be**
A. Prioritisation and scheduling	
1. I am not sure what tasks I have to do each day, I don't make a to-do list.	0 1 2 3
2. When I have finished one job I just go on to the next without checking on my priorities.	0 1 2 3
3. I don't work out which tasks have the biggest gain for me.	0 1 2 3
4. I have difficulty in setting priorities.	0 1 2 3
5. I have difficulty in keeping to priorities or a schedule I have set.	0 1 2 3
6. I am a perfectionist and even if I have several tasks to do I allow myself to spend ages on one task to get it right, which can cause problems in completing my work.	0 1 2 3
7. I often do trivial tasks at my high-energy time of day.	0 1 2 3
8. I don't stop to think when my best time of day is for working.	0 1 2 3
B. Persistence, procrastination and focus	
9. I flit from task to task, starting a lot of things but not always finishing them.	0 1 2 3
10. I feel very intimidated by large important tasks, and don't break them down into smaller ones.	0 1 2 3
11. I put off difficult tasks until the last possible moment.	0 1 2 3
12. I procrastinate, prevaricate and can't decide what to do, nor make decisions.	0 1 2 3

13. I put thing off until the last minute and then I have to work in a rush and panic.	0 1 2 3
14. I allow myself to be interrupted from my work, for example by the phone, talking to others, distractions, new e-mails coming in.	0 1 2 3
15. I spend ages on the telephone, surfing the net, or answering e-mails.	0 1 2 3
16. Once I get started, I cannot stop a task, even if it is taking far too much time and there are other pressing things to do.	0 1 2 3
17. I don't have any protected time in the day when I can get on with my priorities.	0 1 2 3
C. Role definition	0 1 2 3
18. I am not sure what my key objectives are.	0 1 2 3
19. I am unclear of my role definitions and lines of responsibility.	0 1 2 3
20. I'm not sure how long certain tasks take so find it hard to allocate the appropriate time to them.	0 1 2 3
21. I try and do everything myself, and do not consider whether it would be better to delegate tasks, or ask for more help and support.	0 1 2 3
D. Work environment and organisation	
22. My workspace is a mess, I can never find anything at work, and papers pile up around me without being filed.	0 1 2 3
23. I don't know what to do with paper – I just leave it hanging around.	0 1 2 3
24. I don't have anywhere where I can work uninterrupted.	0 1 2 3
25. My work environment is noisy and distracting, and I don't find ways to deal with this.	0 1 2 3
26. If I find myself with free time in the day, for example when commuting, waiting for an appointment, I don't have things with me to do.	0 1 2 3

E.	**Study skills**	
27.	I take ages to read anything, and find it hard to remember what I have read.	0 1 2 3
28.	I'm not sure how to go about academic or work related reading.	0 1 2 3
F.	**Assertiveness**	
29.	I find it very hard to say 'no' to other people.	0 1 2 3
30.	I feel guilty if I am getting on with my own agenda and not focusing on helping others.	0 1 2 3
31.	I spend most of my time doing things for other people, and hardly any time getting on with my own agenda.	0 1 2 3
G.	**Anxiety, stress and emotion**	
32.	I worry a lot and regularly suffer from work related anxiety and stress.	0 1 2 3
33.	I don't feel very confident so I often worry that I'm not doing well or going about my work in the right way.	0 1 2 3
34.	I never have fun at work, I don't enjoy my work.	0 1 2 3
35.	I get very bored at work and this slows me down or allows me to get sidetracked.	0 1 2 3
36.	I find it hard to concentrate.	0 1 2 3
H.	**Life balance**	
37.	I don't have time for exercise, health, leisure, family, I just work all the time.	0 1 2 3
38.	I get very tired and exhausted at work.	0 1 2 3

Scoring

0–38 Averaging 0s and 1s
You are an excellent time manager

39–76 Averaging 1s and 2s
You have some areas to work on but overall you are an effective time manager

77–114 Averaging 2s and 3s
You have a big problem with time management and need to take action now to get yourself more in control of your time (but don't worry – that is what this chapter aims to do)

Below are some common examples of time management problems.

EXAMPLE 2.1 EXAMPLES OF TIME MANAGEMENT PROBLEMS

Work -related

'I work on a project to implement IT in my organisation, but I report to two bosses, the head of the IT Department, and the Project Leader – their demands of me are diverse and sometimes conflicting and very confusing, as a result I get in a mess.'

'I work in an open-plan office. I constantly get distracted by people talking on the phone, chatting across desks, stopping to talk to me. I just cannot concentrate on my work, and I end up frittering my time on superficial tasks whilst at work, and then working well into the night at home to catch up with the tougher parts of my work.'

'I am a design engineer and each part of the work I do seems to take at least three times longer than we estimate it will take, meaning that I spend a lot of time explaining why the work is late and reorganising schedules and activities. This impacts negatively on people further down the development process.'

'I set myself priorities but because I also work as a support service for other people in the organisation, I get inundated by e-mails and requests from others. I spend all my time meeting other people's demands and my priorities go out of the window!'

'Last year I spent ages developing a balanced scorecard system for the organisation to performance manage the managerial team, then a new director was appointed and he pulled the plug on months of work and asked me to set up a totally different scheme. It seems like much of my work is a waste of time.'

Study -related

'I am engaged in a part-time professional development programme 'Into Leadership' where I am attending day release modules, writing coursework assignments both individually and with a group, and am trying to juggle this in between a busy work schedule in my role in the Laboratories of a Government Department. I feel so panicked with all I have to do I end up feeling paralysed.'

'I don't seem to be able to get going early enough on my distance learning course assignments and so I often end up staying up into the early hours to get it in the following morning. The work is rushed and mediocre as a result, and I am then tired for days after.'

'I have young children and I find it impossible to get on with my studying at home. As a result I feel incompetent when it comes to discussing case studies in course discussion because I haven't the faintest idea what they are about as I haven't read them in advance.'

WHERE DOES ALL MY TIME GO? – THE TIME BANDITS AND TRAPS

A time bandit is a work practice, attitude or behaviour that leads to ineffective working practices or your time getting stolen or expropriated away from your core priorities and frittered on less important activities.

Epicurus and the pleasure principle

Think about your own time management bandits and traps, do you see any patterns? One common pattern is to put the fun, exciting, interesting, easy things first, and put off doing the boring, dull, difficult tasks until later. It is a kind of pleasure principle – going for the short-term gains, surrendering to wants and desires as they arise – *immediately*. Epicurus, the philosopher who is attributed with setting up the foundations for a pleasure principle, believed in following desires. However, he is often mistakenly thought to have been a slave to avarice and pleasure, indulging himself in whatever desire arose at a given moment. This is not actually true. Epicurus followed a simple life, one of healthy food, friendship and good company, freedom and thought, not an undisciplined response to every whim and fancy. In relation to your own work or study, following the Epicurian principle will lead you to doing things you enjoy instead of focusing on your priorities.

It is a mistake to think that taking the easy route will improve things in the long run. In reality, giving in to the pleasure principle in the short term results in a mess later on, because over time what happens is the accumulation of a whole mountain of tasks that have been ignored. This can lead to misery, anxiety and depression. A lot of thought and planning went into Epicurus's way of life, and creating time for a balanced, enjoyable life takes planning and self-discipline.

The last-minute rush and adrenaline junky

Some people like to live fast and furiously, and so working in a calm systematic way can seem very boring. Waiting for a burst of energy, or the adrenaline rush that comes with the fear of a deadline looming can become a way of life, but does usually mean that when the job actually gets done, it is done in a haphazard panicky way, leaving the person exhausted after late-night working and long hours in order to finish it on time. In the long run health can be affected, as the fight or flight impulse that triggers adrenaline is intended for moments of danger, not a lifetime of stress.

Hamlet: the procrastinator

'To be or not to be . . .' – 'should I start this paper or go and deal with those statistics, I don't know!' It isn't noble to play Hamlet unless you are Lawrence Olivier! If it can't be faced now, it might be worse later! What is more, as well as getting nothing done, the agony is repeated over and over again, and usually by tomorrow there is no change except the *increased* anxiety of another day gone by without completing the task. There are different reasons for procrastination and prevarication: not having the energy (which is represented by the adrenaline junky above), not having a starting point or the right information (but will you have the information tomorrow?), or being indecisive over what exactly to get on and do. All that happens is that work piles up.

It's all too much

However, for some people, being busy is a way of life. They may ask themselves:

- Where does all my time go?
- Why are there not enough hours in the day?

Typically these people then fool themselves with the thought 'Well, this is just a busy period, once I've got this assignment or deadline over then life will be easier and I can relax'. This is fine if true, but often one deadline out of the way can just open someone up to a new deadline, as they rush from one hectic task to the next. Sometimes this is self-generated: they can't help but take on more and more and more.

Another way they fool themselves is to say 'I'm a no-limit person. I can keep on taking on more and more and more'. No one is superman or superwoman, there are only 1,440 minutes in a day, 1,000 when we deduct sleeping, washing, dressing, eating, etc, etc, etc. In our lives we probably spend six months waiting for red traffic lights to change, two years looking for things, 24 years asleep .... There is only so much time left, and time is not infinitely elastic, we do have limits. After all, no one ever said on their deathbed:

> I wish I'd spent more time at the office!

The headless chicken: action without thought

There may be other reasons for taking on too much work, being too busy or feeling driven. Some people may be working hard but without having clear priorities, and without planning. Spending much too much time on things that are not at all important. Giving the illusion of working hard but not working productively.

The butterfly: flitting from task to task

> Helen arrives at work, puts her coat on the door peg, sits down and turns on the computer. She intends to spend the morning writing the proposal for the new performance appraisal system – a very important part of her job. But first she listens to her telephone messages and realises Gerald wants her to produce some figures for a meeting the following week. She accesses her computer to pull out the figures, and notices she has 21 e-mails, and begins trawling through these. The first few she just looks at and leaves open to come back to later, the sixth one asks her to give some dates for a meeting and she opens her diary to look at dates, and sees that for one of the dates she has a presentation to give on that day. Oh she must remember to take the files home for preparing the presentation so she can do it at the weekend. She gets up and opens her filing cabinet to retrieve them .. ... Oh dear, she is feeling rather giddy, ... she hasn't got anything done and she has been at work an hour already .... Oh she feels so confused, she thinks ... I'd better go and get a coffee ....

One result of not planning or sticking to priorities can be the 'butterfly'. This is someone who flits from task to task in a downward spiral of panic and anxiety, getting in a mess, never getting the boost and closure of completion. Many managers have to be butterflies, for example Mintzberg (1973) and Kotter (1982) showed that managers spend nine minutes or less on 50 per cent of their activities, are subject to constant interruptions and that management is a very fragmented activity. Good time management brings order to this fragmentation, rather than exacerbates it.

Interruptions, interruptions

There are two types of interruptions: interruptions from others that distract us from our work, and 'self' interruptions, ways in which we distract ourselves from our intended activities.

What is your working environment like – quiet and easy to concentrate in, or noisy and busy? Some people work in open-plan office environments where they cannot help but get drawn into conversations with others. Think how you manage your interruptions, what happens if you are concentrating on something really important and somebody starts casually chatting to you as they pass your desk or door?

The proliferation of communication technologies has meant there are a myriad of ways in which we can be interrupted at any time of day. The ding of a new e-mail arriving in the computer, the ringing telephone, the mobile phone, just ensure you are available 24 hours a day 7 days a week. Take the telephone – this is designed for people to contact you when it is convenient for them, not necessarily for you. Some people spend a long time on the phone, not getting to the point, getting sidetracked into idle talk. How long are your phone calls, could they be shorter? E-mail is also a tempter. In some roles people are receiving 50–100 e-mails a day and if every time one arrives on the computer they stopped what they were doing to look at it, it would never be possible to concentrate.

The escapologist: IT and other escapes

However, it isn't just the requirements of others that interrupt us – we also interrupt ourselves. For example, maybe by not being able to resist surfing the Net for another couple of hours, just having a look at a couple more search paths for a holiday or outing.

Some are self-interrupters, maybe finding it difficult to concentrate they just have to go off for another coffee or go and chat to someone else, because they can't quite get down to it. This can be even worse at home – when you spot the washing or ironing or vacuuming out of the corner of your eye. It is amazing how you can suddenly feel the urge to do a bit of gardening or even jobs you normally hate like cleaning the cooker suddenly seem compelling when you are trying to get down to work on a challenging report.

The doormat: yes, yes, yes

One problem can be unassertiveness, or unwillingness to say 'no': This may be because of low internal self-esteem, wanting to 'please others' in order to feel good, or even being too scared to say no. Ironically always saying 'yes' may just mean a person is taken for granted, not necessarily respected and liked. In the end, they can cause more problems for other people, because they become ill or are too busy to do everything to which they have committed, which can be very irritating for others.

Presenteeism

Sam was always first into the office every day and last to leave in the evening. Everyone commented on how committed he was, what a hardworking member of staff. One day Sarah wondered what Sam was actually working on all day at the computer screen, she wandered up to his desk and looked over his shoulder, and found he was playing solitaire!

Being at a desk doesn't mean the same as working – it is passing time instead of spending time. Sometimes the most effective people are those you don't see, maybe they find somewhere quiet to work where they don't get interrupted. Effective people don't necessarily need to impress on others how hard they work – their output is more important than the appearance of work. Some office environments, however, encourage presenteeism – focusing performance evaluation on time spent at the desk, clockwatching, rather than on the quality of work.

Wasted spaces

It has been calculated that people lose up to 20 per cent of their time waiting. All that time spent sitting on the train into work, or waiting for the printer to finish, or a lecture or meeting to start are wasted periods that could have been used to complete a small task, or even begin a bigger one. Do you sit and stare realising you don't have any work at hand for such occasions, or does it even occur to you in the first place to fill these spaces? Sometimes a commuter journey is the ideal space in which to plan the day, write out a schedule, or maybe even concentrate on reading an article or report. Finishing a small task, such as filling in a form, or even beginning a larger task can be slotted into these moments.

Perfectionist

The perfectionist pays attention to detail, agonises over every decision, every word in a report. They must get it right. But what is the point if it is too late, or they have ignored several other things – is it all really necessary? Not all tasks have to be done to the same high standard: writing a routine e-mail for example – does it really matter if the grammar is correct?

Paper mountains

Some people allow a mountain of paper to pile up on their desk, around their floor – a trail of paper that doesn't allow them to be able to find anything they need. They can waste lots of time trying to find things, and the paper mountain doesn't make for good office sculpture, it festers and exudes stress and incompetence.

I'm in a meeting!

Consider the costs of 10 people in a one-hour meeting at £50 per hour each plus all the overheads and opportunity costs, the time spent travelling, preparation – is it worth it? Worse still are those meetings where people are unprepared, there is no agenda; the chair allows the discussion on trivial items to go on for ages without coming to any decisions.

> Heather was chairing a students union General Purposes Committee meeting. The meeting discussed for an hour the subject of what colour the new minibus should be – the Labour Society rep suggested red, the Conservative Group rep blue, the Liberal democrat member orange, and the chap from the Greens said they shouldn't have a minibus at all! Eventually the meeting ran out of time and the main item on the agenda – what to do about the student debt situation never got discussed!

Poorly run meetings are not only a waste of time, but also very demoralising.

D-I-Y enthusiast

The D-I-Y enthusiast thinks they can do everything themselves, never giving a thought to delegation or sharing the work with others. Moreover, when they get into trouble, they don't go and ask for help, they soldier on miserably, not getting anywhere except lost and desperate. If you have too much to do, or are stuck, do you look to see how the work can be allocated differently, do you call in for help or the support of others?

Why oh why do D-I-Y? Refusing to ask for help may be due to lack of assertiveness, but it may also be arrogance – the belief that no one can do it as well, so it is better done single-handed. Other people will never learn the skills if they are not given a chance to start. Delegation is not just a downward action, it can also move upwards, for example where something really isn't a person's job maybe they need to refer it back.

THE CONSEQUENCES

Poor time management is one of the greatest sources of managerial stress. It leads to feelings of incompetence and anxiety. The debilitating symptoms and consequences of stress are discussed more fully in Chapter 9. It also leads to crisis management – where someone responds to whoever is pushing hardest or shouting the loudest. The working environment is likely to be cluttered, with piles of papers on the desk which heaves with awful tasks represented by bits of paper and post-its that decompose or fall off onto the floor. It doesn't just inconvenience the person creating this muddle – it inconveniences others who have to wait for work that is late, or shoddy work that has been done in a rushed way, or invitations that haven't been responded to. Poor time managers may also feel indispensable; so they can't take a holiday or a break, because no one can manage without them.

Given the choice it is unlikely you would decide to work in this way. But you are always given the choice, and the trick is to take back control and make choices that will make you better time managers. But why don't you do that already? It is because poor time management is a habit.

ARISTOTLE AND THE HABIT OF THE GOOD LIFE

It is quite likely that in identifying your own time bandits, you already had an idea what they were. You may even have a good idea of what you should be doing differently. This chapter is not about knowing what to do, it is about putting thought into action, and this requires behavioural change which is a bit trickier to effect.

Aristotle talked about the habit of the good life. The good life is not an abstract idea, it is a habit that is nurtured and acted upon over a period of time. Time management is a habit. It is likely you are accustomed to your habits, may even be comfortable with the way you do things, and they won't be easy to change, because that requires effort and persistence. Therefore it won't be enough if this chapter merely identifies for you what you should be doing differently. You have to break a habit, create a habit, and persevere to maintain it.

Below are some good habits, but for them to work and guarantee you more time, you will need to put them into practice. When we start something new, it is easier to take one step at a time, building up competence and new habits gradually. The personal contract at the end of this chapter will enable you to plan your behaviour change. Glance at this contract now, and you will see it requires you to identify three changes you intend to make, and to put the first step into practice in the following week. As you read through the good habits think which one would be most relevant for you to start with, which will give you the biggest gain, and which relates most closely to the problems you identified in Exercises 2.1 and 2.2.

THE GOOD HABITS OF TIME MANAGEMENT

Habit 1: The 'to do' list

Make a 'to-do' list. This could be either on a palm top or computer, or in a filofax or diary, though ideally this should be portable, as you will want to add to the list whenever you think of a new task and this may not occur when you are at your desk. This will prevent you going 'off task' every time you remember another thing to do. Simply add it to your list and return to the task in hand. This will stop the 'butterfly'. Writing things down will help you remember them and is a better recorder than your memory. You need to devise a system to suit you, but many people have a general list, and then a specific daily or weekly list of tasks to be achieved within a certain timeframe pulled out from the general list. A lot of people find it helpful to rank the items on their 'to-do' list in order of importance. Not everything is of equal importance.

More importantly, ticking jobs off a 'to-do' list can help you see and enjoy your achievements

Habit 2: Clear priorities

Identify your priorities and distinguish tasks that are *urgent* from tasks which are *important*. Urgent_tasks have an immediate impact. Important tasks have a significant impact. Do tasks in this order:

- urgent and important
- urgent (but do them quickly)
- important.

Try to prioritise important tasks. Don't be tempted to fill in odd moments with low-rated tasks. Try and at least start a more important task. If you don't watch out you'll find at the end of the day that you haven't done any of the important tasks but have merely cleared away some of the less important ones!

Be clear what the critical 20 per cent of your tasks are. Pareto's Law suggests that 20 per cent of the work produces 80 per cent of the results. Be clear what the critical 20 per cent of your tasks are and prioritise them.

Look at Table 2.1 below. In which box do you spend most of your time? Too much time in box one means being irresponsible and over dependent, as well as ineffective – you don't get down to anything important or urgent. Too much time in box 2 leads to short-termism and crisis management– you are ruled by urgency but don't do anything that is important. Working in box 3 on a regular rather than occasional basis leads to stress and burnout, as everything you do seems very important and urgent – you are constantly under pressure (see Example 2.2).

Table 2.1   *Time spent on urgent and important tasks*

4 **Not urgent** Quadrant of opportunity ■ development ■ innovation ■ planning	3 **Urgent/Important** Quadrant of pressure ■ crises ■ pressing problems ■ deadline-driven projects
1 **Not urgent/Not important** Quadrant of waste ■ escapes ■ routines ■ office politics	2 **Urgent/Not important** Quadrant of busyness ■ mail and e-mail ■ telephone ■ interruptions

(Developed from an original idea by Covey. S. p151)

Ideally you should be looking to be spending a significant proportion of your time in box 4 where your work can be more meaningful, effective, balanced and disciplined as well as more in your control!

EXAMPLE 2.2   TOO MUCH PRESSURE: SALLY THE SOCIAL WORKER

Sally is a social worker. For the past two years she had worked in a tough inner city borough with a very challenging environment, and above average levels of poverty, crime, drug use and mental illness. She had a very heavy caseload of mentally ill clients, some of whom could have been a danger to themselves or others, and she needed to monitor their position. She felt responsible for their well being, knowing that one mistake from her, and someone could be seriously injured or die. Even worse, there were five vacancies in her department and the council didn't seem able to recruit anyone to fill them. Her managers didn't listen to her view that her job was too much, and certainly didn't give her the support she needed to do a good job. Instead, as a result of the vacancies they loaded her up with more clients to cover the shortfall. She became exhausted, keeping their reports up to date, attending casework meetings, making decisions about their future. She went to see her doctor, as she was not sleeping, worrying about her job, her clients, and her persistent headaches, as well as experiencing palpitations. The doctor refused to give her more sleeping pills, and stronger painkillers, instead pointing out that she was heading for a nervous breakdown if she carried on working in that fashion. When she returned home from the doctor she thought through some of the things he had said and concluded 'I don't have to live like that'. That evening she prepared her cv and applied for a similar role in another borough where she knew the pressures weren't as great, and where there were more staff, greater support, and lower case loads. Two months later she is enjoying her new job and wonders 'why didn't I move before?'

Habit 3: Saying no and delegation

Not all tasks are relevant or appropriate for you to do. Ask yourself what will happen if you don't do a certain task? Does it matter? Some tasks can be deprioritised, or put on hold, or you can say 'no' if you decide not to do them at all. Chapter 7 on assertiveness provides some advice and ways to practise how to say 'no' assertively.

Alternatively some jobs are more appropriate to delegate. As you become more senior you may find you need to change your work role so you are doing less directly yourself, and spending more time delegating work to others. Delegation is not activity dumping, you need to check that the task is suitable for the person, and you need to clarify with them what needs to be done and to what performance standard and check they have the ability to do it and that it is appropriate to their role or development. You may also need to provide them with some coaching and other support, and ensure they have the responsibility and authority required. Many managers are afraid of 'letting go' feeling that they either are the only ones that can do the job effectively, or alternatively it will look as if they are a shirker, continually passing work on to others. This is often not the case, especially if they have considered carefully which tasks to delegate. It is worth examining your job and working out which tasks are most suitable for you to do and which tasks would more appropriately be done by a subordinate, colleague or even someone higher up the organisation.

Habit 4: The best use?

Try not to drift between tasks – as you complete one task don't float onto another. Stand back and ask yourself:

> What is the best use of my time now?

Be honest – it is very unlikely to be something trivial. It is more likely to be getting started on 'the big one'.

Habit 5: Achieving the big one – break it down

Nuclear power stations get built, rockets are launched into space, large, difficult projects happen. How? They are broken down into smaller and smaller chunks until each piece of the project, each stage of the schedule is do-able. The same principle is at work for us on our big, difficult tasks. We often avoid tackling large, important projects because they overwhelm us with their size and importance. If something appears to be too difficult, then the first thing you need to do is break it down into smaller, achievable tasks. These tasks, which you can put on your to-do list, can then be given a schedule, and a priority, as in Example 2.3.

EXAMPLE 2.3   ACHIEVING THE BIG ONE BY BREAKING IT DOWN

Steve had a presentation to do that he was dreading, it seemed so daunting. 200 people would be there, including some very important people, and it would be the culmination of months of work on a project. He decided to brainstorm a 'to -do' list of all the tasks involved in doing the presentation: identify the message, the audience and their needs, key ideas and points for the content, having an introduction, a middle and an end, work out what IT support and other aids he would use, decide on the extra reading and research needed. He then decided to fit all these into a logical order. Instead of panicking, he decided his first hour should be spent that evening at home where he wouldn't be interrupted, with some classical music on the CD, planning it, writing down his key message, followed by producing an outline structure. For the following day at work he scheduled a couple of hours in the afternoon for reading and research, getting the materials together to build up his evidence and information. In a third session he decided to design some slides and pay more attention to making the presentation stimulating for the audience, introduce some anecdotes and illustrations, maybe even having a practice run-through in his head. In a fourth session he decided he would rope in a friend, Tony, get him round for a drink, and get him to listen to him practising the presentation. Tony was an experienced presenter, he would be bound to have some tips, and he owed him one for fixing his computer. In the last session a few days before the presentation he would allow time to redesign his slides, change around the format of the session, and maybe write a short handout to accompany it. That would allow for any slippage should anything go wrong.

Listing out tasks and then making a schedule is an important place to start, because you can get into a mess by omitting to create something tangible and concrete. Having a schedule gives you a feeling of control, and also means that in each session your mind can concentrate on the task in hand, rather than the project in its entirety, facing one do-able task at a time, thus avoiding the feeling of overload.

Habit 6: Do it now: get started!

Of course finding a task too difficult is not the only reason for delay. Procrastination is a great time bandit, and the irony is that all it does is increase feelings of anxiety. Anticipatory anxiety is 9 times out of 10 worse than actually getting on and doing something. Work out where your block is – and gently lift it out of the way.

Think of a child who is scared of the dark, maybe she sees shadows dancing on her bedroom wall, and she starts fearing that a robber is going to come through her window. However, when she turns the light on, she finds the shadows were nothing more than the trees waving outside, and there is nothing there after all. Metaphorically we need to 'turn the light on': getting started means working out what needs to be done and starting, rather than freezing in the headlights of your own fear.

Sometimes it is not anxiety that makes you defer, but indecisiveness. In 95 per cent (at least) of cases you won't have better information later so you might as well begin immediately and clear the task.

A common fear is putting pen to paper, particularly for the perfectionist, yet it is amazing how once you get started, you can even find enjoyment in that difficult job you have been dreading. In any case, a written first draft is rarely very polished, so it may be a good idea to lower your expectations and tell yourself it is more important to finish a draft, however poor, in order to create something to work on and polish, than to not begin at all and miss an important deadline. Beware of disappearing into a lot of unimportant, non-urgent activities to give yourself the illusion of action.

The adrenaline junky mentioned above may need to go one step further and find a way of putting pressure on that bit earlier. One way of doing this is to set an earlier deadline and externalise it. See for example James in Example 2.4.

EXAMPLE 2.4   CREATE AN EARLY DEADLINE

James is a research scientist who has a paper to do for a conference that takes place on 1 May. It is now 1 April. Normally he would spend days avoiding the task, and then a couple of days before the conference stay up all night working on it, arriving at the conference tired and exhausted. Instead James could contact his group manager and suggest that he get a first draft of the paper to him by 14 April, or alternatively suggest he circulate a draft to his research group for comments on that date. By creating an earlier deadline, and then externalising it, he can give himself the feeling of pressure he needs to work, but without having to go through the process of turning into a nervous wreck.

Habit 7: Re-engineer your day, best time for best tasks

Some people are larks – they get up early in the morning, bright and raring to go, yet by mid afternoon they are flagging. Others are owls, they drag themselves out of bed, sit sleepily at their desk in the morning, but then by evening they are ready to work, full of energy, burning the midnight oil. Different people have different 'best times' – what is your best time of day for working? Ideally you should aim to re-engineer your day so that you undertake your critical 20 per cent and your top priorities when you are at your best. Likewise you could save your routine work for when you are tired, and your energy is low.

EXAMPLE 2.5   DAVID HOCKNEY AND THE TEA BAGS!

On a visit to the Tate Modern I looked at a piece of art by David Hockney. It consisted of a packet of tea bags. What made him paint tea bags I wondered? I listened through the earphones to hear the commentary to this painting. Apparently Hockney liked to get up early in the morning to do his painting then, but at that time the café wasn't open so he had to bring his own tea bags into his workplace. By mid afternoon he was often really tired, so regularly he would down tools, pack up and go and watch a film, maybe coming back later, refreshed.

How much more effective do you think you could be if you redesigned your working day to fit with your own natural rhythm. This may be a daily rhythm, or even one over longer periods of time. Certainly some people like to work in quick bursts, others work more steadily.

EXAMPLE 2.6   A LION OR A DUNG BEETLE?

At a talk at Imperial College given by the top biographer Victoria Glendinning someone asked how she worked. Victoria gave the analogy of the lion and the dung beetle. The lion sits there lazily for hour upon hour upon hour, and then suddenly sees her prey and is full of energy, violently chasing and capturing it. A hurricane of energy and vitality. When the activity is finished, the lion returns lazily to sitting and basking in the sun or shade, until her appetite prompts her back into action. On the other hand the dung beetle finds a small lump of dung and laboriously pushes it and pushes it and pushes it, until eventually it rolls over the blade of grass, and it carries on laboriously pushing and pushing and pushing, on and on and on. Victoria said she would really like to be a lion in the way she worked, working with short bursts of high energy. Regrettably she said she was more like a dung beetle, plodding away day after day.

Habit 8: Cut yourself off: find a hideaway

Re-engineering your day also may mean training others to respect your concentration time. This may not always be possible in noisy office environments. You may need to find somewhere quiet where you can work effectively – it may even mean taking work home, or working in a library, or at least away from the office and the distractions of colleagues. For this to be effective, you need to make sure your performance is being judged by outcomes and not process.

EXAMPLE 2.7   XEROX AND RE-ENGINEERING THE DAY

Lotte Bailyn, a professor at MIT helped staff at Xerox to re-engineer their working lives. As well as changing their work schedule, it meant that staff had to learn that others may have times when they weren't available. For this to be successful it also meant that staff needed to provide times when they were available, and advertise these so that they could be contacted.

The principle is that if you remove something, such as your constant availability all times of the day, you need to provide something to replace it, such as office hours when you can guarantee to be available and give others your attention. For example you may decide your best work times are 10–12.00 am and you may hide yourself away at these times, removing yourself from the office or putting up a 'Do not disturb' sign, but in return you say that three days a week you are available 1.00–3.00pm for inquiries. Alternatively, work at home one day a week – this increasingly becomes more possible for more and more people as communication technologies mean you can be reached if absolutely necessary, and you can connect to your workplace by computer.

Habit 9: Wait productively

Now is the time to start using up those odd 5–10-minute slots which everyone has in their days and which we tend to think can't be used productively. They can! If you have trouble getting started on tasks you dislike, use one of the small slots to face up to it. Often knowing that you'll only have to spend a few minutes on it is enough to get you to face up to it. Once you've started it you can usually continue it. Alternatively reading is a good space-filler, and you may find you get to like this habit, looking forward to your commuter journey, and uninterrupted time for reading those books or reports. You just need to make sure you bring the documents with you, but beware, don't cruise with documents, don't become laden down with work to do as you go too and from work. Only take with you what you will need, otherwise the work will become like a millstone you carry around with you.

Habit 10: Killing two birds with one stone

Type A personalities are people who are driving, ambitious, competitive, restless, always liking to be on the go, unlike type B people who are more laid back, calm and take life a bit more easily. These different types are discussed more fully in Chapter 9. Type As like this habit – doing two tasks at once. This works particularly well when you have lots of trivial tasks to do – for example you could be signing letters or viewing e-mails when on the telephone to that manager who does tend to go on rather.

EXAMPLE 2.8   KILLING TWO BIRDS WITH ONE STONE!

Stephanie had a research student, Richard, who wanted her to provide him with some reading on a topic. Stephanie had been asked to do a book review for a journal on the same topic by mid-January, and it was now the middle of December, and at first glance the book seemed to be an-up-to-date review of the literature in this area. Stephanie really didn't have the time to get started on the book review, nor spend time getting more references for Richard. She had an idea – she proposed to Richard that he borrow the book over Christmas to read, and they do the book review jointly, with him making notes on the book over the vacation. Richard was delighted, he had also wanted to ask Stephanie to help him start publishing material, and doing a joint book review seemed a good place to start practising his skills.

Although in Stephanie's case the action meant she had less to do, in some cases it can make you busier. If you are a type A person, don't over do it: type A's are also more prone to heart attacks! Likewise if you are 'a butterfly' don't use this as an excuse to get in a mess, and remember, difficult tasks will require your whole attention.

Another related technique is to take a number of trivial tasks or related tasks and bunch them together. Often you can build up greater speed if you are clearing up several tasks, such as form-filling, at once. Order tasks so you cut down on travelling, for example pick up the office stationery next time you are down in the basement photocopying in the room along the corridor, rather than making an extra visit – it also means you don't just stand at the photocopier staring into space.

Habit 11: Once Is enough

There are four things you can do with a piece of paper: 1: bin it; 2. act on it; 3. pass it on; or 4. file it for use another time. Picking up a note, putting it down again, picking it up later, shuffling it round your desk until the next piece of paper comes in to bury it underneath – is not doing one of those four things. Handle each piece of paper once. This is not easy, but it is rewarding. Why do people let paper hover round their workspace? Often because they are indecisive, they don't know what to do with it. Stop deferring decisions. Don't hoard items to read later – you won't. You never have so far, so it is unlikely you are about to start. The bin is a 'business information neutraliser' that should be used more often, and the 'delete' button on the computer is an underutilised tool – use it, rather than letting clutter build up and paralyse you with a pile of 'indecisions'.

Of course there is some material that doesn't need immediate attention, and you may be about to get started on something important and don't want to allow bits of paper to divert you from that important task. In that case mark the material you need to return to later with the relevant date and put a note in your diary/'to-do' list to remind you. Or set up a reminder system and use recall notes. Sometimes people use computer packages such as Microsoft office and calendar to input dates so that the computer reminds them when to turn attention to a task or activity.

Habit 12: Tidy up

You do need to have a place for everything, and everything in its place. If you have allowed your workspace to become untidy and cluttered tackling it can seem intimidating. It is made more daunting by the likelihood that it is full of those papers you don't know what to do with, are too indecisive to deal with, find too difficult to tackle, so that you don't know where to begin. So how do you start? Habit 11 will have set up the first method – dealing with all new material using the four alternatives idea. As for the rest, you need to schedule a time in your diary, in a low energy time of day, maybe after lunch or at the end of the day to catch up with filing.

Begin by obtaining whatever equipment you need to climb this paper mountain: filing cabinets, files and folders, and try and make them appealing to look at. Then start the climb up the paper mountain by tackling the paper on your desk. Once you have a clear desk you will feel more relaxed at work. Try and move all paper extraneous to whatever you are working on out of sight – it will be less likely to distract you then. Next, move to the other surfaces and then the floor. Horizontal filing (that is, in filing cabinets) is more time effective than vertical filing (piles on the floor). A note on the geology of paper mountains: they form very easily, stroking encourages their formation, dust makes them fester.

If you are still feeling it is all too much to tackle, just imagine what you will feel like walking into a tidy office. Picture how your office could look when you arrive in the morning – isn't that a much more pleasurable start to the day? If you find it very difficult to throw away material, take the *zero based* rule. Imagine there had been a fire in your office, and all the paper was burnt – which files, pieces of paper or data would you really miss? Or imagine this was your first day at work, which bits of paper would you find essential to be able to do your job? This is the information you need and for electronic data make sure you have a copy backed up in a separate place on the computer. Some paper is difficult to throw away because it is represents our history. Other bits of paper may be useful at some point in the future. If you are really not certain, box the material up, label it and put it in a loft or somewhere out of the way, and then see whether you need to get it down over the next year. If you haven't, you could then throw it away.

Habit 13: The electronic battlefield

It is not just paper that can clutter our workspace – there is now the electronic battlefield also, and the never-ending stream of e-mails and SPAM that arrives on our computers. Just because it is in electronic form doesn't mean it's not rubbish. Delete and file as you go rather than letting old messages hang around and clog up your system.

Begin by limiting the times of day you are going to look at your e-mails and stick to them. For many people it won't be more than three times: first thing in the morning, after lunch and when you finish work. When you look at your e-mails skim through them to check if anything is urgent or very important. If it is not, decide a time of day when you can deal with the non-important/urgent messages as a group and make sure it is not your best time!

You could also go one step further and set up electronic folders for your filing to mirror any paper filing system you have. You could even divert your e-mails into these folders automatically, for example anything personal into a separate folder to look at later. Do not let other people's agendas rule your day – immediate responses are not often required.

If you are feeling like taking this even further you could arrange to get yourself training in all the functions of your office software, such as the diary and calendar, many of which are designed to help with time management. Alternatively when you have a free half-hour, explore the functions on your office software, or read the manual, or an introductory basic guide – you may be amazed at what you could do. However, the computer is just as often a hindrance as a help, and there may be times when you need to unplug yourself in order to concentrate and not get distracted from the important task in hand.

Habit 14: Active reading

Students have particular time management difficulties related to reading. It is quite easy for someone to spend hours, even days, reading a book, only to discover a couple of weeks later they can't remember anything they read, their time has effectively been wasted. The situation is made even more difficult with Internet search engines and electronic access to journals, making more books and articles available than ever before. Effectively, the number of publications on any topic is infinite; it is certainly not possible to read everything on a given subject. Reading can become like painting the Forth Bridge, a never-ending activity, unless you prioritise. Therefore you have to be selective and engage in *active reading.*

The first step in active reading is to skim abstracts to see how relevant material is. Go for quality rather than quantity, don't download everything. Is it relevant, is it widely cited, does it appear in a top journal?

Once you have narrowed down the focus for your reading, you can then concentrate on how you read. Skim through first of all to check how useful it is really going to be. Then when you start reading in detail make sure you are actively engaging with the material by asking the following:

- How would I sum up the message in this article in a few sentences?
- What are the key points?
- In what way will I use this article – does it provide me with material for an argument in an essay, an example methodology to use, or what? How can I use this material?
- How would I critique this article – what are its strengths and weaknesses, do I agree with it, how would I classify it in the literature, are there holes in its argument and approach?
- Are there any quotes I need to take down exactly?
- What information do I need about the reference itself?

The third step is to consider note taking. Are you going to use a highlighter pen and jot down some notes in the margin and keep a photocopy or electronic copy of the article? You may decide to keep all your references in Endnote or Reference Manager or some proprietary software for referencing. There is nothing more time wasting than to find you need a full reference and haven't got it, so need to go and track down the source, or the page numbers or authors.

Habit 15: Look after the goose

Steven Covey (1989), in his book *The 7 Habits of Effective People* provides the example of the goose that lays the golden egg. Assume you are the goose, and your work is the egg. If you exhaust yourself, work yourself into the ground, how can you expect to be able to continue to produce the golden eggs? Everyone knows organic, free-range produced eggs are better than battery farmed ones. Why allow yourself to become a battery farmed animal? Take care of yourself, value yourself enough to give yourself time to relax, time off, not life as one hard slog. So work productively rather than to burnout.

This applies especially over exams: working longer and longer without break can lead to exhaustion and ineffectiveness. You deserve a break, and need to keep replenishing your batteries. It is not just long working hours that you need to avoid, but also destructive 'self-talk'. Examine the self-talk that stops you from doing things immediately: 'I can't do this', 'I'm no good', and put in place more constructive self-talk, and find others to reinforce it. You CAN do it!

Address those niggling anxieties and self-doubt. What are they really about?

EXAMPLE 2.9   ALBERT KUSHLICK: A TRULY FALLIBLE HUMAN BEING!

I went to the memorial service for a good personal friend, Albert Kushlick. Albert was one of the most incredible therapists I have come across. Albert, a South African who had come to England to escape the Apartheid regime and imprisonment for his work alongside Mandela, had become an eminent rational emotive therapist. No one who knew Albert was not affected by him. I even chose to spend the night before my own PhD viva at his house, because I knew that if anyone could calm me down and help me feel confident, it was Albert. He made a significant impact on many people's lives and it was not surprising to see so many come to his memorial service to pay their respects. On the front of the booklet for the service there was a picture of Albert, and instead of the expected list of all the amazing deeds he had done in his life, there was the simple statement: 'Albert Kushlick, a truly fallible human being'. That had made me laugh, and remember a story Albert had once told me about how he had travelled across America to arrive at 10 o'clock at night on the doorstep of the therapist he saw as a master of the profession. He was late, but he had travelled for over a day, and when the man opened the door he had grumpily said 'Get lost, you are too late, I'm going to bed!'

We are all fallible human beings, even experts at the top of their profession. Generally we try to do the best that we can. No one has foresight, so all you can do is make the best decisions you can in the circumstances and move on, even if events later prove you to have been wrong. So stop beating yourself up, and do the best you can. Put mistakes down to experience and move on constructively.

Habit 16: Adopt a habit

Time management is a habit. You are trying to change deeply entrenched habits. This takes time. Adopt *one* new habit at a time. Move from theory to practise … practise … practise, dipping your toe in the water and having a go will show you that you can do it …. But before you move on to fill in the personal contract it is worth just having a quick practice at these new skills by using the scenarios below!

TIME MANAGEMENT SCENARIOS

Take 15 minutes to read the following scenarios and to write down what you would do next in each case. You may like to also consider whether what you would really do differs significantly from what you think you ought to do, looking at the habits listed above.

EXERCISE 2.3   THE SCENARIOS

Scenario 1

8.00am Monday morning, uggh! You had a fantastic week away at a conference, and didn't get back until 2.00am last night, having stopped off at a friend's house to break up the drive home, but wish you hadn't. You have got a whole afternoon of meetings, a team presentation to organise for tomorrow to give to another department on the work your team does, and a report to get in by the end of the week. You make your way downstairs to make a cup of tea, and ooooh, there are about 10 letters waiting for you on the doormat. You idly turn on your computer as you wait for the kettle to boil, and your curiosity is aroused by 17 e-mails waiting for you, and one looks as if it is about a possible project idea that you have been pursuing, which might lead to a lucrative new contract. You get out your briefcase, and notice two documents that should be back at your work library in two hours, and it will take you 50 minutes on the tube to get into work. As you open the fridge to get out the milk, oh no, it's stale, and there is nothing else in the fridge, you forgot to shop, and yes, the calendar next to the fridge reminds you that you offered to have your team round for dinner tonight. As you start getting dressed, your heart starts to pump and you can feel that knot of anxiety beginning to clench in your stomach. Oh no not another of those days where you run round like a headless chicken, panicked out and getting nowhere.

How do you spend your first hour?

Scenario 2

11.00am Monday morning, and you are sat at your desk at work trying to get on with your report.

'Hi, how did the conference go? I'm dying to hear all the news, and I've got some ideas on that plan you were presenting.' It's Mike, a member of your team, come for a quiet chat. You would so love to give him the rundown on how it all went, but say:

'I'm so busy.'

'Oh I know, tell me about it, it's so hectic around here, you will never believe what has been going on, I've got a really juicy bit of news to tell you.' And he makes to sit down and start launching into his story.

What do you do and say?

Scenario 3

You are just getting back to your report when you realise that you have left some of the most important statistics that you had downloaded from the Internet, at home. As you search in vain through the pile of papers on your desk, you find a visa card statement that you need to pay off today, and the bank is only five minutes away. You also find that birthday card you meant to send off to your sister, for which you still need to get a stamp. You also feel it would have helped to e-mail your boss to clarify some details about this report, such as how long it should be, and should you focus more on providing one solution to the problem or alternatively provide several options. You are now beginning to feel confused, oh you need a coffee to clear your head, it is spinning, and you haven't put pen to paper yet.

What do you do?

Debriefing

Actually, it is not as easy as you think. It is likely you are torn between what you know you would be likely to do, and that may include bad habits, and what you think you should do having read through the suggested list of good habits. It is likely it will take you a bit more effort to move from the 'should' to the 'do' but that is what the personal contract is intended to do below.

Taking Scenario 1, given the predicament, a good place to start would be writing a long list of things to do, and then prioritising them in a grid identifying urgent and important (see habits 1 and 2). For example in the urgent and important box you could put the presentation and your afternoon meetings, in the important but not urgent box the report, in the urgent but not important box scanning your e-mails and messages, getting the documents back to the library, buying milk, the shopping and the dinner party. In the not urgent and not important box are the letters and many e-mails. Looking at an effective path through this, you could consider beginning by scanning e-mails, then going into work to get going on your report, stopping at the library on the way in. You have a killing two birds with one stone possibility of e-mailing your group before you leave to suggest that you all discuss the presentation over dinner, and a renegotiation opportunity to save time is that you may suggest dinner will be moved to your local pizzeria. The trap is to get caught answering e-mails, but you could print off the project opportunity to read on your commuter journey into work.

Scenario 2 is a common way in which we get interrupted. The sensible approach would be short and sweet and to the point: 'I'm too busy now, but I'd love to talk later, how about we meet for lunch?' Don't get drawn into talking about your busyness because that could mean you just get lost in a moan. Keep it brief and use your body language to confirm your statement. Other techniques people employ to avoid lengthy interruptions are:

- to set a time-limit – 'I have five minutes only'
- set the stage in advance – 'I'm leaving in five minutes'
- remain standing – it is harder to get into a long relaxed conversation that way
- meet others away from your office and workspace – preferably in their office, because it makes your getaway easier and is more difficult to get trapped
- avoid small talk, be ruthless but polite – get them to the point
- don't get dragged into long excuses that open the way to more conversation
- don't get railroaded.

Scenario 3 again places potential interruptions your way – paying your visa and buying a stamp for a birthday card. These are also killing two birds opportunities (on your way somewhere for example) and can also be clustered with other small jobs after you have got on with something more important. Plan when you are going to do these and don't just go off into 'the pleasure principle' of easy fun things like writing and sending a card. Making a note of when you will do thongs can ease your anxiety and stop it buzzing round in your head. Move the pile of papers off your desk to stop them distracting you, make a note of the papers you want to get hold of or download later, and get back to preparing your report. Don't let the lack of certain information stop you getting started. You can always slot it in later, and getting going may help you identify more clearly exactly what additional information you need, and what you may not actually require after all.

Ultimately the best way of dealing with 'busyness' anxiety is to build up your self-esteem, respect yourself enough to enable you to do one job at a time, not run around frantically, protect the other jobs by putting them in your schedule, and focus on the one job you have decided to begin.

SUMMARY AND THE PERSONAL CONTACT

This chapter has identified ways in which you could improve your time management. As time management is about taking control and developing good habits, it has invited you to practise some time management skills. Through changing your behaviour step-by-step, you can become much more effective at setting and achieving priorities and objectives. Enjoy your achievements and learn to work in a calmer more effective way.

Now you have read the chapter and had a chance to learn about your strengths and weaknesses in time management, attempt the personal contract identified in Exercise 2.4 as a way of identifying how you can take action to improve.

In identifying the changes, make sure that these are written *positively:* things you will do, and not things you won't do. For example 'I will tidy up my desk' not 'I won't have a messy desk'.

You may like to consider the SMART methodology in setting your objectives. Check that each objective is:

- **S**– Specific. (Make it a clear specific aim such as 'I will find somewhere to work where I can concentrate for a few hour-periods in the week' rather than something vague and over general like 'I will rearrange my working practices'.)
- **M**– Measurable. (How will you know you have achieved it?)
- **A**– Achievable. (Check that your objectives are actionable and achievable, and you know the steps you will need to take to put them in place, for example: 'To deal with interruptions I will put a sign on my desk "Do not disturb" and wear headphones when I am doing work which needs concentration', rather than 'I will stop any conversation or telephone noises in the office'.)
- **R**– Realistic. (Have you identified small do-able tasks, or are you setting yourself up for failure by making them too demanding?)
- **T**– Time bound. (When will you take action – can you put specific tasks in your diary?)

You are likely to need some support in putting this into action and so you maybe could design or discuss your personal contract and objectives in conjunction with a work colleague, a personal tutor, or even a mentor at work, and include this as part of your CPD.

EXERCISE 2.4 THE PERSONAL CONTRACT

The personal contract

I will make the following change to the way I work and use my time:

1.

2.

3.

I will review these regularly to check that I am making the changes.

I will begin by making the following step within the next week. This could be either 1, 2 or 3 or a step towards 1, 2 or 3.

The first step:

Signed:

Date:

I will also get the following person to support, encourage and help me make this step and check up that I'm doing it.

Support person: ......

REFERENCES AND FURTHER READING

BAILYN, L. (1993) *Breaking the Mold: Women, men and time in the new corporate world.* New York: Macmillan.

CLEGGE, C., LEGGE, K. and WALSH, S. (1999) *The Experience of Managing: A skills guide.* Hants: Macmillan Business. Chapter 31, GRIFFITHS, D. Time Management 285–292.

COVEY, S. (1989) *The 7 Habits of Highly Effective People.* London: Simon and Schuster.

HINDLE, T. (1998) *Manage Your Time.* London: Dorling Kindersley Essential Manager Series.

KOTTER, J. P. (1982) *The General Managers.* New York: Macmillan.

MAITLAND, I. (2001) *Managing Your Time.* London: CIPD.

MINTZBERG, H. (1973) *The Nature of Managerial Work.* London: Harper and Row.

MURDOCK, A. and SCUTT, C. (2003) *Personal Effectiveness.* 3rd ed. Oxford: Institute of Management/Butterworth/Heinemann. Chapter 4, 127–147.

NEENAN, M. and DRYDEN, W. (2002) *Life Coaching: A cognitive-behavioural approach.* Hove: Brunner-Routledge.

WHETTON, D. and CAMERON, K. (2002) *Developing Management Skills.* 5th ed. New Jersey: Prentice Hall/Pearson. 99–100, 113–120, 151–152 or WHETTON, D., CAMERON, K. and WOODS, M. (2000) *Developing Management Skills for Europe.* 2nd ed. Harlow: Financial Times/Prentice Hall, Pearson Education. 93–94, 107–111.

Creativity and ideas generation

INTRODUCTION

This chapter is aimed at anyone who wants 'to think outside the box' in order to generate ideas. The techniques presented are particularly useful for people who do not believe they have time to think differently due to the pressures of daily life. You may think that creativity is something that we have or do not have – there is no point reading about it as it can't be developed. Actually, this is just one further way in which we box ourselves in – there are techniques that can help, whether we use them unconsciously or train ourselves to use them. Creativity is also not something that is in the hands of geniuses alone, it is something everyone can and does utilise everyday – in shopping, cooking, decorating the house, work, leisure, relationships. A good place to begin is for you to think creatively about what exactly is 'creativity'.

WHAT IS CREATIVITY?

EXERCISE 3.1   CREATIVITY AND INNOVATION

a) Identify one creative individual and write down their name. This does not have to be someone famous.

b) Now write down all those attributes of this individual that you believe make them creative.

c) Now identify one innovator and write down their name.

d) List out the attributes of the innovator that make them innovative.

e) Compare your two lists to distil what you perceive to be the difference between creativity and innovation.

f) Now have a go at defining what you think creativity is – in one sentence.

In identifying a creative individual, you may have chosen a famous artist like Pablo Picasso or even just someone known to you – your local florist for example. It is likely that you concluded that creativity is about developing new ideas. You possibly saw creativity as an individual trait, and linked it to concepts such as being open-minded, original, idiosyncratic, flexible, imaginative and having the ability to think freely and abstractly, to fantasise, see possibilities, be insightful, expressive and constructive.

It is likely that you saw innovation as being more of a collective activity, and about implementation – about developing new methods to make the ideas happen in the world. These may be state-of-the-art, revolutionary and groundbreaking developments or more incremental improvements. You may have chosen examples such as James Dyson, or Isambard Brunel as innovators, and people who have designed and built technological feats and products such as bridges, viaducts, cars, and equipment. Innovation requires creativity, but takes it one step further and puts the ideas into action.

One useful way to perceive creativity in the context of this chapter is to see it as described in the definition below.

DEFINITION OF CREATIVITY

The capacity for ideas generation, for looking at problems in new ways and to seek out alternatives.

Put in your own definition of creativity here:

Now you have some conception of creativity, attempt Exercise 3.2 to help you explore your perception of your own creativity, and areas where you think you could be more creative.

EXERCISE 3.2   CREATIVE SITUATIONS AT WORK AND PLAY

Identify some examples of where you are creative in your everyday life, at work, home and elsewhere. This could be something as basic as choosing your clothes, cooking, reading, writing, planning your work schedule or problem solving.

Are you as creative as you would like to be? Identify some situations in which you would benefit from being more creative.

Why do you think you are not more creative more often?

What are your mental blocks to creative thinking?

How can you minimise them?

BLOCKS TO CREATIVE THINKING

In attempting Exercise 3.2 you may have found you have some mental blocks to creative thinking in certain situations. There are a number of reasons we may have difficulty being creative.

Beliefs, thought and intellectual processes

Holding onto certain beliefs can be limiting to creativity, as to be creative we need to allow ourselves to be open-minded. The belief that 'creativity cannot be developed' has already been mentioned, but there are other beliefs that also get in the way. The belief 'I am not a creative person' for example is self-generating; negativity tends to close us down.

A strong belief that 'There is only one right answer' also limits creativity. If creativity is about ideas generation, then focusing on one idea or answer gets in the way of seeing a situation from a number of different angles. It produces tunnel vision which doesn't help us to see the alternatives. Many of the techniques below, such as brainstorming or lateral thinking, are designed to open us up to many possibilities. For example, in relation to the question 'What is a bed' fixing on one answer: 'A place to sleep' will close down other possibilities – such as a place for celebrity romps, a place to rest, watch television, work, recover health, – possibilities and ideas which may lead to new innovations such as a sofa bed, a water bed, a therapeutic bed.

Seeing a situation from one's own perspective, with a lack of empathy for the perspective of others also inhibits creativity. The stakeholder technique below is designed to open oneself up to seeing a situation from new angles.

Judgment and evaluation in particular can get in the way. Evaluating an idea stops us from developing the positive and constructive frame of mind that opens up creative thinking. To be creative we often need to suspend the evaluation to enable the ideas to flow. Likewise our intellect may be powerful, but the over-use of logic may shut down our intuition.

Perceptual blocks

It is not just our thought processes that jump to conclusions and limit ideas generation, but our perceptual processes do so too. Given the mass of information that our senses are bombarded with it is not surprising that our mind automatically builds patterns and tries to make sense of information in a way which prevents us from fully seeing all the alternatives in a situation. For example look at Figure 3.1:

Figure 3.1 *Dots*

In Figure 3.1 it is likely that you see a circle because your mind closes up the dots. More alternatives are available to us if we do not jump to conclusions and allow ourselves to question what we are seeing more often.

Another perceptual problem is difficulty in isolating the problem or issue. You can't see the wood for the trees. This often happens in working on an assignment or coursework, the mass of information required for writing a report or essay shuts down your capacity to think clearly and come up with ideas for writing it. Facing exams can create the same kind of block; the sheer volume of information absorbed in revision becomes a meaningless blur. This often requires the mind to relax in order to be creative – you can get too close to a problem and need 'incubation', a technique discussed below.

To make sense of something, you may place an artificial boundary around a situation, defining it as one problem, when maybe it could be defined in a different way. For example Jacques Derrida has asked the question 'What is a painting?' Most people describe the picture within the frame, identifying the subject matter, Johannes Vermeer's 'Girl with a Pearl Earring' for example. But maybe, as Derrida suggests, the frame is part of the painting, maybe the background in the painting is more important than the foreground, maybe its positioning in the gallery is part of the work of art. Allowing expansion of your perspective and also the question 'What is art' allows for an explosion of ideas. The state of 'undecidability' can be provocative to ideas generation.

Another way we organise our perceptual and intellectual field is through bi-polar thinking. Either/or, good/bad, male/female, black/white, rough/smooth. Philosophers, therapists, theologians and academics through the centuries have commented on the limitations of this bi-polar vision (Soren Kierkergaard, Claude Levi-Strauss, Jacques Derrida, Gestalt psychology and Buddhist philosophy for example). Although this is a fundamental prop to life in the modern world, and a way in which language becomes constructed and the world becomes defined, it is another perceptual limitation. It is a form of stereotyping that, although allowing us to make sense of the world, also gets in the way and is artifice. Exploring the grey between black and white may allow for a rainbow of colours to be perceived – how much more exciting than 'either/or' to allow for 'and/or'. For example a company may be considering taking a diversity management approach, but is also considering setting up an equal opportunities policy. Rather than decide one or the other, maybe they could do both? Some techniques for creativity explore the space that bi-polar thinking ignores.

Emotional

Habit, routine, and laziness all can get in the way of being creative. We adjust to routines, and stop making the effort to change or do something different. As John Maynard Keynes said 'The real difficulty in changing the course of an enterprise lies not in developing new ideas but in escaping from the old ones.' More on the problems of translating ideas into change in practice can be found in Chapter 10.

Another reason for closing down our creative powers is anxiety: we may feel safer sticking in the same groove and find it difficult to tolerate ambiguity. We may fear rejection or ridicule. Creative ideas may not work the first time around and people can delight at your failure. People can be very 'left-brain' dominated (see below) and be very quick to see the problems in rather than the merits of ideas, and this can squash creativity. Being creative may make us stand out in a crowd, for example if we dress differently – just think of the furore when David Beckham wore a skirt. Being creative involves taking a risk and we may worry about making a mistake, or just feel incompetent or useless. One solution to this is to do something different: think of one thing in the day that you always do in the same way – for example travel to work, or the way you cook dinner – and think of a way to change it, upset your routine, as mentioned in the cycle of creativity below.

Lack of emotional resilience can also be problematic – some people give up on a new idea because there are so many problems. Many changes in industry and commerce can be slow, and so people give up trying – see Chapter 10 on managing organisational change.

Cultural/social/personal scripts

We are taught messages about ourselves from when we are very young. Often in families with more than one offspring, children are allocated different roles: 'the clever one', 'the practical one', 'the creative one', for example. This can be limiting as we grow and change, but the messages that parents have passed on to us can be very powerful and impact our identity and sense of self. Our parents may have in words or attitude told us 'You are not creative' and this has become internalised, as 'I am not creative'. Alternatively our parents may have encouraged us not to 'rock the boat'. It may be worth questioning your script to discover what messages you have internalised from your parents. Have you grown up to believe you are creative, or have personal efficacy and the capacity to do something if you put your mind to it? For more about these personal 'scripts' see Chapter 9.

There are also some socially constructed paradigms and beliefs that limit thinking. For example people once believed that the world was flat. For a long time the prevailing scientific paradigm in the West squashed the development of complimentary and alternative therapies from the East, therapies and practices such as homeopathy, shiatsu, and reflexology; claiming they were unscientific and did not meet the standards of modern scientific evaluation, These have, however, more recently been embraced by a significant part of the population.

Environmental

Advertising agencies often utilise the environment in two ways to achieve greater creativity amongst their copywriters: the way the physical environment is designed, and the use of collaboration. Some physical environments stimulate creativity – relaxing, restful places, maybe with sofas and soft colours – others stifle it. Other people can also help or hinder us. To turn creativity into innovation and bring it into existence in the first place requires support. If we are not supported, but squashed at every opportunity, we may not explore our potential for creativity. Ask yourself in what way do you need to change your environment to be more creative in your work, course or leisure? What does your workspace look like, does it help you feel more creative, or distract you or close down your creative processes? Do you have people encouraging you to be more creative, giving you positive feedback for so doing? Work cultures can be very influential, and in particular a 'blame' culture can prevent people from taking risks and being creative, instead encouraging blind obedience or playing safe.

Go back over your statement in Exercise 3.2 on your own blocks to creativity – how many of these reasons apply?

CYCLES AND FUNNELS OF CREATIVITY

There are two processes that can help us examine and tap into our creativity: cycles and funnels. It was mentioned above that we build emotional attachment to habitual ways of thinking, feeling and behaving. In the cycle approach outlined below in Figure 3.1 we can begin by making the familiar strange: break our habits and stereotypes mentioned and open ourselves up to the possibility that our familiar routines are strange; examine our habitual approach to a situation from a different angle – the assumption that this is a strange way to proceed. Then break our connection or attachment to our approach by allowing ourselves to explore some of the techniques raised below. Once we have used new approaches, gradually these strange ways of proceeding may become familiar.

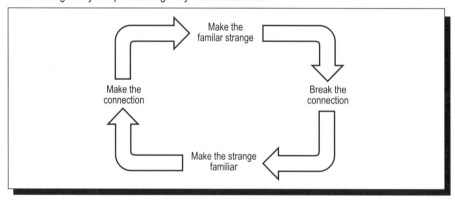

Figure 3.2   *A cycle of creativity*

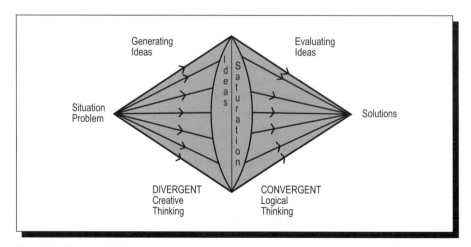

Figure 3.3   *The creative funnel*

If we look at life around us, much change happens in cycles – the seasons for example. One Chinese symbol for change has within it the sign for an opportunity and the sign for a threat. Change is a combination of birth and death, beginnings and endings, growth and loss. The trees and flowers have to die in order for spring to burst forth again. Likewise creativity requires us to relinquish old ideas to allow for new ones to burst forth.

Alternatively, think about your usual approach to problem solving. It is often helpful to begin by allowing oneself to think divergently, and creatively pulling out a variety of alternatives, and the exercises and techniques below help with this process. At some point the ideas generation aspect of the process becomes saturated, and we then move to evaluation: evaluating the options to choose the best one, as in Figure 3.3.

EXAMPLE 3.1   EXAMPLES OF THE CREATIVE FUNNEL

Work-related examples

Example 1 A car company instructed its engineers to spend more time at the front end of the design process being creative in their approach. To do this they brought in a team of multi-functional engineers and also people from production engineering, marketing and sales, to support the design team. The exploration of a wider range of alternatives at the outset followed by detailed evaluation and scrutiny later on led to a much more cost-effective and successful design.

Example 2 Henderson Group One, a marketing and PR agency was designing a brochure for Motorola in the UK to advertise the variety of different organisations and activities of which they were comprised. They spent a lot of time exploring a numbers of new ideas and designs for the cover and content before moving on to evaluate and analyse them to short list the ideas and develop three of them in more detail.

Study-related examples

Example 3 Darren was trying to decide on a project topic for his Masters course. He was absolutely stuck over how to proceed. His tutor suggested he sit down and conducted a brainstorm session (see the section on brainstorming below for technique), throwing down all the ideas however outlandish. Only once he had exhausted all possibilities should he stop to evaluate them and whittle them down to the best idea in terms of how interesting, stretching, useful, accessible it would be for a project.

Example 4 Sheila was embarking on a PhD programme. Her area for study was in diversity and equal opportunities. After two months she was worried that she seemed to be reading a wide range of material and hadn't managed to focus. Her supervisor reassured her that it was normal to feel overwhelmed by a proliferation of material early on in a PhD, and that this wide-range reading and thinking around the topic was a necessary part of the process – focusing down too quickly on her methodology and specific research questions could be a mistake. Sheila was glad when she handed in her thesis that she had allowed herself to think more divergently at the beginning. Her thesis was much more creative and innovative, as she was able to bring in ideas from a wider range of disciplines in order to look at the subject in a novel way.

DEVELOPING A WHOLE BRAIN APPROACH TO CREATIVITY

The human brain is incredibly complex, more so than any computer, and although science has discovered some of the ways it functions, much of it still remains unexplored. Having some understanding of how the brain works, however, can be useful to creativity. In particular, it can help you to develop a whole brain approach and enhance your ability to think more creatively.

The brain has two sides or hemispheres, left and right. Different bodily functions, including ways of thinking, are allocated to each side, although research on stroke victims has suggested that one side can take on some of the functions of the other. Broadly speaking each side plays a particular role and sees the world very differently (see for example Hellinge, 1990: 55–80, Joseph, 1993, Uba and Huang, 1999: 72–74).

Most of us tend to have a side that dominates and this will cause us to think in particular ways. The objective of whole brain thinking is to maximise our thinking potential by encouraging both sides of the brain to work in tandem, communicating clearly and working together to achieve a common objective.

Figure 3.4 provides a simple outline of some of the main differences between the hemispheres.

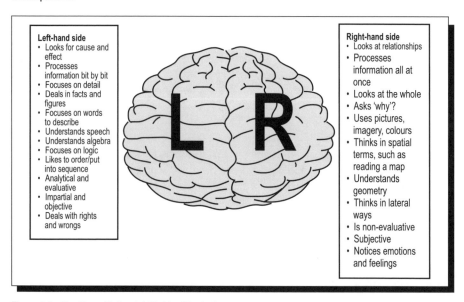

Left-hand side
- Looks for cause and effect
- Processes information bit by bit
- Focuses on detail
- Deals in facts and figures
- Focuses on words to describe
- Understands speech
- Understands algebra
- Focuses on logic
- Likes to order/put into sequence
- Analytical and evaluative
- Impartial and objective
- Deals with rights and wrongs

Right-hand side
- Looks at relationships
- Processes information all at once
- Looks at the whole
- Asks 'why'?
- Uses pictures, imagery, colours
- Thinks in spatial terms, such as reading a map
- Understands geometry
- Thinks in lateral ways
- Is non-evaluative
- Subjective
- Notices emotions and feelings

Figure 3.4 *Functions of left and right side of the brain*

As you can see, the left-hand side (which controls the right side of our bodies), is concerned with our logical thinking, facts and figures. It tends to express itself in words. Our right-hand side (which controls the left side of our bodies), is the artistic side and thinks in terms of pictures and feelings.

EXERCISE 3.3   LEFT- OR RIGHT-BRAIN THINKING?

Imagine that it is the birthday of a niece or nephew or small child you know well. You have given this child a model 'adventure island' as a present. What you hadn't realised is that this model comes in a kit form with several parts. The kit includes step-by-step written instructions, a list of contents, a picture of the completed model (on the front of the box). The child asks you to help make up the kit for them.

Briefly describe the steps you would take to build the model.

There are several ways in which you could tackle the above activity and the approach you take may indicate which side of the brain is the most dominant. For example, if you approached the model methodically and checked to see you had every piece and followed the instructions as they are laid down, you are more likely to be left-brain dominant. Conversely, if you ignored the instructions and simply began to put the pieces together using the picture on the box as a guide, you may be more right-brain dominant. A right-brain dominant person may extemporise, making additions to the model, such as using paper or flowers from the garden or blue-tack. It would also be interesting to examine how you involved the child in this activity: were they your 'apprentice', observing your work while you explained clearly to them your steps and engaged them in simple tasks along the way, inviting them to comment on how successful the model was (left-brain dominant). Or alternatively maybe you let them get stuck in as well, for example encouraging them to experiment, making additions to the model, such as using tissue paper, toys or flowers from the garden (right-brain dominant).

Having a dominant side does not mean that we are unable to use the other hemisphere, but the one that dominates will have the greater influence on how we tackle things and approach life in general. There may also be many external factors that have encouraged us to develop one side more than the other. Schooling, for example, may have placed more emphasis on left-brain subjects. Society will have an influence, as will your job and the people around you.

The rational logic that dominates in many organisations may be sensible for some situations, but in most cases we will be more effective when we take a whole brain approach. This is particularly the case when we want to develop our creative thinking skills. The techniques below are designed to encourage us to use the 'whole brain approach'.

CREATIVITY TECHNIQUE 1: BRAINSTORMING
Background

Brainstorming was an idea originally developed from a Madison Square advertising agency as a technique to come up with new campaigns, slogans and advertising ideas. It is an American idea, attributed to Alex Osborn (see Osborn 1979).

This is a technique that can generate far more ideas and creative ways of thinking/solving problems than would normally be possible using more traditional methods. This is because it helps you to access ideas from both the left and right sides of the brain.

One of the reasons for brainstorming being so effective is that it mirrors or complements how the brain stores its ideas and also how it prefers to work. In particular, it encourages both sides of the brain to work together. It does this by allowing the brain to 'free-fall': that is, work without any constraints; and the left-side is prevented from dominating the thinking process. The brain works in a random fashion, and this is very important because, were the left side allowed to evaluate, reject, judge, etc too early in the process, many good ideas which would have followed later, would have been lost.

DEFINITION OF BRAINSTORMING

Brainstorming comprises a short session (usually about 10 minutes), during which typically a group of people (but it can be done individually) tries to come up with as many ideas as possible about a particular subject, issue or problem. These ideas, however wild or strange, are captured on a flipchart, board or paper.

The method and rules

- blue sky (any idea is acceptable, no matter how outrageous)
- hitch-hike (using the ideas of others as a seed-bed for your own imagination)
- springboard (using one idea as a springboard for another)
- no criticism (criticism closes down imaginative and creative thinking, so at this stage you need to suspend your judgment to enable the ideas to flow)
- no evaluation (likewise evaluation shuts down creative thinking so suspend this also)
- no sequence (do not try to impose any order or sequence, just capture the ideas as they come)
- no linearity (try to avoid writing ideas in a list or linear fashion, as it only encourages the left side to begin to order them)
- quantity not quality (try to think of as many ideas as you can).

The utility of brainstorming

Brainstorming promotes ideas generation and creative thinking at the outset of a problem, and helps to overcome blocks when people get stuck. The evaluation comes later in the process: once the ideas have been captured they can then be put to critical scrutiny. Some uses are for:

- problem solving
- planning an interview or presentation
- planning or managing a new project
- generating more creative or unusual solutions and approaches.

Although you can brainstorm individually or in a group, the group approach is more effective as it enables individuals to spark ideas in each other.

EXERCISE 3.4   BRAINSTORMING

1. Place the problem at the top of a large sheet of paper. Rephrase your problem into a question, for example 'How can I ...?'
2. Start the brainstorm by thinking about the subject/question and writing down all the ideas you have.
3. When you have exhausted all your ideas, you can then begin to order/group your ideas and select/reject as appropriate.

Using six hats thinking in brainstorming

Edward de Bono (2000) identified a way to develop a more structured form of brainstorming, where one thinking mode is used at a time. The six hats, with colours in the sequence in which they guide a group to a solution are identified in table 3.1.

In a brainstorm these thinking modes can be taken one at a time, to enable a more focused approach to brainstorming, particularly if a group is having difficulties with generating ideas. For example, if a group are generally intellectualising about a problem, you could say 'Are there any red ideas on this subject, what do your emotions tell you?' If many of the ideas have been quite conventional you could say 'Now try wearing your green hat, what creative

Table 3.1   *De Bono's six thinking hats (Developed from De Bono, 2000)*

White	Pure facts, figures and information
Red	Feeling, emotions, intuition
Black	'Devil's advocate', negative judgment, what can go wrong?
Yellow	Brightness and optimism, positive constructive comments
Green	Creative, provocative, lateral thinking
Blue	Overview, summarising, what to take forward.

ideas can you come up with?' It also enables a group to think in a different way: for example 'green' thinking allows them to be more daft and playful, without fear of ridicule by others; 'red' gives permission for some emotional issues to be raised, or matters which may not usually be allowed to surface in the work context; 'white' allows a group which has become emotionally attached to and stuck with some ideas to draw on facts, figures and more concrete information to explore these further, in the evaluative stage following a brainstorm; 'black' allows for critical points to be vocalised, which may normally be suppressed to avoid being seen as a 'kill joy', and may stop the development of 'groupthink', which is a process identified further in Chapter 4 and which inhibits creativity and innovation.

Another way the 'six thinking hats' can be used is to separate a larger group into smaller ones, each charged with a different mode of thinking. Alternatively, the 'six thinking hats' can be used to take the ideas from brainstorming and evaluate and reflect further on them. For example getting a 'green' group to generate ideas, pass them on to a 'white' group to explore facts and figures and information about the ideas, then to a 'black' group to explore why the ideas may not work, then on to a 'yellow' group to think of ways round the problems identified or to think of constructive ways to build up the ideas left, and finally a 'blue' group to summarise where the groups have got to with the ideas. Some ideas may be rejected by the black group, others developed by both the white and yellow group may develop into possible courses of action.

CREATIVITY TECHNIQUE 2: MIND MAP

Background and origin

'Mind mapping' has great creative potential. Mind mapping is drawn from the work of Tony Buzan in the 1970s (see for example Buzan 2004). It is a technique, not an end in itself. Its aim is to help us learn non-linearly and take a whole brain approach (Russell 1980). Over time the technique has been refined and in 1995 Mind Map was recorded as a registered trademark of the Buzan Corporation. However, there are a number of variants – for example it is sometimes called a 'spider gram'.

DEFINITION OF A MIND MAP

A mind map or spider gram is a whole brain, pictorial and associative way to capture thoughts and ideas on a problem.

Peter Russell (1980) 'The Brain Book' states:

> The human brain is very different from a computer. Whereas a computer works in a linear, step-by-step fashion, albeit very fast, the brain works associatively as well as linearly, carrying on thousands of different processes at the same time, comparing, integrating, and synthesising as it goes.

> Association plays a dominant role in nearly every mental function, and words themselves are no exception. Every single word has numerous links attaching it to other ideas and concepts.

> When we write, particularly creative writing, we impose order, or structure, before exploring a pool of ideas. This results in drying out of ideas, or missing them altogether, as we do not capture Ideas 'here and now'. Mind map Is a technique to generate ideas as they come, leaving syntax rules aside to help capture and explore ideas.

The large number of alternative approaches may never surface if you approach the problem in a linear way. Useless solutions are not discarded; they are put into the pattern, which may themselves generate useful associations. Keywords are used which help to trigger other associations and thus ideas. These ideas are all captured on a map, a piece of paper, and this visual aspect of the display facilitates the connection of ideas, allowing them to be seen as a whole. It is a more structured than brainstorming, and is more of an individual than a group technique.

Method

An example of a mind map is outlined below. This is a mind map related to this chapter.

Ideally you would have an A3-sized piece of paper, to provide space for the imagination. You start in the centre, the middle of the sheet, not the left-hand corner as is usual. You can use different coloured pens to represent different parts of the map, as colour is associated with the long-term memory and is linked to creativity.

Draw a picture at the centre of the sheet to represent your problem, such as a balloon, a light bulb or exclamation mark, and circle it to separate it from the text, for example by a picture frame, a cloud or plain circle.

Start at the centre with the focal point or problem, like the 'solar plexus', then move out with associations and linkages, writing with keywords.

EXAMPLE 3.2   CREATIVITY MIND MAP

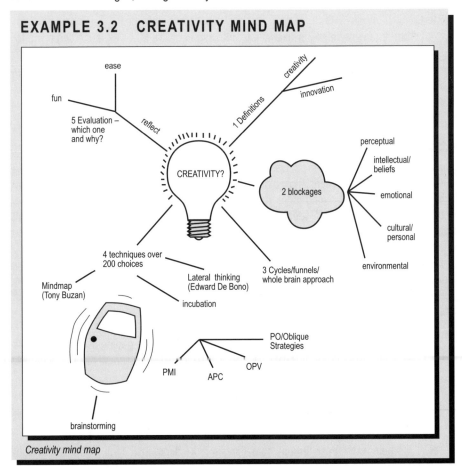

Creativity mind map

EXERCISE 3.5   MIND MAPPING

1. Identify one area in your work where you have been having difficulty with ideas generation or problem solving: for example 'How should I go about reconfiguring this service?', 'How shall I go about writing this article?', 'I have an idea for developing a charity, what should I take into consideration?', 'Why may clients find our service unhelpful and off-putting, how can I make the service more user friendly'. Distil it to the kernel of the concept, and put that at the centre with your 'idea bubble' on a sheet of A3 paper.

2. Put the focus at the centre and ideas branching out from it. Number the ideas and generate sub-branches of ideas. For example if you were developing a charity, you may identify fundraising, linkages with other charities, strategic development, service development, membership support, communication, clients. Sub-branches of fundraising could be private sector partnerships, sponsorship, events, membership subscriptions, retail subsidiaries. You may then number the branches by saying you will start by considering events (1) and then consider sponsorship (2) and partnerships (3).

3. Now make a new mind map drawing on your first ideas, but with one colour for each main branch and sub-branches, and leaving out any ideas you have decided to discard.

Now review how useful this has been:

- What are the benefits (for example for ideas generation, for giving a starting point, for linking ideas together which were previously unrelated, to give yourself an overview)?
- What are the negatives (difficult if you are used to very structured ways of thinking and used to instant evaluation and judgment)?
- What are the applications in your professional and personal life?

CREATIVITY TECHNIQUE 3: INCUBATION

Sometimes the more you try the more you get stuck. Gestalt psychology introduces the idea of the 'paradox of change': the more you push for change or ideas, the more difficult it is to achieve, paradoxically by being more yourself, the more you will change (see further details of this concept in Chapter 10). Ideas are the same – forcing them can just mean that the left brain takes over and the right brain shuts down. The good news is that it may be better to relax and turn off than work hard at a problem.

Many people find that actually 'sleeping on a problem' can help to see things more clearly and to come up with solutions they might otherwise not have thought of. Incubating a problem has a number of advantages:

- It stops you getting bogged down, particularly when you are getting nowhere. In these cases it is often better to come back to a situation later on, when you will often find you can see things from a different angle or a new perspective.
- It provides a mental break and can reduce stress.
- It allows your subconscious to go to work on the problem, seemingly without your having to apply any real effort.
- It will help you to think through something in more depth than if you had acted straight away.

You do not actually have to go to bed in order to incubate a problem! Simply taking a break and concentrating on something else may be enough. Alternatively you could:

- Go for a walk.
- Have a relaxing bath – with candles.
- Take a coffee break.
- Listen to some music, watch a film.
- Use a relaxation technique.
- Go and play a sport.
- Concentrate on another aspect of your work.

Now attempt Exercise 3.6.

EXERCISE 3.6   THE FIRST AID BOX

Draw the outline of a first-aid box with a green cross in the corner. Now draw in this box all those activities you think help you to relax and incubate a problem. Then, next time you get stuck – consult your first-aid box and choose one of these activitie

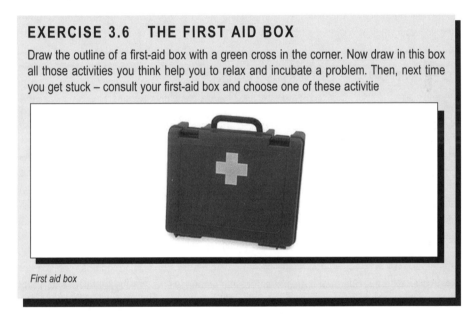

First aid box

We have probably all experienced situations when we cannot remember the name of a place or someone and have tried to recall it without success, only to find that when we stop thinking about it, the name will suddenly come to us. This is an example of the incubation technique working, even though not used consciously.

CREATIVITY TECHNIQUE 4: LATERAL THINKING
Origin

Dr. Edward de Bono coined the expression 'lateral thinking'. Born in Malta in 1933 he studied medicine, and then moved to England and studied at Oxford and Cambridge in the areas of psychology, physiology and medicine. His fame derives from his many books in which he attempts to teach the reader to think clearly.

EXERCISE 3.7   LATERAL THINKING

How many seconds are there in a year?

Solving a problem, in any field, depends on the perspective from which you see the situation; if you can alter your angle of vision, you can contemplate a variety of possible solutions. You cannot do so if you persist in thinking in a single-track way following the most obvious course. Many people would say in answer to Exercise 3.7 (unless it was a leap year), 365 days x 24 hours x 60 minutes x 60 seconds = 31,536,000. Although this is one answer, the right answer in the New Year's Eve quiz I attended, and the answer that would have won a bottle of champagne was, 12 – the 2nd of January, 2nd of February, 2nd March, etc. My daughter had a good alternative – 2 seconds – the time it takes to say 'a year'.

A good example of a lateral thinker is Ernest Shackleton the Antarctic explorer who demonstrated creativity in ways that saved the lives of many men when faced with survival situations (see for example Morrell and Capparell 2001, Shackleton 1999). The packing cases that were full of provisions on ship were converted into sheets to build huts in the Antarctic. When his boat *The Endeavour* had sunk, he used the lifeboats as shelters in their trek across hundreds of miles of ice. Manipulating your mind to look for alternatives through changing your angle of vision is not easy, but there are ways in which it can be developed.

DEFINITION OF LATERAL THINKING

Lateral thinking involves suspending logical linear thinking, instead breaking out of patterns to explore an issue in new ways from new angles.

Lateral thinking can be at the individual or group level. It enables you to cut across patterns and suspend judgment. Edward de Bono identifies two forms of thinking: vertical thinking and lateral thinking. Vertical thinking is traditional logical thinking, characterised by continuity. Lateral thinking is characterised by discontinuity. If creative thinking demands that we break out of established patterns to look at things in different ways, we need to apply lateral thinking.

Lateral thinking is dynamic not static, it jumps from one concept to another looking for movement, not the status quo. It also overrides the binary yes/no thinking that seeks to justify each move before moving on, and also the either/or system of one alternative idea or another, allowing for ideas that may consist of mixing ideas or incorporating both. It is provocative and open-ended.

The process and method

To develop lateral thinking skills it is important to be conscious of the process of how you think and what the results are. Without awareness it can be difficult to change. Time is also needed to generate and explore ideas, developing the habit of 'stepping sideways'. Lateral thinking also relates to attitudes – allowing for flexibility of attitude to enable you to switch into different ways of thinking – for example to think like a child, like an adult, like a leader, like a customer. Tools also need to be developed to enable us to be creative: for example language, mathematics and computers are all tools which help us to develop more complex ideas in different fields.

In the earlier section on creativity blocks, it was mentioned that perceptual patterns can limit our capacity to develop new ways of thinking because we manage our information through pattern recognition. To change these patterns, we need to restructure ideas and escape from inhibitions and self-imposed barriers. The tools suggested by De Bono help to provoke us to disturb our pattern recognition and look for alternatives. Some of the techniques below attempt to do this by using 'chance' as a source of discontinuity, provoking us to make leaps from one idea or concept to another. As well as tools and techniques to support the jump from vertical to horizontal thinking, we need an attitude that promotes awareness of the differences and the courage to practise these new processes and methods.

Lateral thinking tools

Edward de Bono has devised a series of tools to form a 'toolkit' designed to stretch out minds and unclog all the accumulated knowledge. Four of these are presented and developed below: PMI, APC, OPV and PO.

PMI (pluses, minuses and interesting points)

Usually the natural reaction to a new idea or proposal is to like or dislike it right away, to think in terms of 'pros' and 'cons'. If you like an idea, it is unlikely that you will deliberately search for the minus points, and vice versa. It is also rare to pick out points only because they are very interesting. When you use PMI, you delineate the pluses, the good points, why you like something; and the minuses, the bad points, why you don't like something; and those that are so interesting they may lead to a better idea. You can use a PMI as a way of approaching a new concept, suggestion, offer or invitation. You can ask someone else to do a PMI simultaneously when you want to work out a problem that involves both of you.

EXERCISE 3.8   A PMI

Conduct a PMI on the idea that 'all people should work from home'.

P	M	I

Note: most people find it hardest to fill the *interesting* column, but this is the one we should explore more, as the strong likes and dislikes moves us quickly into evaluation. For example a plus might be saving on commuting travel time, and a minus the difficulty separating out work from home, especially for those with little willpower and lots of washing up, noisy children and d-i-y jobs to do. In the interesting column it may lead to changes in house designs, maybe even people moving into streets with others they work with, an engineers' row or dentists' cul-de-sac. Technology would have to improve vastly to facilitate this. The interesting column often produces more creative ideas.

APC (alternative possible choices)

When faced with one of those decisions that seem really tough precisely because you think you have got two opposing alternatives, or only unsatisfactory solutions, APC comes in handy. It enables you to find other possible choices, which is not difficult once you choose to search. An APC can open up a situation into a productive stream of possibilities. To do an APV you effectively brainstorm all the possible alternatives available to you, not just the ones that at first seem the most obvious.

EXERCISE 3.9 AN APC

Assume you have by chance discovered that your colleague, Bob, is working but also claiming benefit and is engaged in multiple fraudulent activities. What course of action is open to you? List out your ideas.

APCs

In Exercise 3.9 it is helpful to explore the grey in between the black and the white, and also the other colours. By moving yourself out of either/or thinking, – should you shop him to the police or not – you may find that you have opened up a creative avenue which may contain some bizarre but also some useful ideas: ask him why, listen to him, lecture him, counsel him, write a story about him, pray for him, even blackmail him, do an ethnographic study of him, join him!

OPV (other people's views) or stakeholding

In any situation in need of a solution, other people and their opinions are important to consider. It is often surprising to see how very differently someone else views a given problem. OPV allows you to get into other people's shoes, and view the world from their perspective. In other words, the situation does not create the opinion, the people involved do. A key factor is the ability to understand how other people think and feel: develop *empathy*. OPV is also a strategy for sizing up others' positions, which can be very useful when entering a conflict situation or negotiation as explained in Chapters 8 and 9. Unlike APC, the OPV does not involve just giving alternative points of view in general. The emphasis is first of all on specific people in specific positions and then a shift to their points of view.

EXERCISE 3.10   AN OPV

Imagine you work closely with a colleague Amanda who has taken up drinking heavily, and you want her to stop. Now consider OPV, by:

a) listing out in one column your arguments and reasons for wanting her to stop drinking

b) listing out in another column your colleague's reasons for wanting to drink.

At this stage it is quantity not quality of ideas that matters.

Now compare the lists.

Your reasons	Your colleague's reasons

In Exercise 3.10 you are likely to find that your reasons are so unrelated to her reasons that by arguing for your rationale you have little impact on her motivation. For example, however much you go on about her health and work performance, it is unlikely she will listen to you if her primary reason is because she has gone through a terrible divorce and feels anxious, lonely and depressed. You may now find that you could open a conversation with Amanda based on alternative ways of tackling her problems, such as seeing a counsellor, or getting more support or friendships and other activities. This may help facilitate a dialogue and communication between you.

Oblique strategies and 'PO"

The BBC have great need of creative talent: to generate ideas for new productions, ways of broadcasting better, new technological developments, almost every department needs creativity. One exercise called 'Oblique Strategies' developed within the BBC aimed to overcome blocks in creativity and encourage lateral thinking. A set of cards with random tenets on them is taken and shuffled. The person with the problem takes one at random, and discusses with the group how this 'tenet' relates to their problem. Some illustrative tenets are reproduced in Exercise 3.11 below.

EXERCISE 3.11   A VARIATION ON OBLIQUE STRATEGIES

a) Identify a problem or block that you have been having.

b) Take the following tenets and at random choose one of them:

mutate and continue

bridges: build? burn?

define an area as safe and use it as an anchor

decorate

discover the recipes you are using and abandon them

faced with a choice – do both

do the words need changing?

is there something missing?

make a blank valuable by putting it in an exquisite frame

not building a wall but making a brick

pay attention to distractions

the properties of water.

c) Either individually, or if you can in a group, consider/discuss how the chosen tenet may give you insight into the problem or block you are facing.

Where oblique strategies involve the use of an unrelated tenet, De Bono identifies a 'PO' word or object to enable the leap in imagination to fit the word to the issue being considered. Why 'PO'? Because in itself it is meaningless and provocative. Using a 'PO" word makes us deliberately escape from one mode of thinking to another. It provides an opportunity to practise lateral thinking.

EXAMPLE 3.3   USING 'PO'

Take the problem 'How could we improve local government?' and identify the unrelated object 'PO'. In this case 'PO' = Curtains.

You could then consider the qualities of curtains: they open and close, they may be colourful or plain, they have movement and flexibility (swinging on a pole, or even automatic), they are functional, they may be bought or self-made, they may insulate, etc. Then relating 'curtains' to the question, this may lead you to think 'open' suggests open government and less privacy and more transparency; 'shut' suggests shutting some departments; 'colourful' suggests more diversity; 'movement' suggests perhaps the activities should move more into the community, or use a community bus; 'swing on a pole' suggests fast track staff; 'automatic' suggests more IT and so on.

There are other similar techniques to 'oblique strategies and PO'. One such technique is 'forced metaphors' where, for example, an animal or creature is taken as a metaphor for the problem you are facing, and the problem is explored with relation to the metaphor. In fact any technique which enables you to make a jump in logic and in some way force a relationship between two unrelated things – the 'problem' and the 'device' – and then solve the problem using the flow of ideas generated from the previously unrelated thing, can be a source for inspiration.

SUMMARY

In this chapter creativity has been defined as the capacity to generate ideas. Although some people are naturally more creative than others, there are a number of techniques we can use to help develop our creativity. At the very least, awareness of some of the barriers to creativity – bi-polar thinking, the dominance of evaluation – may help you side-step these to enable your ideas to flow more easily. Having worked through this chapter you should now be able to identify ways in your own working lives in which you could enhance your creativity. The underlying principle behind many of these techniques is stepping back and looking at a situation from a new angle. However, not all techniques fit all people and situations. Therefore take a few moments to look back over your notes, and particularly Exercise 3.2 to remind yourself of your main blocks and the actions you could take to overcome them, and ways in which the learning from this session could be applied in your working life. If necessary seek out a coach or mentor in your organisation to help you do this.

REFERENCES AND FURTHER READING

ADAMS, J. (2001) *Conceptual Blockbusting: A guide to better ideas.* 4th ed. New York: Basic Books, Perseus.

DE BONO, E. (2000) *6 Thinking Hats.* London: Penguin.

DE BONO, E. (1990) *Lateral Thinking for Management.* London: Penguin.

DE BONO, E (1993) *Serious Creativity.* London: Harper Collins.

BUZAN, T. (2000) *Use Your Head.* London: Ariel BBC Books.

BUZAN, T. (2004) *Mind Maps at Work.* London: Thorsons/Harper Collins.

CLEGG, B. and BIRCH, P. (1999) *Instant Creativity.* London: Kogan Page.

EDWARDS, B. (2001) *The New Drawing on the Right Side of the Brain.* London: Harper Collins.

EVANS, P. and DEEHAN, G. (1990) *The Keys to Creativity.* Middlesex: Grafton Books.

HELLIGE, J.B. (1990) Hemispheric Asymmetry. *Annual Review of Psychology.* 41, pp 55–80.

JOSEPH, R. (1993) *The Naked Neuron: Evolution of the body and brain.* New York: Plenum Press.

KELLEY, T. and LITTMAN, J. (2001) *The Art of Innovation.* London: Profile Books.

VON OECH, R. (1986) *A Kick in the Seat Of The Pants.* Glasgow: Perennial and Harper Collins.

OSBORN, A. (1979) *Applied Imagination.* New Jersey, US: Scribner.

MAJOR S. *The Creativity Gap.* New York: Longman.

MORELL, M. and CAPPARELL, S. (2001) *Shackleton's Way: Leadership lessons from the great Antarctic explorer.* London: Nicholas Brealey Publishing.

POLLOCK, T. *Managing Creativity.* London: CBI.

RUSSELL, P. (1980) *The Brain Book.* London: Routledge Taylor Francis.

SHACKLETON, E. (1999) *South: The Endurance Expedition.* London: Penguin.

UBA, L. and HUANG, K. (1999) *Psychology.* New York: Longman.

VON STAMM, B (2003) *Managing Innovation, Design and Creativity.* West Sussex: Wiley.

Group dynamics and team working

INTRODUCTION

It is likely that at work, in academic study, and in leisure you are a member of a number of different teams and groups. Teams enable you to overcome the limitations you have as an individual and achieve many things you would struggle to tackle alone. Ideally the synergy of a group would mean that not only would you outperform a team's best individual, but as a group your outcomes will far outstrip the sum total of individual members' contributions: $2 + 2 > 4$! Yet strangely some groups can go awry and you may have experienced difficulties in group working. You may have been a member of a group that has been brought down by conflict, sunk into lethargy and despair, or spent ages and ages going round in circles unable to come to a decision. In other teams you may feel you have found your niche, performing well as an individual and enjoying the group experience. This chapter will help you understand a little more about these group dynamics and find ways to improve your team performance and team working skills.

WHAT IS A GROUP? WHAT IS A TEAM?

EXERCISE 4.1   WHAT IS A TEAM?

Which of the following is closest to your ideal of a team?

- women aged 20–30 with red hair
- people in a bus queue
- a theatre audience
- a football team
- 50 people waiting at the airport to go on the same package holiday

Why?

In Exercise 4.1 you may have considered women aged 20–30 and discounted them as a team. If you look at the definition outlined below you will see they do not necessarily interact, share the same values and norms, nor have common goals. They certainly don't perceive themselves as a distinct entity! They are more of a social category than a social group. The people in the bus queue have a common goal – to get on the bus – but consider the situation where the bus is quite full and there are only two places left and ten people in the queue. The goal – 'I want to get on the bus' – may place them in opposition, with some unable to achieve that goal. They may only interact in conflict, elbowing each other out of the way: hardly what we consider team behaviour. Their existence as a distinct entity – a bus queue – is only transient (hopefully!): they don't stay together over a long period of time. The theatre audience do have a common goal – to enjoy the play – and to a limited extent interact to make that possible. The more receptive the audience, the better the actors may perform, particularly in a comedy where the audience's laughter can be infectious and improve the atmosphere. There are some common norms – when to clap, when to go and get refreshments – but these are limited and interactions with one another are transient, as is their identity as an audience. The people waiting at an airport have a common aim – to go on a package holiday – but are likely to interact very little, and then maybe only to get in each others' way, trip over each others' baggage, or for some idle chat. The answer you are most likely to have given is the football team – they have to interact and communicate to succeed and they seek common goals: to win the match or the cup or the league, and are willing to expend massive energy to achieve the goal. They each need to take up different but complementary roles: the striker, the midfielder, the defender, the goalkeeper, otherwise they would all bunch chaotically on the pitch around the ball. Their values and norms also need some congruence: for example acceptable behaviour on the pitch, their behaviour towards their coach, or even the opposition. A social category is not the same as a social group, which is not always the same as team.

DEFINITION OF A TEAM

A team is a social unit or collection of people who interact and communicate with each other, whose behaviour is regulated by shared values and norms, who are willing to expend effort to seek common goals and objectives, who have complementary roles, and who perceive themselves as members of the team.

WHAT ARE THE FEATURES OF A SUCCESSFUL TEAM?

EXERCISE 4.2   FEATURES OF A SUCCESSFUL TEAM

Remember a time when you have been a member of a successful team. It may have been a sports team, or connected to a social activity, a work team, or a course team – to conduct a project or assignment for example.

Now write down all those features of the team that you think contributed to its success.

It is likely in Exercise 4.2 that the features you wrote down fit under one or other of the headings below, for which we can use an acronym: ALPDEC.

A: Aims

Successful teams have common aims, which are discussed, identified and understood by all members who are then willing to expend energy in achieving them. Where the aims are conflicting, teams can be drawn in different directions, and lose time and energy in squabbling and disagreement. Teams need to have processes for reconciling differences in aims, and tackle these differences in a way that, whatever the outcome, whoever's view prevails, all members will work towards it.

L: Leadership

Teams require different types of leadership, and leadership doesn't always have to be taken up by one individual alone. They need co-ordination, which requires a leader to co-ordinate the team's activities, take the chair at meetings, focus on time so it is spent on the important issues, and ensure that the team is working towards its common aims: what in Belbin's team roles (Belbin 1993) is labelled 'co-ordinator'. The type of leader who sets the direction and energises the team to keep it moving in the right way also has an important role in team leadership, one more akin to what Belbin terms a 'shaper'. There are other types of leadership roles that are positive in supporting a group. One is in terms of values and principles, a committed and principled leader who leads by example: a role model, who puts ideas into practice and catalyses a group into action. Likewise a leader who empowers people: a participatory leader who ensures that everybody is heard, has their say, and is empowered to do what they need to, to make the team a success.

P: People

The members of the group and their skills are central to team success. Key qualities amongst the members in their interactions with each other are trust and openness. People are different and have different skills and play different roles, and successful teams need to value these differences and accept each other. They need to listen, acknowledge and manage conflict, but also have the capacity to celebrate when things are going well. And above all else, to have fun!

D: Design and delivery

To be successful the team needs to be able to define success in terms of key result areas and performance levels and standards: what constitutes good performance? To manage their activity towards these outcomes they need to plan, establish a schedule with milestones, and develop skills and decision-making capabilities in order to achieve these.

> ## EXAMPLE 4.1 EFFECTIVE DESIGN AND DELIVERY OF A TEAM TASK
>
> The syndicate group for conducting the 'entrepreneurial challenge' project agreed to divide the work into three chunks: market analysis, competitor analysis and customer analysis, each to be researched in pairs. They would meet weekly over the next month to assess each others' performance, and bring together the material to enable them to draw up the business plan. Two people were allocated the task of producing the presentation and the final report. They agreed performance criteria for the work being done and allocated a coach to advise on the financial parts of the assignment and evaluate their work, and another adviser on utilising their statistical information.

E: Environment

Many people in doing Exercise 4.2 find it quite easy to apply their ideas to the first four categories, but often have not considered these last two: environment and change. Yet these are also crucial to team success. Teams need to be aware of what is happening outside of their team: are competitors developing products or ideas that would somehow invalidate the work of the team? Are there potential allies or other teams that could work together in partnership, sharing information, or maybe even merge? Are there experts outside of the team that could help? A team also needs to evaluate opportunities, threats and potential trends, as well as gather information about customers, if they have them. They need to be aware of all their stakeholders and their interests and have plans for meeting their needs. For example, a team working on improving video technology may need to reassess its aims if the competition and market are moving to DVD technology, or a team working to develop new text mobiles would be foolish to ignore the competition's development of picture/text mobiles.

C: Change

Change is another issue that can get overlooked in teams, and yet can be critical. Teams need to reassess their aims and their raison d'être continually, and encourage the creativity and flexibility to develop and change what they are doing. Personal behaviour may need to change to adapt to group norms and teams need to assess constantly whether they have defensive routines which prevent them learning and changing. They may also need to accept the loss of some members and deal with the incorporation of new ones. In some cases teams may need to question their need to continue to exist at all. Otherwise teams can disintegrate into obsolescence, or become plagued by group think and other negative processes: see below.

GROUP DEVELOPMENT AND CHANGE MODELS

Table 4.1   *Three important models of group development and change*

Tuckman (1965), Tuckman and Jenson, (1977)

Forming	Storming	Norming	Performing	Adjourning/ mourning
Testing and dependence	Intra-group conflict	Group cohesion	Functional role relatedness	Celebration of success, dealing with loss, saying goodbye

Bion (1961)

Dependency	Flight then fight	Unite

Schutz (1958)

Inclusion	Control	Affection
Insiders and outsiders	Who is powerful?	Who likes who, forming bonds

(For further information see Jaques 1995.)

Tuckman's five stages

There are many group development models, and three have been chosen in Figure 4.1 to represent some of the stages of group formation commonly identified. For the management development and business community, Barry Tuckman's model is probably the most commonly used and easiest to assimilate. It assumes that groups go through five main stages, beginning by *forming* when the group focuses around the question 'What shall we do?' At this stage individuals are likely to be polite with each other, guarded, testing the ground. Often at this stage group members are dependent, looking to others for direction. The second stage, *storming*, occurs as conflict gradually emerges as differences between individuals and their aims become apparent, and there is some challenge for the leadership. There may also be despondency and low moral as initial optimism is overridden by the discomfort of the confusion and conflict. The third stage occurs as the group starts to develop trust and cohesiveness, open exchanges occur as feelings start to be expressed and discussed, and the group moves from storming to *norming*, identifying common ground, group norms and working practices. Moral and productivity improve and the group enters the *performing* phase, where trust and energy, clarity of roles and mutual understanding means the group becomes highly productive as it focuses on the task. The final stage, *adjourning* or *mourning* occurs as the group achieves its task and maybe finds it is time for individuals to leave or the group to change or disband. Of course these stages don't always happen in order, and problems and difficulties can easily push the group back into a storming phase as disagreement and new leadership challenges take hold. Each of these stages requires different styles of leadership, with more emphasis on clarifying the focus earlier on, then facilitation skills to deal with conflict and team building, followed by coaching and performance management as the group performs, with a gradual move away from giving direction, to supporting self-empowerment as the group becomes more mature. In industry and business, and particularly where teams have evolved to maturity, or are comprised of professionals, teams are self-managed. This approach to leadership is particularly pertinent where members are self-motivated, skilled, confident and have worked through the earlier stages of team formation.

Bion and the Tavistock model

The work of Wilfred Bion and the Tavistock model is more commonly highlighted in therapeutic groups where psychological group dynamics become more the focus.

Bion (1961) assumes that groups work at two levels:

The work group. Here the aim is to meet to perform specific overt tasks, such as set up a new project, new IT system, new department;

The basic assumption group. Here the tacit aim is to preserve the group and alleviate its anxieties and satisfy the needs of the members. The group behaves as if it shares a number of tacit assumptions and notions.

There are three main basic assumptions the group may share: dependency, fight or flight and pairing or hope (a fuller discussion of this can be found in Stokes 1994). If the group is dominated by *dependency*, then the group behaves as if its primary task is solely to provide for the needs and wishes of its members and looks to the leader to look after, protect and sustain the members, rather than present them with the demands of reality. The atmosphere is one of passivity, as the group awaits direction from the leader who will provide the solution to its problems. This is commonly found at an early stage of group formation, but can also be found in certain organisational environments. For example, in medicine and certain health professions a group of patients may be encouraged in the basic assumption of dependency, passively relying on the doctor to save them. To some extent airlines may encourage the dependency of passengers on the crew.

A second basic assumption is one of *fight or flight*. Here the group behaves as if its primary task is to take action to deal with an internal or external enemy. The leader's task is to devise courses of action to lead the group into attack or flight, and the group's task is to follow. An atmosphere of paranoia can prevail, and actions can be without recourse to practicality or effectiveness. The army, social work and investment banks are all work environments that can encourage the fight or flight mentality in a group. As Bion suggests:

> The individual is a group animal at war not simply with the group, but with himself for being a group animal and with those aspects of his personality that constitute his 'groupishness' (Bion, 1961)

The third basic assumption that can prevail in a group is one of *pairing or hope.* The group behaves as if its primary task is to create a better future in which a solution will emerge which will save it from its current difficulties. The atmosphere is one of hopefulness and the group watch and wait to see which leader will come forward. Sometimes a pairing occurs where two members of the group debate or fight out the alternative plan of action or for leadership of the group, while the group waits with bated breath for the leader or victor to emerge. Hope is a feature of groups found in therapeutic circles, and in advertising and PR agencies. Many clients attend therapy in the hope that their problems will be dissolved and their lives made happy, and expect the therapist to make this possible.

Bion's theory is quite complex and it is not possible to do it justice here, but it is worth considering whether you have had a group experience where the group has sat and passively waited for the leader to tell it what to do, as in the dependency basic assumption. Maybe you have been in a group which has taken flight, and run away from the project in hand, avoiding the task which might appear insurmountable and instead taken refuge in displacement activity, such as gossiping, joking and talking light heartedly, or over intellectualising, and talking very abstractly. Alternatively the group may have become dominated by attacking and blaming behaviour, looking for a scapegoat (see below) or an enemy to fight to deal with their anxiety. Dependency is more common early on in group formation, whereas fight or flight comes later as the group begins to experience difficulties with the task. You may have experienced a hopeful group, awaiting a saviour to be born or an unrealistic Utopian solution to be found, colluding with each other in the illusion that the perfect solution is possible. The model of group development provided in Table 4.1 with relation to Bion suggests that initially groups are dependent or try and escape their problems, then enter a fight stage over how to deal with them, followed by uniting to take action: again this roughly follows the Tuckman stages.

A good team co-ordinator may be able to pick up some of the basic assumption behaviour, and find ways of surfacing the underlying anxieties whilst gently but firmly bringing the group back to the work task in hand.

Other psychotherapeutic processes that occur in groups are:

Introjection. This is where someone internalises whole comments made to him or her without critical reflection. These comments may reflect the views of parental or authority figures from their past and so carry some resonance. For example, someone may say casually 'You really are stupid' meaning it in a joking way, but another group member may internalise this and feel that they genuinely are stupid, and this may continue to affect and inhibit their group behaviour and performance. This can also lead to a group member acting out the role of *victim* in a group, taking any blame whether or not it is warranted.

Projection. This occurs when someone projects onto another group member parts of themselves that they feel uncomfortable about. For example a member may feel afraid but instead vocalises this to another group member, as 'You are scared to do the presentation'. This may lead to the person assuming the role of *persecutor*, attacking the others for their faults or even blaming them, which is easier than self-castigation. Sometimes this projection can occur in a caring way where an individual in the group may become a *rescuer*, or compulsive carer, looking after other members of the group as a way of dealing with their own anxiety.

Transference. This is where a group member transfers onto another the characteristics of an important person from their past, usually a parental figure. For example one group member may be rather remote and aloof, and another may develop an intense reaction to their behaviour, with feelings catapulting out of control, with distorted perceptions of the other's behaviour and exaggerated attributions, such as seeing them as rejecting, cold and insensitive, whereas in fact they may only be shy and retiring. This is because feelings for the parental figure get inadvertently transferred onto the group member.

EXAMPLE 4.2   BION'S BASIC ASSUMPTIONS AT WORK

A female headteacher behaved like a strong matriarch, a mother figure to her governing board, treating them all as children. The basic assumption became one of dependency, where the normally mature and responsible governors became like children, either obediently following her lead, or sometimes giggling and misbehaving like primary school children. However, the governors became irritated with their matriarchal leader and although compliant in the meetings, complained and moaned about her outside of them. The governing body were very ineffective, as the group passively listened to the reports of the head and nodded through decisions without any critical discussion.

Occasionally some group members would unwittingly try and change the basic assumption to one of pairing or fight and flight. On one occasion the meeting was discussing the production of the annual report, and the chair, the local vicar, diverted into a discussion about the Bishop's visit. This was in part avoidance behaviour, as he had been reticent in working on the annual report, but also it was an indirect attack on the headteacher. The headteacher responded by saying she would be far too busy to meet the Bishop because she would be tied up with other matters, such as the annual report. The chair responded by saying he would be unable to help with the annual report because he would be too busy dealing with the Bishop's visit. The ensuing battle for control watched by the other governors (mere observers to the spectacle) was a metaphorical jousting match, ending with the capitulation of the chair to work on the governors' report with the head graciously agreeing to meet the Bishop, but clearly showing it was low on her list of priorities.

Schutz on inclusion, control and affection

The last framework for group development identified in Table 4.1 is that of William Schutz (1958), who highlighted issues of inclusion/exclusion, power and control, and affection. Although these are placed in sequence and to some extent relate to Tuckman's model, they can also be examined as independent constructs and processes that can crop up at any time.

Observe the children's playground in a primary school, or talk to children when they return from school and you will find that a preoccupation within any group or gang is that of insiders and outsiders: who is a member of the group, who is excluded? Even in adult groups the process of exclusion or peripheralisation can be an extremely painful and rejecting experience. Who can forget the feelings provoked by being on the margins, ignored or picked upon by other members of the group? Early on in group formation issues of inclusion and exclusion come to the fore. Often an inner core develops akin to the 'kitchen cabinet' of political ministers and regimes. The few members that seem to be at the centre of things, that have power, are feared or envied by others. After inclusion come issues of power and control. As Tuckman's model implies in the storming stage, preoccupation with power, leadership and control can tie up a huge amount of emotional energy as well as divert the group from its primary tasks. For some groups, power is distributed fairly evenly and democratically, for others power becomes captured or attributed to one or a few individuals. The behaviour of domination, often associated with those seeking to force themselves into the centre to take power over the group, is one behaviour that can cause much friction and bad feeling within groups. The third stage of Schutz's model – affection – is also very important to group members' experience: who likes who, am I liked by others or disliked? After the conflict can come harmony, as individuals get to know each other better, and hopefully enjoy each others' company, despite their differences.

EXAMPLE 4.3   INCLUSION, AFFECTION AND CONTROL

A syndicate group of students, assigned to working together on group assignments on a business studies course found themselves bedevilled by petty squabbles and conflict, seemingly unable to get on with the task at all. They sought the help of their personal tutor, a member of the faculty at the college. The tutor asked to see the students individually.

The first student, Amanda, complained angrily that the others were wasting time, wouldn't get on with the task, spent all their time moaning and griping, and wanted the tutor to help her establish control over the group. She had not come on a management course to waste time in petty discussions and pointless conversations.

The second student, Banji, cried in the session with the personal tutor. She felt that Amanda picked on her and ridiculed her and it made her feel dull and stupid. She didn't want to be part of the group anymore.

The third student, Chi, seemed depressed. He felt isolated in the group and struggled with the language, often feeling a few step behind the discussion on the assignment. He found it hard to be included in the discussions, as by the time he had formulated what he wanted to say the discussion had moved on. He was also bewildered by all the heated argument going on around him.

The fourth student, David, had spent years working in an engineering company, had come on the course as a mature student and found the group a shambles. Every time he tried to co-ordinate its activities and bring in each member to elicit their opinion and identify which part of the task they could perform, Amanda would interrupt and tell everyone what they should be doing. He was used to working democratically, and found Amanda loud and obnoxious.

The fifth and sixth group members, Eva and Francis, turned up to see the personal tutor together. They were enjoying the course and had quickly become friends and spent much of their time out socialising. They weren't very worried about what was happening in the group and seemed uninterested in doing anything about it. They thought some of the conflict was amusing, but felt the foreign students Banji and Chi could make more of an attempt to participate in the group's activities and get involved, and complained that they never entered into the social life of the group, for instance coming down to the pub.

Phew – the personal tutor was perplexed, what on earth was going on with the group? What could she do to help?

NEGATIVE GROUP PROCESS CONCEPTS

Lack of synergy

Synergy is where $2 + 2 = 5$. That is where the sum total quality of the decision-taking outperforms the sum total of the contributions of each individual. This occurs when the group dynamics enable each individual to stretch and produce more ideas than they would if left to their own devices. The sheer combination of individuals' talents leads to superior performance. However, teams are often less effective in their decision-making than individuals. Take for example, the many 'survival' games used by trainers in team dynamics: 'lost in the desert', 'lost on the moon' or 'lost at sea'. In these games teams score points for identifying in a correct order the items that would be most useful to them. I have run these exercises many times, and it is not unusual to find that the team score (such as 16/20) may be better than the average individual score (9/20) and the best individual score (15/20), but this is not always so. Generally the team score is not as good as taking the correct answers from all the individuals in the team (which may lead to a score of 18/20). Why would this happen? This may be because of poor team dynamics, where the loudest member prevents the ideas of a quiet but bright member from being heard. This is why the meeting skills mentioned in a section below are so important.

Social loafing

Max Ringelmann, a German psychologist in the late 1920's found that if we have a group of people in a tug of war, pulling with all their might to win the game, it is likely that their total force exerted in pulling the rope (in the research this was 53 kg each, 159 kg in total), is less than the sum total of their individual strengths if each person was measured pulling the rope alone (in the study each person was able to pull 65 kg, Kravitz and Martin, 1986) later experiments and studies have confirmed this finding (for example Liden et al, 2004). It is inevitable that once individuals enter a group, some will take the opportunity to become a slacker, making less effort than if they were attempting a task on their own. In extreme circumstances this leads to a member becoming a free rider, expecting the others in the team to do all the work. Why do some individuals contribute less to the group than others? Some do not perceive the task as important, or may not feel their contribution is recognised. Alternatively they may be lazy and opportunistic, or an individualist who serves their own self-interested agenda but who is not a team player. This can cause much resentment and demoralisation within the group, and needs to be tackled both by the co-ordinator, and collectively by group members, as it is very easy for one individual social loafer to slide the group into a more general cultural morass of apathy and unproductiveness. This plagues both academic course groups and work groups, particularly where the group is evaluated on group performance, and where some individuals feel they end up doing all the work. Tackling these issues head on and early on is essential, and it can be helpful for a group to set the ground rules for contribution at the outset, and discuss this issue, even before it raises its ugly head.

Scapegoating

A scapegoat is someone made to take the blame or punishment for the errors and mistakes of others (Chambers Study Dictionary 2002). William Tindale, in a translation of the Hebrew, formed the word from *escape* and *goat* in the sixteenth century. The word has a fascinating derivation. It originates from early sacrificial and purification rituals performed in Greek and Roman societies, as well as appearing in the Old Testament:

> And Aaron shall lay both his hands upon the head of the live goat and confess over him all the iniquities of the children of Israel, and all their transgressions in all their sins, putting them upon the head of the goat, and shall send him away by the hand of a fit man into the wilderness: And the goat shall bear upon him all their iniquities unto a land not inhabited: and he shall let go the goat in the wilderness. (Leviticus, *16, 21ff,* and see Bremmer 1983: 299).

EXAMPLE 4.4   A SCAPEGOAT – THE WICKER MAN

In the film 'The Wicker Man', the police sergeant Neil Howie, played by Edward Woodward, is enticed into a community on a remote Scottish Island, Summerisle. He arrives to investigate the disappearance of a missing girl Rowan, unaware he has been chosen as scapegoat for this pagan island's misfortune and the failure of its harvest.

In this film we see many of the classic characteristics of the scapegoat. Ideally a scapegoat has to be a part of the group, in this case the pagan islanders. Howie is briefly assimilated into the group through the bogus investigation of the missing girl, Rowan. He has the status required of a scapegoat sacrifice: a policeman representing the rule of law and authority, second only to Lord Summerisle himself. He also possesses innocence and virginal qualities, demonstrated by his resistance to the attempted seduction by Willow, played by Britt Eckland, on his second night on the Island. Through calling door to door around every member of the community looking for the missing girl he unwittingly enables the sins of each member of the community to transfer to him, and mimics the traditional circumambulation of the city of the chosen sacrificial animal or person. In classic rituals, the scapegoat was supposed to accept its role willingly, often duped by having water splashed onto its head to make the head bob as if in assent. Howie steals the garb of Punch to join the May Day procession believing himself on a quest to save Rowan, not realising that his voluntary participation in the festival adds to his own precarious role as scapegoat, dancing to his own sacrifice.

The film ends with Howie's dramatic sacrificial death, ablaze in a wicker cage on the clifftops as an offering to appease the gods of this pagan isle, with the community grouped dancing and singing around him.

(notes drawn from James, 2004)

In many ancient Greek rituals, the scapegoat known as the *pharmakòs,* would be used to purify the community by carrying away their woes as it was expelled from their midst, or even burned to death. Often the goat would be whipped on its way with twigs from the wild fig or willow tree. Sometimes a human sacrifice would be used, a young man feasted for a year and then cast out or thrown into the sea, taking with him plague, famine and drought (Bremmer 1983: 299–320).

Groups, when beset by difficulties, can respond by projecting these onto one of its members, blaming that person for all its ills. The person subconsciously labelled the 'scapegoat' can find the experience traumatic, and in extreme circumstances may be expelled from the group. Many writers on group dynamics, including Bion (1961) and Janis (1982) cite this as a crucial process used to protect the group from its own discomfort, but ultimately to undermine successful decision-making and performance.

Example 4.5 lists a number of contemporary examples of scapegoats from business, industry, politics and sports, drawn from a search of the media for the term 'scapegoat'.

EXAMPLE 4.5   MODERN-DAY SCAPEGOATS

Sport
Rio Ferdinand, the Manchester United football player, was claimed to have been scapegoated when he was penalised with an eight-month suspension for failing to turn up to a drug test, thus missing playing for England in Euro 2004, only returning to play for Manchester United in September 2004.

Politics
George Tenet, CIA Director resigned on 3 June 2004. According to *The Independent* (4 June 2004) he was 'the Bush administration's de facto scapegoat for the fiasco of Iraqi weapons of mass destruction and the heavy loss of US credibility that followed'.

Business
After the Hatfield train crash, where huge concerns were raised over Railtrack's safety record, Railtrack was taken into special measures by the then transport secretary Stephen Byers, and some media coverage at the time suggested that Railtrack was scapegoated, and that the blame lay elsewhere, such as with the government for years of under-investment.

Martha Stewart is a former stockbroker turned 'style guru' in the US, who was convicted early in 2004 on various counts of lying to investigators and obstructing justice about the sale of particular stocks. She was sentenced to several months in jail. Some media coverage at the time suggested that she had done no worse than many others who hadn't been prosecuted, and was prosecuted because of her celebrity status, thus a 'scapegoat'.

What is interesting about many contemporary examples is that there is often a grain of truth, or a basis in fact, for a person to be penalised and scapegoated, leaving some doubt in the mind over their innocence. For example George Tenet, as Director of the CIA is surely responsible in part for the CIA's poor intelligence?

Group think

Group think can be defined as 'a deterioration of mental efficiency, reality testing and moral judgement that results from in-group pressures' and 'the psychological drive for consensus at any cost that suppresses dissent and appraisal or alternatives in cohesive decision making groups' Janis (1972/84, 1988). Irving Janis studied political decision-making fiascos (for example the Bay of Pigs Invasion, and the escalation of the Vietnam war) and found that a number of negative group processes could develop which together formed a phenomenon he called 'group think'.

Symptoms of group think include:

- illusion of invulnerability
- rationalising away data that deny group beliefs
- unquestioned belief in group's inherent morality
- stereotyping competitors/dissenters as weak, evil, stupid
- direct pressure on deviants to conform
- self-censorship by group members
- illusion of unanimity
- self-appointed 'mind guards' who protect group from disconfirming data.

EXAMPLE 4.6   THE CHALLENGER SHUTTLE DISASTER

A good example of group think in action was in the case of the Challenger shuttle disaster in 1986. The flight readiness review assessing whether to go ahead with the launch of the shuttle had developed a feeling of invulnerability: the previous launches had gone ahead without problem. So could this one. The problem raised by engineers such as Boisjoly, that the O ring sealants wouldn't be able to work at the low temperatures forecast for that cold January day, were rationalised away, and dissenters like him were stereotyped as techies who were pedantic and didn't appreciate political and managerial concerns. Pressure was put on dissenters to conform – the group were told to take off their engineering hats and put on their managerial hats – the launch must go ahead, the president himself was awaiting the chance to talk to the teacher in space, it would be a political disaster not to go ahead and moreover would jeopardise the space aviation industry in America. Despite their concerns, group members eventually agreed. The flight should go ahead.

Good leadership and co-ordination can prevent group think if the leader ensures that silent members all get a chance to speak and voice their concerns without prejudice or where individuals are encouraged to give voice to problems, rather than them being swept under the carpet. How many times have you been in a group where, in the urge to seek resolution, the chair has asked 'Is that agreed' and taken silence as assent? Rarely is silence agreement: often it can mean members are disengaged, bored, not understanding what is going on, or vigorously disagreeing with what is being said but lacking the courage to speak up. Where there is real agreement it is more likely that individuals will positively give their assent in speech or body language. Certain values can help a group avoid group think: for example valuing diversity. A spread of different group roles as discussed below also helps here: members who seek out information from outside the group (eg a resource investigator) can help prevent the group avoid becoming too inward –looking, avoiding uncomfortable information.

Obedience to authority and group pressure

Stanley Milgram's controversial electric shock experiments (Milgram 1974), initially at Yale University, illustrated how far people will go in obeying authority when they are asked to do things that may counter their own morality. In one experiment, 26 out of 40 subjects (65 per cent) administered (or at least they thought they did), the most potent electric shock available as part of what they thought was an experiment into the effect of punishment on learning (with psychiatrists predicting only 1 in 100 would do this).

Soloman Asch (1951) designed an experiment where groups of six (five plants, one volunteer) were asked to identify a line, from several others, which matched the length of another line. In the first session all members answered correctly, in the second where group plants deliberately gave an incorrect answer, 32 per cent of the genuine volunteers went along with the wrong opinion despite initial hesitancy.

These examples seem staggering, and when I ask a class what they would predict would be the extent to which individuals would go along with authority and group pressure in these cases most people vastly underestimate the percentage. Yet these individuals were ordinary people like you and me, Milgram's subjects were not monsters hell bent on sadistic punishment. It takes a great deal of courage and self-assurance to defy authority and group pressure.

Risky shift and caution shift

Groups tend to polarise and be more extreme than individuals in both directions. Stoner's experiments (1961) found that groups of management students took riskier decisions, although the research was criticised for lack of realism. On the other hand Myers and Lamm (1976), investigating 'risky shift', also found that some groups tend to be over cautious and found polarisation in both directions. Why? Individuals may feel abnegated from the responsibility of a decision when that decision is shared in a group. Alternatively individuals may get bogged down in agonising over decision-making, because of the disagreement and different points of view. Some of the challenges of managing meetings to prevent a group either rushing to a foolhardy decision, or alternatively spending hours agonising over insignificant decisions, are raised in the next section.

MEETINGS

One reason why groups are considered to be particularly ineffective is that they are always in endless meetings, wasting everyone's time. It has been said 'A camel is a horse designed by a committee!' Some of the main reasons for meetings being ineffective and one of the biggest time wasters in companies are:

- The purpose of the meeting is unclear, or, worse, is held to satisfy a timetable only.
- Too many people are present.
- Some of those present would rather be elsewhere.
- The agenda is vague or non-existent.
- People do not prepare items for discussion.
- Time-keeping is poor and the meeting overruns.
- It is poorly chaired.
- Minutes are late or inaccurate, and do not identify what action should be taken by whom.

Chapter 2 identified some ways in which time management could be improved. However, there are also a few simple principles for running effective meetings.

Consider a meeting that you might chair. Firstly think through the purpose of the meeting. Meetings should take place for one or more of the following reasons:

- to progress and co-ordinate projects, activities and people
- to brief people and exchange information
- to build team morale
- to solve problems
- to make decisions
- to share risks and sensitive or difficult decisions
- to announce decisions
- to generate ideas.

Reconsider your reason. Are you sure there isn't a better way to achieve that objective? For example, are you certain the meeting will enhance morale and not just cause further demoralisation? Could talking individually to people be more effective in providing support to morale than holding a group meeting? Likewise, meetings can be problematic when it comes to making decisions: often it is better to make a decision as an individual, rather than go through the complexities of meetings where everyone volunteers their point of view in order to assert their status, and the decision becomes enmeshed in politics, and finding the lowest common denominator, which nobody can object to (as in the case of the minibus example in Chapter 2).

Once you have identified a purpose, make sure this is clearly and simply stated at the outset of the meeting, as well as in advance.

In relation to meetings you already chair or attend fill in Exercise 4.3 terms of time allocation.

EXERCISE 4.3   MONITORING YOUR MEETINGS

List out in the following table all the meetings you have attended over the last month, identify their purpose, how long they took, whether they achieved their objectives, and ideas as to how they could have been improved.

Meeting and purpose	Time taken	Objectives achieved	Improvements?

A particularly pertinent issue is the *'opportunity cost'*. If you identify all the costs of holding the meeting, the cost of administration, the room and resources, travel, the cost of the time taken by all the participants to attend (which in a meeting of managers could easily amount to £50 per hour × 8 people = £400 per hour). This figure could easily be £600 per hour. Associated with this figure are all the other things the managers could have been doing with their time. Then ask is the achievement of the purpose of the meeting sufficiently important to outweigh these costs (assuming the purpose is achieved)? It is always worth paring down the participants to a minimum and keeping them focused on the purpose, which requires good chairing skills, or the evocation of a good co-ordinator (a team role which is outlined in the next section). The chair, or co-ordinator, should utilise an active agenda where the purpose is identified and time allocated for each item listed. They need to circulate the agenda and information required for the meeting in advance, as well as advise participants on preparation of items, and make the agenda and time allocation clear at the outset of the meeting. Chairing skills are vital. The chair facilitates and controls the meeting, keeping the discussion relevant and on task and on time, and ensures a balance of contributions from each participant. They steer the meeting through the agenda, summarising decisions and each topic as they go, and always ensuring that the minutes are circulated after the meeting with a note as to what action should be taken, when and by whom.

However, the success of a meeting is not all down to the skills of the chair. It also related to the behaviour of participants. At a meeting participants should:

- suggest ideas if they have them
- control their contributions, confining themselves to what is relevant, making a positive contribution but not speaking unnecessarily
- listen carefully and follow the discussion
- clarify other people's contribution and build on their ideas, taking a positive, constructive 'can do' attitude
- accept decisions, even if they conflict with their own view
- review the success of the meeting afterwards, and remember that it is not just the work which is conducted within a meeting that makes it achieve its purpose. Most of the work associated with meetings occurs before and after the meeting, which merely serves to focus the attention.

What participants should not do is:

- interrupt
- dominate the discussion
- be hostile or a silent detractor
- arrive late, leave early, rustle through papers or read messages on their mobile at the meeting (appearing too busy or important to give the meeting their full attention). This can be very distracting and undermining
- whisper, gossip, pass secret messages, or in other ways distract the meeting from its purpose.

TEAM ROLES

Meredith Belbin working within the Training Research Unit at Cambridge conducted research into team roles. Over a number of years he looked at teams in a business game setting and experimented with constructing teams of different types and qualities to see whether he could

EXERCISE 4.4 PREFERRED TEAM ROLES

1. Tick 12 words from the column below that most describe yourself and your attitude towards working with others in a team.	2. Tick 6 words from the second column below which you think most describe your weak points in a team.

Clarifies goals (CO)	Manipulative (CO)
Dutiful (IM)	Impractical (PL)
Challenging (SH)	Uninspiring (ME)
Unorthodox (PL)	Over stretches self (RI)
Expertise (SP)	Over conservative (IM)
Thrives on pressure (SH)	Impatient (SH)
Reliable (IM)	Pedantic (CF)
Painstaking (CF)	Over critical (ME)
Individualistic (PL)	Erratic (PL)
Explorative (RI)	Over delegates (CO)
Unemotional (ME)	Unresponsive to new ideas (IM)
Imaginative (PL)	Ignores big picture (SP)
Involves others (CO)	Short term horizon (RI)
Innovative (PL)	Unambitious (TB)
Intuitive (PL)	Over optimistic (RI)
Dynamic (SH)	Authoritarian (SH)
Orderly (CF)	Negative (ME)
Analytical (ME)	Worrier (CF)
Resourceful (RI)	Preoccupied (PL)
Specialist (SP)	Meddlesome (CO)
Diplomatic (CO)	Indecisive (TB)
Sociable (TB)	Jargonistic (SP)
Courageous (SH)	Easily influenced (TB)
Opportunities Orientated (RI)	Hurtful (SH)
Co-operative (TB)	Inflexible (IM)
Driving (SH)	Anxious (CF)
Develops contacts (RI)	Contributes on narrow front (SP)
Without prejudice (CO)	Unimaginative (ME + IM)
Takes up challenges (RI)	Obsessive (CF and SP)
Self starter (SP)	Impatient (SH + RI)
Prudent (ME)	Uncritical (RI + TB)
Listens well (TB)	
Meticulous (CF)	
Knowledgeable (SP)	
Discerning judgement (ME)	
Resilient (SH)	
Creative (PL)	
Accurate (ME)	
Timely (CF)	
Purposeful (CO)	
Perfectionist (CF)	
Friendly (TB)	
Single minded (SP)	
Enthusiastic (RI)	
Organised (IM)	
Sensitive to others (TB)	
Shrewd (ME)	
Brings people together (TB)	
Practical (IM)	
Promotes decisions (CO)	
Predictable (IM)	
Conscientious (CF)	
Hard working (IM)	
Dedicated (SP)	
Supportive (CO + TB)	
Steady (ME + IM + CF)	
Intense (SH + PL)	
Skilful (SP)	

3. Look at the words you have ticked in both columns and put a tick next to each of the initials which are listed below if they are also in brackets next to the words you have ticked.

CO

SH

PL

RI

ME

TB

IM

CF

SP

predict team success. In particular he tested team members for intelligence and their personality characteristics and over time found that what emerged was a number of team types or roles. Most people had a preferred team role and a secondary role which they used if no one else fitted it or someone played their preferred role better. A fascinating finding of his research was that teams of similar individuals do not necessarily perform well. In fact, Apollo teams populated by highly intelligent people often under performed. More successful are teams which contain a balance of different team roles and types. Table 4.2 identifies a summary of the typical features, qualities and weaknesses of each of the nine team role types identified by Belbin. Before you look at Table 4.2, you may like to identify your own preferred team roles through Exercise 4.4 (note: Exercise 4.4 is a succinct way of identifying possible team roles; for a fuller explanation of the roles read Belbin 1993. There is also a *Team-Role Self Perception Inventory – Revised Edition* produced by Belbin).

Take your two highest scores in terms of the initials and look at Table 4.2 to see which your preferred team roles are.

Knowledge of your preferred team roles can help you in a number of ways. It can enable you to appreciate your likely contribution to a team. You can also use it for development to practise roles you do not normally perform. When constructing a team you may be able to ensure a variety of team roles are covered. When you are working in a team the whole team may be able to evaluate which roles are covered and which tasks and roles may be missing from the team and take action to fill the gaps. For example, if you find that you have no completer/finisher in your team but several co-ordinator types, you could make sure one of the co-ordinators manages the time schedule and pays special attention to the final stages and completion of the work. If a team seems to be experiencing certain problems you could explore whether this is to do with the mix of types in the team. For example an indecisive team is populated by resource investigators and plants; a low morale team may be full of monitor evaluators, completer finishers and shapers; a slow team could be dominated by monitor/evaluators, implementers and completer finishers; a directionless team may have an excess of implementers.

Table 4.2 *Belbin's nine team roles*

Type	Symbol	Typical features	Positive Qualities	Possible Weaknesses
Coordinator	CO	Calm, mature, self-confident, Controlled.	Welcomes all potential contributions, treats on merit and without prejudice. Good chair, clarifies goals, objectives, promotes decisions, delegates well.	Can be seen as manipulative. Delegates personal work. No more than ordinary in intellect or creative ability.
Shaper	SH	Highly strung, out-going, dynamic, challenging. Thrives on pressure.	Drive and courage to overcome obstacles. A readiness to challenge inertia, ineffectiveness, complacency or self-deception.	Proneness to provocation, irritation and impatience. Hurts other people's feelings.
Plant	PL	Individualistic, serious-minded, unorthodox.	Creative and imaginative genius, solves difficult problems.	Up in the clouds, inclined to disregard practical detail or protocol. Too preoccupied to communicate effectively.
Resource Investigator	RI	Extroverted, enthusiastic, com-municative.	A capacity for developing contacts and exploring new opportunities. Responds to challenge.	Overoptimistic. Liable to lose interest once the initial fascination has passed.
Monitor/ evaluator	ME	Sober, unemotional, prudent.	Judgment, discernment, discretion, accuracy, hard-headedness.	Lacks drive and the ability to inspire others. Overly critical.
Team Builder	TB	Socially orientated mild, sensitive to situations.	Co-operative, perceptive, diplomatic. Listens, builds, averts friction, calms the waters. An ability to respond to and promote team spirit.	Indecisiveness at moments of crisis. Can be easily influenced.
Implementer	IM	Conservative, Dutiful, disciplined Predictable.	Organising ability, Practical common sense, turning ideas into practical actions. Hard working and reliable.	Inflexible, unresponsive to unproven ideas and new possibilities.
Completer/ finisher	CF	Painstaking, orderly, conscientious, anxious.	A capacity for follow-through. Perfectionism. Searches out errors and omissions, delivers on time.	Tendency to worry about small things. A reluctance to 'let things go'. 'Nit-picker'.
Specialist	SP	Single minded, self-starting loner, dedicated.	Specialist, provides rare knowledge and skill.	Contributes on a narrow front. Dwells on technicalities, overlooks the 'big picture'.

SUMMARY

This chapter has helped you identify positive behaviours and roles that promote good team performance. It has suggested that groups develop and change over time and that there are a number of ways in which underlying emotions and drives can impact their development: feelings of inclusion, power and affection for example. It has also unveiled some negative group dynamics that can obstruct team performance, and it is important that you can understand and recognise these.

It is worth reiterating what you can do to improve your constructive contribution to a team or group and maximise team performance. The following are constructive team behaviours that make for good team relations:

- understand own roles and accountabilities
- collaborate effectively with other team members
- make the team goal a higher priority than conflicting personal objectives
- be willing to devote effort to achieve team success
- be willing to share information, perceptions and feedback openly
- provide help to other team members when needed and appropriate
- support team decisions
- demonstrate courage of conviction by directly confronting important issues
- respond constructively to feedback from others

Next time you are in a team situation, remind yourself of these behaviours and try to put them into practice. Even better, bring these to the attention of your team, and see if you can persuade all of the members to sign up to this way of behaving. Some teams even put their desired team behaviours on a list and post it up on the wall or in the agenda, to remind each other of their intent.

Finally, it might be helpful to write your own action plan on team working to help you review the insights you have gained from this chapter and ensure they are put into practice. An outline is provided in Exercise 4.5, and you might like to discuss this with a mentor or coach.

EXERCISE 4.5   AN ACTION PLAN ON TEAM WORKING

Identify three main insights you have gained from this chapter and explain how and where you are going to put them into practice in your academic study or working life.

You could choose ideas with relation to:

- effective performance in teams: ALPDEC
- dealing with different stages of team development as a leader or participant
- dealing with issues arising from 'basic assumption' behaviours, or dealing with issues of inclusion, control and affection
- preventing negative group processes such as lack of synergy, social loafing, scapegoating, group think, obedience to authority and group pressure, risky or caution shift
- handling meetings either as a participant or chair
- knowledge of your preferred team roles or team roles exhibited in your group.

1.

2.

3.

REFERENCES AND FURTHER READING

ASCH, S. (1951) Effects of Group Pressure upon the Modification and Distortion of Judgment, in GUETZHOW, H. (ed) *Groups, Leadership and Men*. New York: Carnegie Press.

BELBIN, M. (1993) *Team Roles at Work*. Oxford: Butterworth Heinemann.

BION, W. (1961) *Experiences in Groups*. London: Tavistock.

BREMMER, J. (1983) Scapegoat Rituals in Ancient Greece. *Harvard Studies in Classical Philology*. 87, 299–320.

JAQUES, D. (1995) *Learning in Groups*. 2nd ed. London: Kogan Page.

JAMES, P. (2004) Ritualistic Behaviour in *The Wicker Man:* A Classical and Carnivalesque perspective on 'the true nature of sacrifice'. Unpublished paper. Milton Keynes: Open University,

JANIS, I. (1982) *Victims of Group Think: A psychological study of foreign policy decisions and fiascos*. 2nd ed. Boston MA: Houghton Mifflin.

JAQUES, D. (1995) *Learning in Groups*. 2nd ed. London: Kogan Page.

KRAVITZ, D. and MARTIN, B. (1986) Ringelmann Rediscovered: The original article. *Journal of Personality and Social Psychology*. May, 936–941.

LIDEN, R., WAYNE, S., JAWORSKI, R. and BENNETT, N. Social Loafing: A field investigation. *Journal of Management*. 30(2), 285–304.

MILGRAM, S. (1974) *Obedience and Authority*. London: Tavistock.

MYERS, D. and LAMM, H. (1976) The Group Polarization Phenomenon. *Psychological Bulletin,* 83, 602–627.

SCHUTZ, W.C. (1958) *FIRO– A Three-dimensional Theory of Interpersonal Behaviour*. New York: Holt, Rinchart and Winston.

STOKES, J. (1994) The Unconscious at Work in Groups and Teams: contributions for the work of Wilfred Bion, in OBHOLZER, A. and ROBERTS, V. (eds) *The Unconscious at Work*. London: Routledge. Chapter 2.

STONER, J.A.F. (1968) Risky and Caution Shifts in Group Decisions: The Influence of Widely held Values. *Journal of Experimental Social Psychology*. 4, 442–459.

TUCKMAN, B. (1965) Developmental Sequences in Small Groups. *Psychological Bulletin*. 65, 384–399.

TUCKMAN, B. and JENSON, N. 1977 Stages of Small Group Development Revisited. *Group and Organizational Studies*. 2, 419–427.

WEST, M. (2004) *Effective Teamwork: practical lessons from organizational research*. Oxford: Blackwell.

Communication and interviewing skills

AIMS AND LEARNING OUTCOMES

This chapter is designed to improve your communication and develop your interviewing skills. More specifically it will enable you to become a better listener, and learn to communicate in a clear and effective way.

When you have completed this chapter you will be able to:

- appreciate the different components of the communication process

- identify barriers that can develop and impede communication

- be aware of the pitfalls in electronic forms of communication, and use communication technology wisely

- understand the skills needed to be an effective interviewer, and develop these into practice, in particular being able to build rapport, use appropriate question-asking skills such as probing; and make appropriate use of reflection, paraphrasing and summarising.

This chapter will raise your awareness of *how* we communicate, not just *what* we communicate, and this includes an appreciation of non-verbal communication, paralanguage, proxemics and kinesics, terms which you will be introduced to below.

INTRODUCTION

Communication is something we do all the time, generally without even thinking about it. Yet when you stop to analyse it, there are a number of complex processes occurring. This chapter begins by exploring the elements in the communication process, and barriers and problems that can develop and lead to miscommunication. Communication is challenging, because to do it successfully we need to develop more self-awareness and awareness of others, how we impact on others and how others perceive us.

Although much communication is face-to-face, the growth of information and communication technologies has meant that increasingly we are communicating by telephone, fax, and e-mail. These forms of communication set us particular challenges and allow for misunderstandings arising from the lack of body language and other signals. These are addressed below.

A hugely important communication skill within work organisations is interviewing. It is not the same as every-day communication and it requires particular techniques. Interviews are used for a variety of different reasons and these also require us to adapt our style to the situation. In this chapter we will explore the skills necessary for effective interviewing.

THE COMMUNICATION PROCESS

Management communication is often developed into a particularly complex process.

EXAMPLE 5.1A   USUAL PROCESS FOR RAISING A FIRE ALARM

FIRE!

1   Raise the alarm.

2   Go to a place of safety.

3   Call the fire brigade.

EXAMPLE 5.1B   MANAGEMENT COMMUNICATION FOR DEALING WITH FIRE

FIRE!

1   Network with colleagues and neighbours.

2   Technical discussions and consultations over ignition devices, oxidising processes, flammable materials, optimal evacuation paths.

3   Focus groups formed to test ideas for evacuation, market research initiated on alternative approaches.

4   Solutions implemented – Contact call centre located in Lahore, activate counter-action and back-up. Negotiate strategic partnership with Royal Air Force for launching rescue. Privatise fire service. Put in insurance claims. Staff to work from home, when in office to wear full safety boiler suits.

5   Evaluate solution. Sack the consultants.

In management communication things are rarely simple, and there is a tendency for communication to become unnecessarily complex with many different parties getting involved and a variety of opportunities for information and perspectives to become distorted. Your task in this chapter will be to seek out ways to communicate in a clear and effective way.

Think of a recent interaction you had at work with another person. What were you focusing on in this interaction? Nine times out of ten, we focus our interactions on what we want to say and what information we want to convey. We focus on ourselves as:

- **'the sender'** of a message and
- **'the message'** itself.

However, there are five other key components in the communication process (for further discussion of this see Daft 1993, Chapter 16, or Buchanan and Huczynski 2004, Chapter 6). These are often explained using the analogy of old telecommunication and transmitter systems, or the analogue radio, and according to Buchanan and Huczynski the origins of this model derive from Shannon and Weaver's (1949) work on signal processing in electronic systems. These components include:

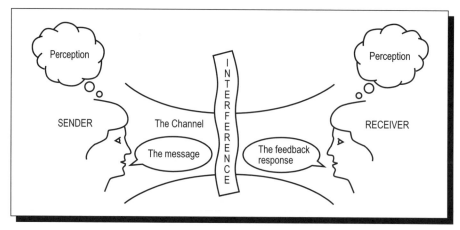

Figure 5.1 *Components in the communication process*

- **'The receiver'** who has to decode and interpret our message, requiring them to listen.

- **'The channel'** which is the path the message follows, for example upwards, downwards, horizontally, formally or through the grapevine, verbal or written, handwritten or electronic, etc.

- **'Feedback'** which is the response given.

- **'Perception'** which is the meaning given to the message by both the sender and receiver. If perception differs, which is inevitable, then there is the potential for miscommunication.

- **Interference'** are the barriers that obstruct or distort the communication.

Of course most interactions are a much more complex interplay and interchange between the two or more people in the communication process. At any one time we are often giving out and receiving, encoding and decoding information. Communication therefore is as much about listening as it is about speaking or sending information, it is a two-way process. Huczynski and Buchanan (2001, 179) jokingly define conversation as 'a competitive sport in which the first person to draw breath is declared the listener'.

EXERCISE 5.1   ANALYSING A CONVERSATION

In the following conversation identify:

a) What channel is being used for communication? Is it appropriate?

b) What is the message the sender (Chris) is conveying?

c) What feedback is Chris receiving from Lesley?

d) What appears to be the sources of miscommunication and different perceptions involved?

In staff coffee area at work:

Chris [going past the room, arms full of papers, sees Lesley and pops his head round the door to speak to her]: Oh I'm glad I bumped into you [moving closer to Lesley]. I wondered if I could send you a load of e-mails that have got client names and addresses in and could you extract them from the e-mails and enter them on the database? I'm so rushed, I haven't time!

Lesley: I'm just getting myself a cup of tea [in a querulous high pitched voice and bending over the fridge getting out the milk], sorry what did you say it was . . .?

Chris [abruptly interrupting]: If I send you some e-mails can you enter the names and addresses on the database? Sorry to interrupt you, I'm so busy (making to leave).

Lesley: Hang on [louder, and sounding upset and cross]. I don't think I know what you mean, can you say that again slowly, you are confusing me.

Chris [sounding impatient and harassed]: I need some information taken off some e-mails and put into the database, it is dead simple, honest, if I just send them to you, you will see what I mean, it's easy!

Lesley [speaking rapidly, gabbling]: Is this one e-mail, or several, how do I know which are the names and addresses you need? Actually I'm really busy with work for Pat at the moment [starting to back towards the door].

Chris [exasperated]: Look it's obvious, I haven't got time to explain it more now, I'll talk later. I know your busy, I really appreciate it, thanks . . . [looking at Lesley's retreating back as Lesley leaves the room, then saying to self] God she is so useless, she has got no work to do, and she can't even do simple things and the rest of us are rushed off our feet. Gosh secretaries are so dumb!

Lesley [saying to self]: I can't hear what he is saying, I go into a fog when he talks to me, all rushed and panicky, I can't cope, I want to resign [swallowing tears and returning shakily to making her tea, then spends the next 30 minutes having tea and moaning to a colleague about how stressed she is and how unreasonable the managers are].

There are clearly a number of ways in which in Exercise 5.1 Chris and Lesley miscommunicate. This exercise demonstrates that non-verbal communication is as important as what we say. Non-verbal communication includes body language, physical body posture, gesture, facial expressions as well as the way we speak. The study of body language has been termed 'kinesics' and incorporates the movement of the limbs, touching and posture. Where body language conflicts with what we say – for example Chris's impatient demeanour contradicts his statements of appreciation for Lesley – greater emphasis is usually placed on the non-verbal message, in this case, his exasperation with Lesley.

The lack of congruence between what we say and how we say it can be unconsciously duplicitous. *Paralanguage* describes the way we speak rather than what we say. It covers voice quality, its pitch, coughing or groaning, vocal qualifiers, such as variations in the volume or pitch, and vocal segregates, such as pauses and interruptions. In the interchange it is paralanguage that communicates Chris's anxiety and irritation (speaking loudly and interrupting) and Lesley's nervousness (when speaking rapidly and with high pitch), confusion and anger.

Non-verbal leakage also gives clues to our thoughts and feelings. In a game of poker a player who brashly throws the chips on the table may be masking a weak hand. Deception can be masked by jerky movements and nervous tics that are unconscious and automatic. Non-verbal leakage is particularly prevalent when we are lying, so, for example, when we are giving insincere praise we may deny the praise by shaking our head, crossing our arms or any number of small involuntary signals. Unconsciously we pick up the underlying message that may be hidden from us, and Lesley's response to the interchange by her negative retort and passive aggression (through avoidance of her work) demonstrates her receipt of the slight. We have to be careful, however, how we interpret non-verbal leakage, for example lack of *eye contact* may mean someone is lying, but also may merely be because that person is shy, lacks confidence or comes from a culture where maintaining eye contact with someone senior could be considered insolent. Body language only gives us clues to, not evidence of, true feelings.

A positive example of the power of non-verbal communication is in *postural echoing* where people mirror and recreate the posture and body language of another as a sign of empathy and agreement. You will notice that when two people are communicating well, this mirroring occurs, but when it is mismatched, as in Exercise 5.1, there is a lack of mirroring. Chris could have spent more time getting in tune with Lesley through mirroring her and responding to her defensive cues, and through more active listening (covered below) to find a way to communicate without Lesley feeling so threatened.

Proxemics is the study of the communication function of space and the way people unconsciously structure their space, such as through distance and closeness. Chris closes in on Lesley, trapping her in the staff coffee area, and Lesley retreats to hide in opening the fridge, and then scurries away out of the room, and this reinforces a 'persecutor' 'victim' (see Chapter 9) exchange. Chris could have used the space in a less threatening way to enable Lesley to feel more confident, making a positive exchange more likely.

Think of shopping and how, when looking in a shop window and another person comes and stands close by, we may unconsciously move away. There are four zones of personal space: intimate, personal, social and public. Poor communicators often infringe others' space boundaries, or alternatively put too much distance between themselves and the person they want to communicate with. It takes judgment to find the appropriate distance to use, and this is even more important when communicating with people from different cultures who may have very different expectations of what is appropriate and comfortable in terms of the space between communicators. For example, many European and American cultures prefer proximity, but this may seem rude in far Eastern, Asian and Chinese cultures.

Before moving on to the next section, check your understanding of these aspects of the communication process by attempting Exercise 5.2.

EXERCISE 5.2   COMMUNICATION PROCESSES

Define in your own words each of the concepts below, and give an example from your own experience of when this has been an important aspect of communication. Draw from exchanges you have had or situations in which you have found yourself. If you need to, re read this section.

a) kinesics

b) paralanguage

c) non-verbal leakage

d) postural echoing

e) proxemics

There are clearly a number of other ways in which in Exercise 5.1 Chris and Lesley miscommunicate, and in the next section we will look at some of the barriers and ways in which these may arise.

BARRIERS TO COMMUNICATION

There are a number of ways in which 'interference' can get in the way of communication. Typically this includes:

- lack of clarity in message
- complexity of the message
- jargon
- lack of trust in relationship
- defensiveness
- dismissiveness of the other
- failure to listen
- poor attention span
- emotions
- conflicting assumptions
- attitudes to tasks/people.

Review your answer to Exercise 5.1 and see which of the above issues got in the way. Also think of situations at work/college or at home where there has been a breakdown in communications. What were the reasons? In Chapter 9 we will be exploring some of these interpersonal and intra-psychic issues in more detail, but in this chapter we will focus on building competence in communication for the more general interactions we have in the workplace and particular skills for particular situations.

There are also a number of perceptual processes that create barriers to communication, two of which are:

- stereotyping, prejudice and bias
- halo/horn effect.

Stereotyping is where we place someone in a category to which we ascribe often negative characteristics – in this case Chris may have the stereotype that 'all secretaries are dumb' for example, and Lesley 'all managers are unreasonable'. Our assumptions often lead us to prejudge people and impact our behaviour in a way that makes it more likely for our assumptions to be realised.

The halo/horn effect is where we take one action and magnify it to represent our whole image of the person. It would be quite easy for one poor piece of communication, such as in Exercise 5.1, to lead to Chris and Lesley seeing each other as a 'bad' manager and secretary respectively for evermore, despite later behaviour showing that Chris, when not under pressure, acts patiently and Lesley competently. These processes become particularly important when we are communicating with someone in order to interview them, particularly when it comes to judging and evaluating them, as in selection and appraisal. These processes lead to the five-minute effect – where we sum up a person and make a decision, for example to select or reject them, within the first five minutes of the interaction, rather than being more open-minded and waiting for further evidence before coming to a judgment. Good communication requires us to be more open-minded about people, not rushing to quick judgments but being more open to a person revealing other sides of their personality.

The channel of information impacts the nature of the information we absorb and also our perceptions of the meaning of that information. Face-to-face communication is the richest channel, and best for non-routine, complex, difficult and ambiguous messages. Think back to the communication incident you were asked about at the beginning of this chapter – in what ways did you receive the information? One study by Albert Mehrabian has suggested that in spoken face-to-face communication, and specifically with relation to first impressions, verbal impact (ie what you say) accounts for only 7 per cent, vocal impact (ie the tone of voice, and way it is said) 38 per cent, and facial and physical impact (ie body language, including posture, gestures and eye contact) 55 per cent of the information interpreted

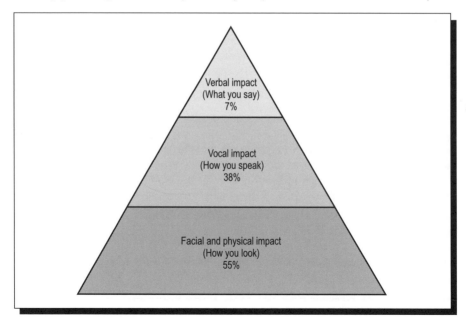

Figure 5.2 *Impact of face-to-face communication*

(Mehrabian 1971, and also quoted in Daft 1993, 557, O'Connor and Seymour, 1990, 35). See also Figure 5.2.

Many channels filter out these other information sources. The telephone and electronic media still enable some limited interaction, but memos and letters tend to be quite a static form of channel, and fliers, bulletins, and general reports are the most impersonal, static and least rich channels of all. However, the latter can be useful for conveying exact and factual information, where accuracy is important. In face-to-face interaction our memory can easily omit key information, such as the time or place of a meeting. A game of 'circular whispers' illustrates this point well. Try out Exercise 5.3 with some friends – you will be amazed at how the message gets distorted. This can be a salutary lesson for busy managers like Chris in Exercise 5.1 who insist on throwing out complex factual instructions in a casual verbal way. Imagine how much more difficult it would be to get correct decoding of the message if there was a lot of background noise, and all the people concerned were busy, involved with other thoughts and activities. No wonder so much communication goes awry!

EXERCISE 5.3   CIRCULAR WHISPERS

Sit in a circle with several friends, colleagues or family members. One person then passes a message on to the next by whispering, and they pass it on to the next and so forth, until the message returns to the first person. The last person to get the message should state it out aloud, followed by the first person repeating the original message.

Try this with the message 'Meet Steven James and me in reception at his office at number 15 Victoria Place at 1.00. If I don't get there in time, say within 10 minutes, you and Steve go on to Sartre's Restaurant on Durant Street. Get the drinks in but wait for me before you order lunch. Mine is a gin and tonic but don't forget Steven doesn't drink alcohol.'

NON-FACE-TO-FACE COMMUNICATION

Twenty years ago the author did not have e-mail; now she is getting approximately 80 e-mails a day. How many e-mails a day do you receive? Add to that telephone conversation, texts, and use of the fax, and you will realise that increasingly your communication is not face-to-face, but mediated through advanced technologies.

We spend a lot of time coaching people in interview skills and face-to-face communication skills, but the use of e-mails is a relatively recent and unexamined phenomenon. On the one hand it seems likely that they save much time and wasted effort by enabling information to be sent to many people at once at the click of a mouse. However, there is also growing evidence to suggest that they may lead to inefficiency. Take for example the growing practice of copying everyone in on an e-mail. As we become more and more inundated by floods of e-mails, the endless and often irrelevant chains of discussion that get peddled round and round can become a drain on resources. It can result in us paying less attention to the information than perhaps it requires. It fills our in tray with rubbish. Instead of a cycle of satisfaction being developed through e-mail chains on a particular policy or debate, we may just end up in a cycle of frustration and misunderstanding as everybody puts in their pennyworth and becomes part of the confusion and chaos. Laziness and the speed at which we are pushed into churning out e-mails may lead to further confusion, which can take several further e-mails to sort out – points that one telephone call could have resolved. How many times have you received an exhaustive sequence of e-mails, only to find you have to telephone the person sort the matter out: an action that takes five minutes, after many more having been wasted on e-mails. Chapter 2 on time management demonstrated how we can easily be led into ineffective behaviour in our use and abuse of e-mails.

Consider what the strengths and weaknesses of using e-mails are. They are useful for the quick communication of factual information to a range of people. They are not so useful for more sophisticated interactions of complex ideas. Are you and your colleagues playing to their strengths or their weaknesses? Attempt Exercise 5.4 to assess their utility.

EXERCISE 5.4   USING E-MAIL

Part A

1. Take the last 10 e-mails you received (or a sample of 10 typical e-mails). Categorise these e-mails according to the following criteria:
   - importance (rate each e-mail 1 = unimportant, 2 = fairly important or 3 = very important)
   - urgency (1 = very urgent, 2 = quite urgent and 3 = not urgent)
   - utility (1 = useful to you/your work, 2 = quite useful, 3 = very useful)
   - identify the e-mails according to their *type* and purpose:

   provision of information

   request for response/information

   work-based discussion, problem-solving, decision-making, analysis

   social and personal chat and gossip

   unsolicited mail, advertising, marketing mail.

2. Now examine these e-mails and their method of communication. Note down:
   - the level of *formality* (1 = informal, 2 = quite formal, 3 = very formal)
   - your emotional *response* to the e-mail (did it make you feel interested, irritated, angry, upset, happy, etc?).

3. Look at the potential for misunderstanding in the e-mails and note down where this may take place and how.

4. Look at what you decide to do with each e-mail (see Chapter 2):
   - act on it
   - file it
   - delete it
   - reply to it.

5. Now re-examine each e-mail and identify whether the mode of communication was the most appropriate for its purpose (ie e-mail versus leaflet, letter, telephone call, face-to-face etc). Did it achieve its objective? If not, why not?

Part B

6. Now take a sample of 10 e-mails you have sent. How important, urgent, useful were they? What purpose and type were they? How formal or informal were they? Read them from the point of view of the recipient – what potential for misunderstanding and miscommunication may there be in them? What do you think the recipient will do with them? For each e-mail, do you think this was the most efficient and effective form of communication?

In attempting Exercise 5.4 it is particularly interesting to explore your use of e-mails with relation to the conveying of complex ideas and information and for discussion. The room for misunderstanding and confusion may be greatest in this area. Although an informal culture has developed around the use of e-mails, there are times when this becomes inappropriate or may be misinterpreted as insult. The reason for this is the much more limited signals and cues provided in communication through e-mail. For example if we are talking to someone face-to-face we can check out whether, when they say 'you are useless', they are joking or serious through their facial expression – are they smiling or serious, their gestures – are they pointing threateningly at you, or clapping you on the back – and their body language – is it relaxed or uptight. In an e-mail there is very little to go on, just the words on the screen, and so one casual word 'useless' can take on greater significance. The opposite may also happen: with the mass of e-mails and over-use of the 'urgent' exclamation mark, truly urgent messages, such as 'Turn up at 9.00 am tomorrow for the interview' may be buried. For this reason it is likely that face-to-face and traditional forms of communication will continue to be important in work, and also why, when we communicate through electronic methods, we may need to be more careful of what we say and how we say it.

INTERVIEWING SKILLS

Communicating is concerned with giving and receiving information, talking and listening. Interviewing is one process where communication skills become absolutely critical, because most interviews utilise the communication process to enable evaluation, assessment, or decision-making. Although the information conveyed varies depending on the type of interview (and below we focus on selection, counselling and appraisal interviews), there are still a number of common skills which underlie all. These are highlighted under the five headings of contact, conduct, content, control and capture.

Contact

An interview only succeeds if we can build up some kind of rapport with the respondent. They need to relax and to be put at ease, and at the same time engage with you in communication. One reason why many interviews start with informal talk and chat is to build a friendly trusting environment, to get people talking and settle them down. Through building trust and a rapport we can establish a 'working alliance' with the subject and give our objectives a chance to be realised.

Table 5.1 identifies the ways in which we can use clues to assess whether the interviewee has been put at ease.

Table 5.1 *Building rapport*

Evidence of rapport	Evidence of a lack of rapport
The subject is at ease, talking freely	The subject has clammed up and is speaking monosyllabically
The subject is doing most of the talking	You are doing most of the talking
There is supportive body language – the subject is smiling, the body posture looks relaxed	The subject looks tense and worried, their body looks taught and rigid
The subject is using cues appropriately: nodding using eye contact reflecting body language (for example posture, hand movements, leg positions)	The subject is not using cues effectively: head immobile lacking eye contact, looking away defensive body language, hunched, crossed and not reflecting yours
The subject is responding to non-verbal signals, for example: stopping talking and listening as appropriate	The subject is ignoring or not picking up on non-verbal signals, for example: continues to talk when you have signalled you want to move on talking over you

However, there are other factors involved in making contact with the person being interviewed, and at the outset it is up to you (the interviewer), to clarify the purpose of the interview, how long it will take, what form and so on.

Conduct and questioning techniques

In conducting the interview, the interviewer needs to create good *questions* to encourage information sharing. Different types of questions elicit different responses. Firstly there are open and closed questions.

Open questions

These get the interviewee talking and so are helpful for developing the rapport and opening up the subject, particularly if they are reticent. They also give you (the interviewer) a chance to sit back and listen to the subject, take stock and gather general information from them. They provide the subject with freedom to develop their ideas and express themselves. Examples might be:

> 'Tell me about your experience over the last year' or 'Let's explore some of the difficulties you have been facing, perhaps you would like to outline these for us to explore.'

Closed questions

These provide you with specific information or enable you to clarify a point. They are useful for closing down a verbose subject, and as a precursor to moving on to another topic, particularly when you have limited time. For example:

'How long were you working on that project?' or 'Who was in your team?'

Next there are *probes*. Open questions are a form of probing – they encourage the other person to talk more deeply and freely – but there are other ways to ask probing questions:

Elaboration

These questions are designed to elicit more information from the other person. Such as:

'That is really interesting, can you tell me more about that?' 'What do you mean by that?' or 'Let us unpack that a little further. . . .'

Behavioural anchors

It can be very helpful to get illustrative examples from the person being interviewed, ones which relate to their experience rather than hypothetical situations. This is particularly the case in selection, appraisal and promotion interviews. For example:

Interviewer: You say you are extremely good at working in a team – can you give me an example of a team you have worked in, and what team behaviours and roles you displayed in that team?

Repetition

Sometimes the respondent finds it difficult to answer the question, or may even evade it, so repetition can be a good way of not being fobbed off. If at first you don't succeed, try and try again! For example:

Interviewer: Why did you leave your last job?

Subject: Oh for a lot of reasons really, there wasn't one, but I was really glad to then move on and I'm happy in the work I do now . . . .

Interviewer: So why did you leave the last job?

Subject: It's difficult to say, but I'm much happier here.

Interviewer: 'I appreciate it may be difficult to articulate why you left your last job, but please try.

Subject: Well I guess I just didn't get on with the others, they wound me up, and I didn't feel at all motivated . . . .

Follow-ons, storytelling and mutual musing

One way to keep the interviewee talking and to keep the focus on them is to use follow-ons:

Interviewer: Then what happened?

Asking the interviewee to take you step–by-step through an incident. To tell a story narratively, often chronologically, again enables a greater depth of information:

Interviewer: Can you take me through the process leading to the decision to change the supplier?

Alternatively a reflective way of enabling your respondent to think deeply and have time to reflect on a situation before speaking is to ask questions in the manner of mutual musing, such as:

Interviewer: That is very puzzling, I wonder why that might be?

This is a less direct and less threatening way of introducing a question, and the respondent may not feel put under such pressure or on the spot, and again this may enable them to talk more freely.

Of course not all interventions and probes you make are questions. There are a number of other valuable interventions that are ways of demonstrating active listening. These include:

Reflecting back

Here you are providing a mirror for the other to see the words they have used, their meanings and feelings. If you reflect these back to them, it gives them an opportunity to check that they have said what they meant to say, and also to delve a bit deeper into the issue. So for example the exchanges could be:

Subject: No one has been listening to me.

Interviewer: You really don't feel you have been listened to.

Subject: No, and it's made me feel so powerless . . . .

Or

Subject: It is really worth proceeding with this project.

Interviewer: You believe we should go ahead with the project.

Subject: Yes, it is a brilliant opportunity for the company to get into this growing market . . . .

Paraphrasing

Paraphrasing is similar to 'reflecting back', but instead of repeating the words of the subject, you may put them in your own words. Again it keeps the focus on the subject and keeps the flow of information coming from them, not you. So for example the exchange could be:

Subject: I really would like to be given some more difficult tasks, ones that I can really get my teeth into, I'm getting fed up in my current work.

Interviewer: So you feel you are ripe for taking on a more challenging role. You sound frustrated with your work now.

Subject: Yes, I'm so ready for a change, I've been in my job for years . . . .

Summarising

Of course giving subjects a chance to talk allows you to listen, but there may come a time when you need to summarise what they have said to check your understanding, before moving on. This is particularly useful when a respondent seems to be going on at great length and is having difficulty focusing – it gets them and you back on task and feeling competent. Otherwise it is easy for the conversation to drift and the candidate to trail away into silence, losing energy and interest in the discussion, or allows them to avoid difficult issues. Sometimes an interruption with a summary can be a good way of keeping in control of the interview.

Subject (having gone on at length already): So I really think I have done a fantastic job this year, despite the hitch over the new contract, and I get on well with everyone, and I really enjoy the work, and . . . .

Interviewer (interrupting): If I could summarise your feelings about your performance, you feel you have done a good job and enjoy it, but there was one hitch, perhaps we could move to look at what happened with the new contract, and why that was difficult for you.

Although summaries are extremely useful in interviews, the summary doesn't have to be provided by you – it is something that you could ask the subject to do:

Interviewer: You have told me many things about your work over this year, overall how would you summarise this experience, what is your overall impression of how you are doing?

Clarifying

We don't always understand what the subject is saying in an interview, so seeking clarification is useful for you and also them. After all, if you don't clarify your understanding of what they are saying, what is the use of the information that is being provided? For example:

Subject: I have been feeling really bad a lot recently . . . .

Interviewer: Can you just say what you mean by bad, do you mean low?

Subject: Sort of, well actually it is really a feeling of anxiety, a knot of panic that sits in my stomach, it almost paralyses me.

Interviewer: And by a lot do you mean it happens all the time?

Subject: No, it is worse in the mornings, it gets better when I get into my work and get something achieved.

Interviewer: And this is just recent.

Subject: Well I guess it really started when we merged the companies and I took on a lot more work.

Not all ways of probing relate to what we say – they may relate to what we don't say. Often an inexperienced interviewer may find dealing with silence very awkward, and feel compelled to jump in when there is a silence. Actually it may be more effective not to speak, or to use body language to encourage the respondent to take their time, and to go deeper.

Minimal prompts

It may sometimes be better to respond with minimal prompts such as nodding, smiling and making noises of encouragement, rather than feeling you need to always make a more elaborate intervention. Allowing a respondent the space to talk without interrupting, constant questioning or judging is particularly important in counselling and appraisal interviews. In fact it can be a profoundly meaningful experience for someone to talk and be actively listened to, to have their thoughts and feelings witnessed. There often isn't space in organisational life for a manager to take stock and actively listen to their colleagues, and the power of this to motivate others should not be under estimated.

Some interviewers, often through nerves or the need to prove themselves, jump in to make suggestions or move the topic on or make other interventions where minimal prompts would work better.

For example instead of:

> **Subject**: I feel so overwhelmed and upset . . . . [silence]
>
> **Interviewer**: Oh you poor thing, lets look at what we can do to make things better.
>
> **Subject**: I can't carry on.
>
> **Interviewer**: Oh dear, well lets turn to look at how you did last year.

A better exchange could go thus:

> **Subject**: I feel so overwhelmed and upset . . . . [silence]
>
> **Interviewer** nods sympathetically and looks attentive
>
> **Subject**: I just feel so frightened of Mr. Wager, every time he comes over he just criticises my work, and he's always putting me down in front of everyone else . . . . [silence, but looking as though she has something else to say]
>
> **Interviewer**: Mmm [sounding empathetic, and clearly paying attention, sitting forward in seat confidentially]
>
> **Subject**: . . . and he keeps putting his hand on my knee when there is no one in the office . . . .

Many people find silence difficult to endure, but an expert interviewer will be able to listen to the silence and get an impression of what is behind it. See Table 5.2 for the different types of silence.

Table 5.2 *Different types of silence*

In answer to the question:	Some possible answers could be:
'Why are you upset?' it is likely there may be a silence before the person answers. There are a number of different meanings this silence could imply. Brainstorm your ideas about what a silence could mean, and then identify ways in which you could identify the meaning of the silence.	a) feeling overwhelmed by different things to say, having too much to say b) feeling blank, vacant and empty, having nothing to say c) feeling confused, not knowing what to say d) feeling angry or resentful, not wanting to say anything e) reflecting, wanting to take time choosing the right thing to say f) feeling overcome by emotion, unable to say anything. Of course there are many other responses, we may get clues from body language and non-verbal cues, but we would need to check these out rather than jumping to our assumptions which may be incorrect.

Active listening

Although question-asking techniques are extremely important, communication is a two-way process, and active listening skills are equally vital. Cameron (2002, 184–187) identifies some features of active listening: suspending judgment, concentrating on the speaker, watching body language, avoiding interruptions, seeking clarification, acknowledging feelings, allowing silence, encouraging and prompting, avoiding opinions, not offering 'solutions'.

Holding back on one's own evaluation is important in order to hear what the other person is saying. Of course we may often have a view on something, but active listening requires us to 'bracket' this view – hold it in abeyance – in order to enable us to hear better what the other person is saying. Bringing in your own evaluation too soon closes down the speaker and prevents you hearing what they have to say. Listening means putting the focus on the speaker, and not over-interrupting what they are saying or throwing in your own opinions. However, at the same time we need to show our interest by our body language, and also by observing their body language. Listening means paying attention to all aspects of their communication: listening to their emotions and feelings and picking up clues from how they are talking. We may even need to go further and seek more clarification where we don't understand or are not sure about something that has been said, or we want to check out that our information, and impressions are accurate. We also need to encourage them to talk, prompting when necessary. All the time we are doing this we are registering information, impressions and ideas.

There are times when our evaluation is important (for example in an appraisal interview) but these evaluations need to be made after the person has been fully heard, and jumping in with your own judgments too soon will not enable that to happen. Some interviews can be very emotionally charged, for example when someone is nervous in a selection interview, or is being assessed on their performance. In jumping in too quickly and not engaging in active listening it is more likely the other person will resort to impression management – distorting the information to make a better impression on you – or defensive behaviour, neither of which enables useful communication.

Techniques for active listening can be supplemented by 'supportive listening' techniques identified in Whetton and Cameron, (2002, 220–248). Supportive communication is aimed at enhancing a positive relationship between the communicators and is particularly useful where the interview is dealing with problems, and giving difficult feedback. One of the features of supportive listening is that it is problem orientated rather than person orientated. It is much more helpful to focus on problems and issues, which can be changed, than people, their personalities and characteristics, which can't. Likewise it should be specific and not global, as has been mentioned with relation to SMART objectives in Chapter 2. In listening, voice and body language, thoughts and feelings should be congruent, so if you say you are upset, you look it. A particularly interesting aspect of supportive listening is the need to be descriptive rather than evaluative. A message is much easier to accept if you describe what happened and your reaction to it, instead of jumping to a judgment. However, you should also own the communication, and not make it some general truth – this is specifically your view, not an abstract person's view. Communication that is validating is very helpful, for example where you show respect for the other person and involve them: 'I've mentioned some of my ideas, but I'm sure you have some of your own ...'. Finally you should also build on what the other person says, not ignore their comments or make big leaps onto other topics or foci.

Content

If we pay too little attention to the process of the interview then it is likely that the content of the interview – the information we want to convey and receive – will get lost. To enable you to ensure that this doesn't happen, it is important to have notes of what you want to cover, (information capture is discussed below). Also you will need a structure outlining when each aspect is to be raised. For example, for a selection interview you are likely to have a pro forma of the areas you want to explore, and you may also have an evaluation area for comments which relate to the person specification in these areas. The selection interview may cover: qualifications, employment history, current role, skills utilised, future career plans, reasons for wanting the new position, views on their own strengths and weaknesses, etc. It is important to have documentation on this because you will need to demonstrate fairness in the process: that you have assessed all candidates in the same way, and also be able to justify your decisions. Other interviews may be less structured, such as in a counselling interview, but you will still need a plan as to how to navigate through the areas you wish to cover. Of importance here is how you handle closure, so that when somebody has unburdened personal information you don't just leave them feeling vulnerable and insecure as they go back to their job. You need to have an idea as to how you are going to end the interview: summarise, maybe reiterate learning points, ideas for action, or even reaffirm their value as a human being and your respect for them and the feelings they have been experiencing.

Giving feedback

Of particular concern is the issue of giving negative feedback and how that can be handled in an interview. You may have decided to raise the problem, ask for their response and 'listen', discuss the problem further and invite them to examine how they can improve and move towards joint problem solving for a course of appropriate action. Sometimes these problems are raised in the context of an appraisal discussion or even informal discussion on someone's performance. There may be negative feedback to give but the aim is for it not to become demotivating and debilitating. A positive way of putting this is:

> commend – recommend – commend.

For example

> I really liked the way you handled the client and listened to their issues. It would be even more helpful if next time you could give them the protocol and go through it at the start of the work. However, overall I think the client's views are very positive about the way we are handling the contract.

It is often considered constructive in appraisals to begin by giving positive feedback, then to cover the more negative feedback, and at the end return to the positive: the nettle sandwich. This enables the person's ego to be protected and makes them more likely to be able to hear and respond less defensively to criticism. However, for some interviewers, the desire to bury the nettle in the bread means that the critical message is so difficult to decode that it gets missed entirely. Motivational interviewing techniques suggest that it is often easier to get the respondent (rather than you) to elaborate on and introduce the difficulties and problems as well as suggest possible ways in which they could be rectified. This makes it more likely that they will take responsibility for them and take action in this area. Also getting the respondent to summarise the outcome of the interview can help reinforce message and future actions, and is a good way to check that you are both perceiving the information in the same way. Some hints on giving feedback are listed in Table 5.3, and dealing with 'giving criticism' is discussed in Chapter 7.

Table 5.3 *Giving feedback*

Here are some tips on giving feedback:

Be specific. Vague generalities do not help: 'You are no good at running meetings' should be replaced by 'Your handling of the meeting on Thursday, and in particular the way you let it overrun, was a problem'

Be timely. When is the appropriate time to give feedback? Now may not be appropriate. Weeks later may mean the incident is forgotten.

Be objective. Focus on facts, observations, needs, values: 'This has happened three times this week.'

Be and speak for yourself. Do not hide behind an anonymous 'we'. Speak from your heart, even if it means declaring your emotions, such as 'I felt very hurt'.

Be balanced. Rarely is something all bad or all good. Therefore mention mistakes *and* good points.

As a gift. Feedback should be a gift – so make sure that you are giving it for the benefit of the other person, not just yourself. Think how they would want to receive this feedback.

Control

An interview needs to be controlled in two ways. One is through planning prior to the interview, and the second is through the conduct of the interview itself. In planning an interview you need to establish its purpose. Do you want to counsel, evaluate, support, develop, chastise? You need to consider what you want to accomplish and what will be the outcome of the interview: a decision on whether you want to recruit or reject a candidate, identify a person's development needs, evaluate a person's performance for the purpose of feedback, and so on. There are other underlying objectives also: maintaining and enhancing the subject's motivation and self-esteem for example.

In conducting the interview itself, you, the interviewer, need to maintain control. That means not letting the respondent divert you from meeting the objectives of the interview, or getting and giving all the information necessary. Sometimes we mistake talking for being in control. Interviewers often wildly underestimate the amount of time they spend talking. You should never be doing more than 50 per cent of the talking, and for some interviews, such as selection and counselling, you should be intervening significantly less than the respondent, maybe as little as 10 per cent of the time. Some of the techniques for probing help us prevent being distracted from our agenda.

Capture

An interview can be a stimulating and profound experience, but it is not enough to feel satisfied with the performance you, as the interviewer, put in, if the information that is needed from the interview has not been captured appropriately. There are effectively two main ways in which the information can be captured: note-taking and electronic means.

Note-taking is simple, but has the disadvantage of being distracting and preventing good eye contact. It can create gaps in speech, making it more difficult for the interviewer to manage the interview effectively. He or she can become distracted from questioning and the actual content of the dialogue by the desperate need to write it all down. It can easily produce inaccurate recall, as writing is much slower than speech. Accuracy may be vital, for example in the case of a research interview where the interviewer wants exact quotes and the volume of information to be accumulated is high. One alternative is to have a structured pro forma that enables succinct, focused note-taking. This is particularly helpful for a selection interview where interview notes can be used as evidence in subsequent discrimination cases. A selection interview is likely to contain the headings around which the person specification has been written, with room for a candidate to be graded against the criteria (for example: meets criteria, exceeds criteria or lacks criteria, or a numerical grading system) and space for the provision of evidence and notes. If you cannot take notes in the interview itself it is vital to set aside time immediately afterwards to fill in your impressions and notes. It is amazing how quickly the memory of the interview fades, particularly if you have one interview after another.

An alternative which is utilised more in research interviews is to tape record an interview. The advantages of tape recorded interviews are they allow the interviewer to concentrate on what is being said and to use exact quotes. However, they can distract a respondent and inhibit the dialogue. Transcription itself is laborious – the approximate rule of thumb is six hours transcribing for every hour taped – but this can be speeded up with a transcription machine. However, some people use the tape recorder selectively, using a tape counter to identify the really important points in an interview and note these down and transcribe selectively rather than verbatim. Another way is to use it as a back-up, in case your note-taking and memory fail. Tape recording is used for telephone as well as face-to-face interviews, and the equipment for this is very reasonably priced and discreet, but it is vital to obtain the prior permission of the respondent and this should not be done covertly – you are not MI5!

The content of the interview is not the only information you may need to capture. It is likely that for many interviews, such as selection or appraisal, you will need to capture decisions and actions agreed. It is vital in the conclusion to the interview to sum up or ask the interviewee to sum these up: for example agreed development activities and training, changes in behaviour or the way a job is conducted. These also need to be written down.

To help you digest the information from this section and relate it to real life situations, you could attempt Exercise 5.5.

EXERCISE 5.5   OBSERVING INTERVIEWS

If you have the opportunity to observe an interview in your workplace then arrange to do so. However, it is likely you will need to gain permission from the subject and provide them with confirmation of your willingness to keep the information confidential.

Alternatively if this is not possible, see if you can obtain one of the many videos/DVDs on interviewing skills that are available and include mock interviews. It is likely your human resource department or training department have access to such videos. They can be obtained from companies such as Video Arts, and Fenman.

Watch or observe one interview and record the evidence of contact, conduct, content, control and capture provided, and its implications. Focus particularly on the questioning techniques used, the use of probes, and the amount of time the interviewer and interviewee are doing the talking.

1. Contact
   - Has the interviewer established a rapport? How?
   - Introduction – clarified purpose and structure.
2. Conduct: evidence of the use of appropriate question-asking techniques and interventions
   - open
   - closed
   - probes:

     elaboration

     repetition

     reflecting back

     paraphrasing

     summarising

     clarifying

     minimal prompts and silence.
3. Content
   - evidence of planning
   - purpose clear
   - constructive feedback.
4. Control
   - structure
   - percentage of the time interviewer speaking / interviewee speaking.
5. Capture
   - Has the interviewer captured the information they need from the interview in the most appropriate form?
   - Has the interviewer clarified what happens next, points for action.

SUMMARY

Communication is on one level intuitive: we do it automatically. However, we can train ourselves to be more effective communicators by putting into practice the skills and suggestions made in this chapter. In particular these relate to focusing on clarity, identifying your purpose, choosing the right medium, and developing your question-asking and active listening skills, as well as devising appropriate ways to capture information and clarify action that needs to be taken. Increasingly managers and learners are faced with communication overload, and so you may need to take action (see Chapter 2 on time management) to limit the amount of communication input you are receiving to clear space for high quality purposive communication.

REFERENCES AND FURTHER READING

BECK, A., BENNET, P. and WALL, P. (eds) (2003) *Communication Skills: The Essential Resource.* London and Oxford: Routledge.

BUCHANAN, D. and HUCZYNSKI, A. (2004) *Organizational Behaviour: An Introductory Text.* 5th ed. London: FT/Prentice Hall.

CAMERON, S. (2002) *Business Student's Handbook: Learning Skills for Study and Employment*. 2nd ed. Harlow, Essex: FT/Prentice Hall Pearson.

O CONNOR, J. and SEYMOUR, J. (1990) *Introducing Neuro Linguistic Programming*. London: Mandela, Harper Collins.

DAFT, R. (1993) *Management*. 3rd ed. Orlando and London: The Dryden Press, Harcourt Brace Publishers.

HARGIE, O. (ed) (1996) *The Handbook of Communication Skills*. London: Routledge (Taylor and Francis).

MEHRABIAN, A. (1971) *Silent Messages*. Belmont, California: Wadsworth.

PONT, T. and PONT, G. (1998) *Interviewing Skills for Managers*. London: Piatkus Books.

SHANNON, C. and WEAVER, W. (1949) *The Mathematical Theory of Communication*. Urbana, Il: University of Illinois Press.

WHETTON, D., and CAMERON, K. (2002) *Developing Management Skills*. New Jersey: Prentice Hall.

FURTHER INFORMATION

Videos and DVD's on interviewing can be obtained from:

Fenman Professional Training Resources (Training Videos)
Fenman Ltd, Clive House,
The Business Park, Ely, Cambridgeshire,
CB7 4EH
Tel +44 (0) 1353 665533
Fax +44 (0) 1353 663644
E-mail: service@fenman.co.uk
http://www.fenman.co.uk

Video Arts Ltd:
6–7 St. Cross Street,
London, EC1N 8UA
Tel: +44 (0)20 7400 4800 / 0845 601 2531
Fax: +44 (0)20 7400 4900
http://www.videoarts.com

Verbal and written presentation skills

INTRODUCTION

Many people, when faced with a presentation, when standing up in front of an audience, or writing a document whether it be for students, tutors, managers or clients, focus on *what* they want to say: the content. In this chapter your attention will be drawn to *how* you want to deliver the information: the process of giving or writing presentations. This will make the material you deliver much more palatable, interesting and relevant to your audience. The shift of emphasis is from what you want to say or write, to what they want to hear or read. To do this, you will have to move away mentally from yourself as the giver of information, and step into the shoes of those on the receiving end of your presentation. Begin by imagining this now. Take one presentation you have given and step into the audience – it is from this perspective you need to tackle this chapter.

EXERCISE 6.1   TODAY'S JOURNEY

Write a short piece (one or two paragraphs) telling the story of your journey to work, to your course, or to the local shops – in fact anywhere you may be going today. Tell it in four different ways from the following angles:

a) a report for a committee
b) a letter to a newspaper
c) an e-mail to a friend abroad
d) a story for a child.

Exercise 6.1 will be the basis from which you can check and practise your written communication skills.

WRITTEN PRESENTATION SKILLS – PUTTING PEN TO PAPER

Getting started

So where did you start when writing your story? The hardest part is getting started and there are a number of barriers to deal with before you even begin: you may think you cannot write or that writing is difficult. You may find it difficult to believe in what you have done or that anyone would be interested. It is also likely that you do not have time, it takes so long you keep putting it off. Getting started is a big hurdle for any writer. Where to begin?

Begin by thinking of your audience. There are four questions you needed to ask yourself: what is the story, who are your readers, what is in it for them, what is the message *for them*?

Knowing your audience

Exercise 6.1 requires you to think about different audiences. You may find you have to write *down* to your audience, making your ideas simpler, as in the story for a child, or alternatively write *up* as for a report, make it appear professional and authoritative even if you don't believe this to be the case. You therefore need to separate what you are writing about from who you are writing for. As in Exercise 6.1 the same story can appear very different for different audiences.

For example your story may have begun by you getting out of bed. To a child, a bed is a piece of furniture to sleep in, be read stories in and kissed goodnight in or woken in the morning, a place for dreams and nightmares, a place to keep teddies, even a den. To your friend it may represent a figure in their credit card statement, or a stylish addition to an interior design. To a newspaper it may be the venue for celebrity romps, and for a technical journal or catalogue or a hospital performance measure it may be:

> A device or arrangement that may be used to permit a patient to lie down when the need to do so is a consequence of the patient's condition rather than a need for active intervention – such as examination, diagnostic investigation, manipulative treatment, obstetric delivery or transport.

It is quite likely that you will have to write for many different audiences in your life. Think of the range of different types of writing:

- e-mails
- letters
- reports and executive summaries
- meeting minutes and reports
- essays and assessed assignments
- papers for conferences
- articles
- editorials
- reviews, book reviews
- viewpoints

They all require very different styles of writing.

Knowing your purpose, angle and message

You cannot do everything in one piece of writing, so you need to work out what is your angle or your distinct contribution, and what is the piece for? What is your principle message, is the message worth saying, is it generalisable and interesting? What is the story?

If you are writing a management report, is it to provide information, to provoke discussion, to persuade others of the wisdom of a decision? If it is an assessed piece of work for a course, what are the criteria for assessment? Critical analysis, application of appropriate theory to practice, evidence of knowledge of the literature, intelligent answering of the question? Moreover, have you provided a clear rationale for any conclusions you have come to?

If you are writing up research for publication, is it a report, a review, a 'how to do' piece or opinion viewpoint? What is the angle or contribution: is it new methodology, a new application, a gap in existing work, or new ideas or conceptual framework?

Look back over the four short stories you produced for Exercise 6.1 above. How do they differ? It is likely that the committee report is written in a drier more formal style, but containing facts and evidence, and the message may be to advocate a policy, for example on transport in London. The letter to the paper is more likely to be provocative, maybe even emotional, engaging the reader in an argument that may or may not be backed up by evidence. The aim is perhaps to entertain or maybe to persuade others to appreciate your point of view or get a grievance aired and off your chest. The e-mail to a friend is more personal and intimate, and may be more convoluted and rambling, with the aim of keeping in touch. The story for a child is likely to be more imaginative and descriptive, as well as easily understood by anybody. The purpose is to entertain, but there may also be a message in it 'Do not talk to strangers' for example. Which of these did you enjoy reading and writing the most? It is highly likely you plumped for the child's story. This suggests an important lesson. Whoever the audience, we are most likely to be interested if it is written in a clear and interesting way, including description and maybe some puzzles to engage our mind, and permission to be creative and have fun.

For any piece of writing for presentation do check by using 'the message test': read it and check you can summarise the message in a few sentences. You could even show it to a friend and see if they can see the same message: is it conveyed from your head to that of the reader or listener? Where many novice writers go wrong is that the key message is buried under a mass of data, red herrings, and superfluous information. If the writing is a tapestry of ideas, facts and information, there should be an overall picture, not just a jumble of stitches, that can be seen when you look at the complete tapestry. This can be a matter of confidence; hesitant writers may try and demonstrate their worth by throwing in too much data, too much information. Go back to being the reader: what will the reader remember of this report, assignment or article in a few weeks' time? Very little, and it is better that, if they only remember one thing, it is your key message, rather than one of your asides.

Intelligibility and jargon

Whatever the audience, intelligibility is important; no one is impressed by a surfeit of jargon. Look through your stories in Exercise 6.1. Did you include any jargon, are the sentences intelligible? Could any of the sentences be phrased in a simpler, more direct way? Use English, plain English, and avoid long sentences. Use one word if it can replace two.

It is more likely you included jargon in the report to the committee, and sometimes when you are writing technical documents or reports, a certain amount of jargon is necessary, but that is not an excuse to become incomprehensible. Clarity is always important. If you are writing for journals and professional publications you do need to understand the discourse that is employed in that field, the abbreviations, and the ways in which ideas are conveyed. So if you are submitting a paper to a journal you need to check the format and writing style, as well as the referencing system and readership.

There are three types of writing that particularly worry managers and students: effective report writing, writing for assessment, and writing for publication. These we will take in turn below.

EFFECTIVE REPORT WRITING

Table 6.1 identifies the key components of an executive report.

Table 6.1 *Key components of an executive report*

Title	A few words indicating the subject of the report
Executive summary or abstract	Outline of key points from main body, conclusions and recommendations. Or abstract – usually one paragraph including aims, method and findings
Table of contents	List of main headings of report and page numbers
Glossary	If necessary and explanation of key terms and abbreviations
Introduction	Introduces the topic of the report more fully, its remit, aims and objectives, and explains the report's structure and value
Aims/terms of reference	Often included in introduction, but may separately outline the purpose and area of investigation
Main body	The main content of information, analysis and discussion
Conclusions	Indicating main issues, findings and decisions required
Recommendations	Points of further action suggested (if required by terms of reference)
Appendices	Detailed information referred to in main body
Bibliography or references	Bibliography is the list of books, articles, etc. *used in research* References are all the sources actually *referred to* in the text

It is always preferable to put the executive summary at the beginning of a report (although it is written last) so that a busy reader can focus on the important parts first and then decide whether to read the whole document.

Reports are usually requested by others and should have agreed 'terms of reference' indicating the subject to be examined and the reason for the report. Even if you decide to prepare a report on your own initiative, it is necessary to set your terms of reference and purpose. Reports should be directed to a particular reader or group of readers.

Language, headings and style

The language used in a report may be determined by your organisation's 'house style'. This indicates whether you write directly and in the first person ('I suggest you do this …') or in the third person ('It is suggested that these actions are appropriate'). Whatever style is favoured, the writing should be clear.

As a report may be a lengthy document, it is important to have headings and subheadings that guide the reader through a logical structure. These headings need to be numbered and highlighted (underlined, capital letters, italic, etc). There are several conventions used to number headings and subheadings. Main headings can be numbered 1, 2, 3, etc with subheadings as 1.1, 1.3, 1.3, 2.1, 2.2, 2.3, etc. Alternatively headings can be 1, 2, 3, etc, with i), ii), iii) or a), b), c) indicating subheadings. It is important to be consistent in numbering throughout a document.

Standardisation and navigation are important issues which enable reports to be read and digested quickly. Increasingly reports are produced and sent electronically, and therefore familiarising yourself with the electronic formatting and templates available on your word processing package is essential. Using these can enable you to format your document headings and subheadings more easily and also help the reader navigate through the document, for example enabling the reader to click on a section in the contents to move straight to the section in the text is very useful.

Diagrams, tables and graphs will help in presenting detailed information and indicating significant points in your analysis, but you must refer to them in the text, and label them effectively.

Most reports benefit from revision and editing. The principle of having a clear structure to follow is important. One approach to report writing is to begin with the structure as a series of subheadings and then build up each section in turn, trying to complete, if not a whole report, at least discrete sections in one sitting. This approach prevents you from going off at tangents, and keeps the writing on the focus of the report.

Probably the most widely used book on structuring presentations is Barbara Minto's 'The Pyramid Principle' (2002), which has been used to train many management consultants in firms such as McKinsey's. The reason it is so popular is its logic and clarity – a good role model for any business presentation. The guiding principle is that the mind automatically sorts information into distinctive pyramidal groupings in order to comprehend complex information. Ideas are easier to follow if they are presented in this logical pyramid structure under a single summary thought. The structure of the pyramid is reader focused, following the questions that the reader is likely to raise in the order they arise.

To use the Minto Pyramid Principle approach you need to follow a few basic rules: see Example 6.1.

EXAMPLE 6.1   THE PYRAMID PRINCIPLE: GUIDING RULES

Ideas at any level of the pyramid must always be summaries of the ideas grouped below them.

Ideas in each grouping must always be the same kind of idea.

Ideas in each grouping must always be logically ordered:

- eductively (in argument order: major premise, minor premise, conclusion)
- chronologically (if cause-effect then in time order, first, second, third)
- structurally (UK, France, Spain)
- comparatively/categorising (the most important, the next most important).

The pyramid structure establishes a question/answer dialogue using the questions that are likely to be in the reader's/listener's mind. For example, if at the top of the pyramid you have the statement 'X company should set up a home delivery service' the question is likely to be 'Why', so at the next level of the pyramid there are answers, such as 'Because this is more convenient for the customer.' The next question may be 'In what way is it more convenient?' and the next level of the pyramid may answer this question: 'Because many of the customers are physically disabled and cannot get to a shop easily' and so on. Going vertically down the one line of the pyramid is driven by these question and answer exchanges. The purpose is to follow the logic of the reader in raising and answering their questions as they arise and putting them into a pyramid following the logic of each. Every sentence leads automatically to what comes next. The pyramid should fall into place with each level becoming a question and answer leading up to the core topic

The introduction needs to introduce the question and answer dialogue by starting with presenting a situation and then providing a complication that would lead to the question

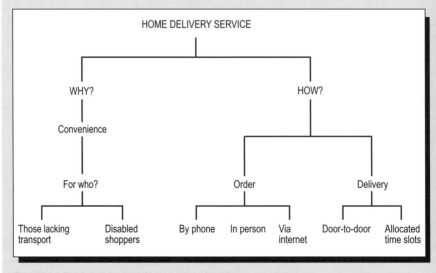

Figure 6.1 *Example of the pyramid approach to preparing a presentation*

and answer dialogue. This generates the reader's/listener's interest. Ideally the situation should be something the audience would agree on. For example 'There has been much dissatisfaction with the current performance management system, and so the time is right to revise this. We are developing a new system, but you may have some concerns and would like to know more about the way it works. For example whether it will be fair . ..' and so on.

You could try to use this approach with a presentation you are preparing to see if it works for you.

Read Chapters 2 and 3 of *The Pyramid Principle* for more information (Minto 2002).

Even if you feel you have managed to settle on a way of structuring your presentation and feel you have accomplished a good format it is wise go through more than one draft, especially if it is a report. The first draft should be put aside for a day or two then a second and final draft prepared by:

- checking that conclusions and recommendations stem logically from the main report
- editing and improving the style
- checking spelling and grammar
- checking the numbering of headings and that they agree with the table of contents page
- pruning out irrelevant sections.

This moves us on to 'bullet points'. If you are merely writing an executive summary, then reducing the report down to bullet points may be appropriate. However, if it is a longer report, and particularly if it is for assessment for your course, then it is likely to require more in-depth analysis than just a few words.

WRITING FOR ASSIGNMENTS AND ASSESSMENT

There are some very basic things you need to check even before you start:

- Check the *deadline* and work back to the present to plan your time in a sensible schedule, allowing for redrafting.
- Check the *word length* requirements, many tutors penalise you for not keeping to these.
- Check the *referencing style*. This is likely to be either:
    - the Harvard system which lists all the references you have used alphabetically according to the author's surname at the back of the text. The surname is followed by initials, date in brackets, title, place of publication and publisher, thus: Winstanley, D., (2005) *Personal Effectiveness: A guide to action.* London: CIPD. In the text itself the reference would then be '(Winstanley, 2005: 121)'. This book uses the Harvard system so look at the list of references at the end of this chapter as a template or
    - the Vancouver system, where references are numbered in the text and listed in numerical order at the end.

Don't forget when you are reading your material for the assignment to take down the full reference of all materials used. There is nothing more irritating than finding these incomplete when actually writing your assignment and then having to spend hours tracking them down.

Table 6.2 *Prescription, description and analysis*

Prescription	Description	Analysis
Advocating a position Prescribing a course of action Normative and persuasive	Clearly explaining or expounding a theory or position. Summarising or précising a theory or idea Giving a definition	Classifying approaches Evaluating strengths and weaknesses Comparing and contrasting theories or viewpoints Providing a commentary

For people who have moved from managerial roles back into formal training and education, writing an academic assignment can seem daunting. There is a difference between a management report and an academic report. This is usually concerned with the extent to which prescription, description and analysis are required, and these terms are summarised in Table 6.2.

A work-based report may require some analysis, but often the point to be highlighted is the prescription, the course of action to be taken: for example which new IT system to adopt, and how this should be handled. Some reports are evaluative, with more analysis, for example evaluating the impact of a new performance management system on staff morale. Academic reports take analysis to another realm. They may also require practical application, but there is usually a requirement for an analytical theoretical discussion of the literature. Here a body of knowledge referred to as 'the literature' is searched, surveyed and drawn upon. Often academic assignments require a topic to be evaluated from the view of classifying different literatures about the topic, evaluating the strengths and weaknesses of key writers and theories, comparing and contrasting these to develop an argument with relation to a question. This argument may be in terms of the value of the theory or even its application to an area of practice. For many students, the grading of their assignment reflects the extent to which they have been analytical in the discussion of the topic. A student may spend hours of hard work on an assignment, reading the literature, identifying key points and writing an assignment, only to find their grade is poor because they have been descriptive with the literature rather than analytical: summarising it but without providing evaluation. Evaluation based on uninformed opinion is also unacceptable. Instead the views expressed should be backed up with *evidence*: quotes, ideas, theories from the literature, statistics and factual information, case study information – all fully referenced to avoid plagiarism.

Plagiarism is passing off the ideas or writing of another as your own, and is severely penalised. Many academic institutions have software to check for plagiarism and will identify any passages that replicate those in textbooks and articles. If in doubt, cite the author in the text, and fully reference the author in the list at the end of the assignment.

Analysis is a tricky concept, and if you are not sure of the difference between description, prescription and analysis, attempt Exercise 6.2.

EXERCISE 6.2   DESCRIPTION, PRESCRIPTION AND ANALYSIS

Against the following statements, mark whether you think it is description (D), prescription (P) or analysis (A).

i)   It could be argued that both Maslow and Herzberg are preoccupied with self actualisation and humanising work practices, but if we compare the 'hierarchy of needs' with 'the two factor theory' we can see they contain significant differences.

ii) Maslow's 'hierarchy of needs' contains five levels: physiological, safety and security, belongingness and love, esteem and self-actualisation'

iii) Herzberg's ideas for job enrichment and enlargement are very appropriate for making routine boring jobs more stimulating and interesting.

iv) Stakeholding should be put into practice in all companies, whether public or private.

v)   Suggesting that stakeholding should be adopted because it is good in itself is very different from suggesting that it should be taken up, because it leads to superior performance as is implied by the Centre for Tomorrow's Company Report.

vi) Stakeholding means taking into account the views and needs of all those who can affect or are affected by an organisation's policies and actions.

Review your answers to Exercise 6.2 and justify your decision. ii) and vi) are descriptive, as ii) is providing a summary or précis of a theory, and vi) is providing a definition. Description is essential in a report, but on its own is not enough. iii) and iv) are prescriptive statements, and these can be used in a report when you have built up evidence for making your argument (whether through your own statistics and data or through the arguments and studies of others), and should come late on in the report after building up your case and exploring the evidence. They should not be used as 'Joe Public' comments and are not an opportunity to vent your own views, built on 'emotivism', prejudice or general knowledge. i) and v) are both analytical statements because i) goes beyond describing the authors' views to invite us to compare and contrast them, and v) because it begins to make distinctions between different perspectives which could form the basis of a classification or model.

WRITING FOR PUBLICATION

Publishing a presentation, particularly in the academic context requires a number of extra considerations. Writing for academic journals these days is a minefield.

Format, style and audience

The first consideration is the choice of journal, as each journal has a different style, format and target audience. Most journals produce notes on their web pages about the kind of articles they seek to publish. For example, if a student wanted to publish their project in a human resource management journal they may consider *Human Resource Management Journal* which is for both academics and practitioners, tackles current issues in employment and expects excellent data tied to theory and previous research, usually of 4,000-8,000 words. This is very different to the requirements of *People Management*, which focuses on relevance for practitioners, short pieces of less 2,000 words with topical updates and key practical points. Therefore it is important to know the requirements of the journal before you waste time submitting your work to the wrong place.

Reputation and impact value

Reputation of the journal is also important and increasingly journals are ranked according to their impact value, which is a formula based on the citations made to articles from the journal over a set period of time. Many publish their impact values. Alternatively a search through Web of Knowledge can identify these. Increasingly academic departments publish their own lists and rankings of the most prestigious journals in which to publish, usually ranked from 1–5, with 5 representing journals of international and highest reputation.

The process

Some articles are submitted by invitation, which is gratifying, but many more are submitted on spec or in response to a call for papers around a theme, or deriving from a conference. Surprisingly articles have a higher acceptance rate sent on spec than in a call for papers. Submitting an article is not the end of the process. Initially the editor will view the article and if they think it is worth consideration will usually send it to academic review. For some journals only a fraction of articles get this far. Many academic journals have this peer review process, where typically two, but maybe three, academics review the article 'blind' and anonymously: neither they nor you know each other's identity. This review process rarely takes less than three months, and again many articles are rejected at this stage, and seldom is an article accepted without minor or major amendments. This can be an eye-opener to the uninitiated, as reviewers' comments can sometimes be contradictory and you should seek the editor's advice in how to deal with these. It is worth checking with the editor which suggestions from reviewers should be taken on board, and, when articles are resubmitted you will need to explain how you have responded to the reviewers' comments. After that comes copy editing and proof reading. All in all the process can take up to a year, and for some journals there is even a subsequent delay and it can take up to two years to publish in the journal! Resilience and non-defensiveness are important to survive this process. Many good papers get rewritten and submitted successfully elsewhere and if the reviewers' comments are handled positively and proactively the review process can raise the quality of the paper.

THE ART OF VERBAL PRESENTATION

There is a presentation paradox when we give verbal presentations.

The presentation paradox is:

> We deliver presentations *verbally*, but we prepare presentations by *writing them*. Yet the written and the spoken word are different.

To illustrate this difference pick up a piece of work you have written, such as an essay or executive summary, or even just pick up an article in the newspaper, and read out the first few lines as if you were giving a verbal presentation. It doesn't sound quite right does it? The written word when spoken can be dry, rambling and lifeless. We therefore have to put a lot of thought into two key components to convert our ideas into speech:

- preparation and support
- delivery.

By addressing these areas, it is possible to transform what could be a turgid, rambling, incoherent presentation into one that is stimulating, clear and relevant.

Preparation

Good preparation means that you do not have to worry about *what* you are saying, and can focus on the *how* of the next section. A lack of preparation can result in a rambling presentation, due to unclear objectives and focus. Worse still, you can dry up as you lose yourself in the structure, or forget what you are going to say next. The presentation can come across as unstructured with an unclear message.

EXERCISE 6.3   PLANNING A PRESENTATION

Either:

Tackle this exercise when you have a presentation to give.

Or:

Imagine yourself as a 'toastmaster' introducing yourself to an audience giving a three-minute introduction to you and your work.

Take each of the paragraphs below and follow the advice for that section. By the end you should have a well-prepared presentation and be ready to practise delivering it:

- preparation objectives: why, to whom, what
- key messages: no more than five
- organising the structure: use cards or PowerPoint,
- support: any slides, handouts or artefacts
- preparing for delivery: introduction, main body and conclusion, what should you include?

Or

Go back to the section on written presentations and utilise the Minto Pyramid Principle illustrated in Example 6.1.

Preparation objectives

Begin by asking yourself 'why am I giving this presentation?', 'Who is the audience, what are their expectations and knowledge?', 'Where will I be giving my presentation, how many people will be there, when will it be, how long will it take?' Most importantly you need to ask 'What are its objectives?' Ask yourself 'As a result of this presentation the audience will ....?' What? Work harder, learn, be convinced, be inspired, buy, sell, join, leave, see it my way? Now try and summarise the objectives in one line. From this, identify what are your key messages.

Key messages

Recall the last presentation you attended: how much of it do you remember? Very little! People forget most of what they hear in a presentation, so keep your key messages short, sharp and few in numbers. Don't confuse *volume* of information with *value* of information. It is often tempting to demonstrate how much you know on a subject, but remember you are usually building a case, not proving you have done a lot of work.

The key messages are going to be the skeleton of your presentation, so use them as a framework to structure it. If you are having trouble identifying them, try brainstorming them by putting everything you can think of down on a piece of paper, and then go back and select some from this list.

Organising the structure

Now review the content of your presentation, isolate all the key points you want to make. You could put these onto cards or cut and paste them in a document, by sorting them into themes. It may help to summarise the presentation in five sentences, and put the information into sections relating to key messages. Find a way of ordering these logically. Do not hold back on parts of the puzzle. A bit of history and context can help. Review your structure and metaphorically return to that seat in the audience. What questions might go through your mind as you view the presentation that could get in the way of your understanding? An alternative method is to follow the Pyramid Principle mentioned in the previous section.

Support

There are now an amazing number of ways in which you can support your presentation: slides, overheads, PowerPoint and other IT-based presentation equipment, video, CD or DVD clips, pictures, artefacts, handouts, flipcharts ... the list is endless. It is important not to use too many different forms of illustration, as this will just confuse your audience and distract them further from your points. Beware too many distractions, and don't hide behind them. They should be an aid only, don't let the message get lost.

EXAMPLE 6.2 TECHNOLOGY GETTING IN THE WAY?

A group of first year aerospace engineering students spent many hours preparing a presentation on a SWOT analysis of Boeing. The PowerPoint presentation started with curtains opening to an aeroplane zooming across the screen. Unfortunately, as the presentation progressed, noises crashed, bells rang out, bullet points flew cross the screen in a rainbow of colours, appearing, disappearing, transforming. After 5 minutes and 40 slides the audience were left reeling as the presenters popped into view to ask if there were any questions. The audience sat dazed and silent!

EXAMPLE 6.3 USING A WELL-CHOSEN ARTEFACT

A group of trainee presenters were asked to give a five-minute presentation on a special person or a place. One presenter brought out a rock and passed it round the audience. She proceeded to talk about the caravan she had stayed in as a child, placed in derelict slag heaps left from a tin mine amid the cliffs high above the crashing sea. The rock was a mass of quartz and fool's gold that as a child she had excavated from this special holiday place. This had led to her love of mineralogy later in life. Another presenter showed a photograph of his Grandma in her garden outside her house, holding a pair of secateurs. It was her love of gardening and her growing arthritis that had prompted him to enter a design competition with a design for a gardening implement for the elderly. When asked weeks later which presentation the group remembered, they all remembered the rock and the memories associated with it, and also the grandma and her secateurs.

However, most people do expect you to use either slides or 'PowerPoint'. These enable you to present your message visually as well as verbally, and can convey complex information and data, as well as adding interest and directing attention away from you.

In preparing slides:

- avoid small font
- use a clear layout, and choose an appropriate one
- don't place too much information on it
- use whole numbers
- use lower case after the heading
- use the T-shirt or billboard rule.

The T-shirt or billboard rule suggests that less is more – and you use phrases and words, not complete sentences. What you put on the slide should be no more than you would put on a T-shirt or a billboard: it should be the highlights, not the detail.

One problem with slides and PowerPoint is that they can make the presentation very inflexible and static. Sometimes in a presentation you want to be able to ad lib, recap, explore a point in more detail and respond to the audience in a more off-the-cuff way. In these cases it can be more useful to use a flipchart, a whiteboard (whether electronic or manual) or notes that can be written on a visualiser as you go along. All of these methods enable you to stop mid presentation and involve the audience, for example through capturing points they may make about an issue, or through visually explaining an illustration. The act of producing the material in front of the audience can be captivating and energise a presentation, although if you take too long with your back to the audience, scribbling indecipherable scrawl on the flipchart, it can appear amateur and over casual.

Look at the presentation you have been preparing for Exercise 6.3: what artefacts, slides or other forms of support might you use?

Delivery

There are three main sections of your presentation:

- the *introduction*: where you tell them what you are going to tell them, and you capture their attention
- the *main body*: where you tell them, you deliver your key messages
- the *conclusion*: where you tell them what you have told them, and restate your message.

Introduction

Beginning with the introduction, think about what your audience needs to know. They want you to introduce yourself, explain your purpose. They perhaps want some indication of length and format of the presentation: how long are you going to take, can they ask questions? Maybe you even want to give them a taste of the key messages. This takes care of the formalities, but underneath, the main consequence you are developing is 'attachment': you are getting their attention and interest and building a rapport, so try and engage their mind. For example, you could pose them a question or puzzle, so they are motivated to find the answer. You don't want a passive audience, sitting back as if they are watching TV – 'Entertain me'. You want them to be actively engaged, so find a way to motivate their mind to listen actively to the presentation with all their senses.

The main body

Each section of the main body of the presentation needs to be signposted, related to the key message, and summarised. Just as attention is drawn through posing the audience a puzzle at the beginning, so in the middle they need reassuring that they are following what is being said, they are competent listeners. This builds up confidence in your audience – you don't want them 'tuning out', thinking the presentation is going over their heads, or feeling inadequate because they cannot follow what is said, or worse still, bored stiff.

The conclusion

A presentation shouldn't finish with a jolt, nobody likes a sudden stop. You need to plan a conclusion that will be clearly signalled before the end. Attention curves are the highest at the start and at the end, so the signal should recapture their attention if it is wandering. There should be no new material in the conclusion: instead make a restatement of key messages to ensure the audience has picked up these up.

However, delivery is much more than placing the right pieces of the puzzle in the right places. Consider Exercise 6.4.

EXERCISE 6.4   WHAT MAKES A GOOD SPEAKER?

Think back over speeches you have heard, whether they be work presentations, political speeches or after dinner speeches and ask yourself 'What makes a good speaker?' Brainstorm a few ideas and write them down.

Although you may have mentioned in response to Exercise 6.4 the need for the speaker to have a clear message, well organised thoughts and a well structured presentation (points raised above), it is also likely that you have concentrated on other aspects of the delivery: their presence and charisma, confidence, voice projection, the ability to communicate thoughts and feelings, being tuned in to an audience, making a link with the audience. There are six key areas which will help here:

- posture and breathing
- body language and gestures
- voice tone and variation
- eye contact
- handling nerves.

Posture and breathing

To maximise your impact and projection, it is beneficial to consider how the body and our breathing can work for rather than against us. Matthias Alexander was an actor who kept losing his voice, but he discovered that by making changes to his posture, and in particular the relationship between his head, neck and spine, he could make significant positive improvements to his voice, and this became known as 'the Alexander Technique'. Consider how you stand when you give a presentation (refer to Chapter 7 on assertiveness and examine the posture for assertive behaviour). An alternative is to consider the mountain pose in yoga. You should be standing in a relaxed way, feet hip width apart, arms, shoulders, hips, jaw-line relaxed, the backbone lengthened. It can help to go round the body clenching and relaxing each muscle group; this way you can find out if there is any tension anywhere you can let go. If it helps you can do some basic warm-up exercises like half-neck rotations, shoulder circles, hip rotations.

Breathing is equally as important. Concentrate on breathing from the lower belly rather than high up in the throat or upper abdomen. Exercise 6.5 provides some examples of ways you can ensure you are breathing correctly. Take five minutes out of your day to practise these.

EXERCISE 6.5   BREATHING FOR EFFECT

1. Breathe in and out slowly and deeply using the nose and mouth and an open throat. As you do so place your hands gently over your belly and feel the belt area expand and contract in a relaxed way.

2. Now breathe in and count to 20 and then let go, 3 times.

3. *Dog panting:* imagine you are a dog on a hot day and pant rapidly from the lower abdomen, watch your belly go in and out.

4. *Cat on the flowerbed:* imagine you have a prize plant and a cat is just about to dig it up and make use of your flowerbed as a toilet. Go 'pssst' very loudly, making a sweeping hand movement to scare it away. Walk around the room going 'pssst' louder and louder each time, clearing the cat away with a sweep of your arm. Again the 'pssst' should come from very deep in the abdomen.

(with thanks to Piers Ibbotson)

You may feel very silly doing Exercise 6.5, but the more you can practise breathing deeply and issuing your voice from deep inside the more you will be able to project it, and it will sound more solid and confident. Actors do such voice training for a reason!

It is not just your breathing that should come from deep in your belly, but also your centre of concentration. Many people, when they panic, move their focus up to their heads where the thoughts are buzzing around. In fact you will feel much more confident and grounded if you move your focus and centre down to the centre of your body – that is where the presentation should issue from.

Body language and gestures
An audience focuses mostly on how you speak and how you look, rather than on what you say, so your attention should be on your voice, gestures and body language. It is worrying, but we all have personal ticks and habits, such as putting our hands in our pockets, waving our arms around, jangling keys in our pockets, playing with an earring, or even pacing up and down like a lion in a cage. What are yours? You could get yourself video recorded and watch yourself to find out.

EXAMPLE 6.4   USING BODY LANGUAGE

My father, as a politician, used to give the same speech over and over again, especially in elections. As a child I was dragged around countless draughty halls to listen, often I used to sit outside the doors and look in through the window to see where he was in his speech. I could always tell. When he sliced through the air with the side of his palm he was 'dividing up local government', when he was placing his hands down as if to put money in piles he was 'allocating money to childcare and education.' He was a skilled orator, but I grew to realise that much of his communication was through his gestures.

It is not just your own body language that you should be paying attention to, but the audience's also. Noticing whether they are attentive or yawning and falling asleep can help you change the tempo or adapt what you are doing to meet their needs. For example, if they are looking puzzled you could slow down and provide more examples.

EXERCISE 6.6   KING LEAR IN THE STORM

Either: take an excerpt from a speech, for example from a Shakespeare play such as the one below taken from King Lear, Act III, Scene 11: Lear in the storm on the Heath:

> Rumble thy bellyful! Spit, fire! Spout, rain!
>
> Nor rain, wind, thunder, fire, are my daughters:
>
> I tax you not, you elements, with unkindness;
>
> I never gave you kingdom, call'd you children,
>
> You owe me no subscription: then let fall
>
> Your horrible pleasure; here I stand, your slave,
>
> A poor, infirm, weak, and despis'd old man.
>
> But yet I call you servile ministers
>
> That will with two pernicious daughters join
>
> Your high-engender'd battles 'gainst a head
>
> So old and white as this. O, ho! 'tis foul.

Or: take an excerpt from the presentation you have been preparing in Exercise 6.3.

Stand in front of a mirror or in an open space and concentrate on giving the presentation using exaggerated body language and gestures. Then try again and see if you can mime the presentation.

What you are trying to practise in Exercise 6.6 is getting used to using your body to emphasise the points you make. Watch any actor and you will see they use every muscle of their body to good effect. If much of our impact is through gestures and body language this can make the difference between a lifeless presentation and a truly enthralling, engaging one. Giving a presentation is giving a performance, so if it helps consider yourself Lawrence Olivier or Dame Judy Dench.

Voice tone and variation

One key to making a presentation lively is to vary the tone, speed and pitch of your voice.

- **Speed.** Exercise 6.7 is intended to enable you to learn to slow down or speed up, depending on your needs. Most novice presenters go too fast so it is likely B will be most helpful to you.

EXERCISE 6.7   GOING FASTER OR SLOWER

Take the material you have planned for Exercise 6.3.

a) If you are naturally a slow speaker, practise delivering this presentation as if you were a commentator for the Grand National horserace, ie very fast.

b) If you are naturally a fast speaker, and gabble your presentations, practise delivering this presentation as if you were a commentator for the funeral of the Queen Mother, ie very slow, deliberate and seriously.

c) Now vary the speed of your presentation, and decide where it is appropriate to slow down and where to speed up. Here you could start slow and speed up, as if you were the footballer Beckham taking a penalty.

Learning to control the speed and timing of your delivery is a great talent: in fact you will notice that great speakers make tremendous use of timing. They learn to deliver a line just at the right time. Try and get in tune with your presentation and discover its own natural rhythm. Generally if you are in doubt, it is better to go too slow than too fast. There are other rhythms and devices you can exploit also:

- **Repetition.** Notice how politicians often repeat something again and again for effect, for example Churchill's famous post-Dunkirk Second World War speech on 4 June 1940, in the example below. In Churchill's case Grint (2000: 371) calls this in Greek *anadiplosis* or 'double back' where the repetition of the words or phrase used is at the beginning or end of each sentence. Interestingly Grint (2000: 371) claims that this speech was delivered in a flat and monotone way, its power lay in the repetition. Grint also mentions *chiasmus,* or word inversion as an alternative to repetition, for example the famous Kennedy's 'Ask not what your country can do for you; ask what you can do for your country.'

EXAMPLE 6.5   REPETITION – WINSTON CHURCHILL 'FIGHTING ON THE BEACHES' EXTRACT

We shall go on to the end, we shall fight in France, we shall fight on the seas and oceans, we shall fight with growing confidence and growing strength in the air, we shall defend our Island, whatever the cost may be. We shall fight on the beaches, we shall fight on the landing grounds, we shall fight in the fields and in the streets, we shall fight in the hills; we shall never surrender.

- **Silence** as well as slowing down before stating something really important. You can leave a silence ... this builds up anticipation.
- **Volume** sometimes going from loud to very quiet can compel the audience to listen very carefully. Conversely in the Winston Churchill extract above he gradually raised the volume to build to up a crescendo at the end.

Eye contact

EXERCISE 6.8 EYE CONTACT

Next time you are relaxing somewhere informal with a friend, in a bar or café, try to converse with them for two minutes where you break eye contact and look down or away every two seconds.

Consider the impact this has on the conversation and rapport between you.

It is likely in doing Exercise 6.8 that you found that the conversation became disjointed, contact was broken, your friend may have found this irritating and you nervous, disinterested or aloof. In fact it is very difficult to sustain good communication with someone who doesn't make eye contact, or who is constantly breaking it.

Why is eye contact so important to communication and for giving presentations? Because it is the medium through which we make a connection with our audience, and once this connection has been made it is the way we can check their reaction to our presentation – are they nodding in agreement, or looking puzzled, fascinated or bored? Eye contact shouldn't be a fixed stare on one person in the audience as that will make them feel really uncomfortable. Instead you should slowly scan round the room, noticing everybody. It is surprising how often a speaker focuses on a few people in the middle of the room, leaving many at the side out of their gaze and consequently feeling abandoned and left out. Try to make contact with all your audience, however briefly, but in a relaxed and interested way – don't rove your eyes round like a lecher viewing attractive talent at a nightclub!

Handling nerves and worst fears
Even just reading this chapter is likely to have awakened some fears in giving presentations, and you may already be feeling nervous about your next presentation. It is unusual not to at least feel some butterflies in the stomach or anxiety before a presentation. Examine what your fears are. Common fears are of:

- drying up
- losing your place
- dropping your notes
- having your slides in the wrong place
- boring your audience
- handling the difficult question
- speaking in English as a foreign language.

Much of this can be prevented by good preparation and practice: maybe have a practice run through. Also the breathing and posture exercises mentioned above should help.

However, some nervousness is advantageous to a presentation: like a good racehorse, to perform really well it is helpful to have some adrenaline rushing through your veins. The difference between good and poor speakers is not whether they feel nervous or not, it is how they view these nerves: fear is very similar to excitement, and so if you view it as a form of stimulation to get all your senses working, then it is something you can harness to your benefit.

However, there are two specific issues about which speakers worry: if the audience gets bored how can they keep their attention; and what if someone in the audience ask a difficult question?

Getting and keeping the audience's attention

We listen at 500 words per minute, we speak at 125–250 words per minute, so clearly the average listener's thoughts have time to wander off, however interesting the speaker! Although attention curves vary, there is also a natural attention curve where the listener tunes in at the beginning, drifts off in the middle, and then returns at the end. You need strategies to capture and recapture attention. You could make some dramatic gestures, change your voice pitch, tone and modulation, inject humour and make a joke, or give signposts. Think about what strategy you would be comfortable using.

Knowing your audience is vital for keeping their attention – speak to the audience you have not the one you wish you had! That means you need to stress FAB: the Features And Benefits, of your presentation or whatever issue you are dealing with for them. For example if you are talking to an audience of GPs about a new form of treatment, stress what features and benefits the GPs need to be aware of and the ways the new treatment can help their patients and carers. In knowing your audience you have to empathise with them, step into their shoes; provide examples that will mean something to them personally. If you are an expert on a particular subject, remember *the facts don't always speak for themselves,* you may need to simplify what you say for the audience, and explain. However, beware of patronising them, nobody likes to be spoken down to.

The difficult question

One of the worst fears is being thrown a question you can't answer. *Handing the difficult question* is tricky – imagine what the difficult question might be in your presentation. There are at least six responses you can make, other than stunned silence and stuttering, that are perfectly effective and reasonable. You can:

> **Throw it back to the questioner.** What do they think? It is interesting that a lot of people dress up a point they want to make as a question. Therefore you can convert it back to the point and get them to state it. For example, if in your presentation on competences the question is 'Aren't competences just a bureaucratic waste of time?' instead of looking at them blankly, you could ask them 'What makes you think that is the case?' It is quite likely they will go on to make a point such as 'Well at my last company the list of competences were put in the filing cabinet after the consultants left and it was never opened again.' This has then given you more material to go on and time to think, so you could answer 'Yes, if competences stay in the ownership of the consultants then that is a danger, to counter that you need to make sure that people in the organisation are more actively involved in drawing them up, putting them in their own language, piloting them, etc, etc...'.

> **Invite others to respond.** Usually people get quite bored just sitting and listening, and presentations come alive once there is more debate, so it is perfectly acceptable to open up an idea and ask 'What do others of you think?' Most people in your audience will have a perspective on what is being said, and some will be itching to show they are on the ball.

Ask for clarification. If you don't understand the question, rather than bluffing, you could ask them to expand and explain their point further. So in answer to the first question above you could say 'Are you suggesting that sometimes bureaucracy can make them less useful, or that they shouldn't be used at all?' Sometimes when people rephrase the question this gives you more 'anchors' to go on, so they may respond with 'Well actually they do seem to take up so much managerial time that could be utilised better elsewhere', which may lead you to say 'Yes the start-up time can be costly, but with the right system, you may end up by saving time when they become second nature . . .'.

I'll deal with that later. Some questions are really a diversion from your main messages, and it would be damaging to pursue them. They may relate to a very narrow area of interest of the questioner in which case you could say 'Perhaps we could pursue that at the end of the presentation, or over coffee'. Other questions require you to have information at your finger tips that you just don't have available such as 'What percentage of companies are using competences in recruitment?' To this you could say 'I haven't the information with me right now, but give me your e-mail address and I'll send you the data tomorrow'. There is always the classic 'I don't know but I know a man who does' or in the phrase from 'Who wants to be a millionaire': 'I'll phone a friend'. All these responses buys you time to go and seek out the information you need.

Bridging. Some questions move you away from the focus of what you are trying to say. In this case an alternative to 'dealing with it later' is to use a technique called 'bridging.' In this case you acknowledge the point that has been made, such as 'Yes, that is a good point,' or 'No, I don't believe that', and then use the bridge phrase such as 'but more importantly' or 'We believe' and then move on to communicate your original key message.

I don't know. Better than blustering and drawing attention to your nerves, it sometimes is just better to give a straight 'I don't know' and move on 'Next question please'. An audience will respect the fact that you haven't wasted their time with waffle, and that you are honest and open. Nobody really likes a know-it-all anyway, and they may even like you the better for it.

Cultural issues: English as a foreign language

Many of these worst fears may be magnified if English is not your first language. Some publications are particularly orientated to giving presentations in your second language (Powell 1996 and Comfort 1995 are particularly good for this). Here are some options you may like to consider:

- Find out **difference** between your own culture and the norms of the culture to which you are presenting. In particular pay attention to the level of formality expected, forms of greeting, expectations to do with audience participation, style of dress expected. One way of checking this is to find a friend or course-mate that is more familiar with the culture and ask them for some guidance.

- **Prepare well**: you may need to give some extra time to preparation and also to rehearsing and practising your presentations. Again if you can find a friend who is willing to hear you run through your presentation this can help.

- Use a **graphics package** such as PowerPoint: having a structured slide show can help you structure the presentation and makes it easier for you not to get lost within it.

- **Introduce your status** as an 'English as a Second Language' speaker. You could say something like 'You may find it difficult to follow some of my presentation, please bear with me as English is my second Language, I'm from . . . .' Sometimes bringing the fear into the room and out into the open can dispel anxiety.

■ You could also focus on **relaxing the audience** and yourself by saying 'If there is anything you don't follow, I'll come back to it at the end'. Give them a clear message that shows you understand they may have difficulties following your talk, but also that you intend to do what you can to address any problems they may have in understanding you.

PRESENTATION PITFALLS

By now, you should have a firm grasp of what to do in your presentation, but before you start, just beware a few common pitfalls:

The walking telephone directory
This occurs when you write what you are going to say in longhand and read it out: IT IS SO . . . . BORING! What is more, you cannot even make eye contact. So why do people do it? Because they are nervous and worried that they will forget everything.

HINT: list topics with key issues only on your cards, one for each topic as this helps you structure your notes. Or do the same using the PowerPoint notes to accompany each slide, or write your extra notes on a hard copy of your slide. Never read your presentation.

The mouse
The mouse avoids eye contact with the audience and hides behind the equipment. Why? Because he or she is scared.

HINT: take a deep breath and relax and look at them and smile (but not with a fixed grimace). The worst thing they can do is turn off, and they will definitely do that if you don't look at them.

The fidget
Here you jiggle about like a cat on a hot tin roof. We all have some mannerisms, but some are more distracting than others.

HINT: relax, don't let your body tense up. Also do Exercises 6.5 and 6.6 above.

The station announcer
Here you mumble, mumble in a boring monotone: 'The next train from platform 4 mumble mumble . . .'. We can't hear you, and if you speak fast we can't follow you.

HINT: vary your pitch, speed, and volume for effect. Use a pause . . .. Before speaking s-l-o-w-l-y in a *clear* voice for important points. Practise projecting your voice. Use breathing exercises and breathe from the diaphragm.

The encyclopaedia
A font of knowledge – do you think we will really remember all 172 points? And what about the detail? Did they go on, and on, and on

HINT: limit your presentation to a few key points and highlight these points and summarise them in the conclusion.

The anarchist
No structure, no introduction, no conclusion. Why are you here, what are you talking about?

135

HINT: introduce yourself, state for how long you will be talking, when people can ask questions, give them signposts on what to expect.

The spider
Great slide show – if only we could see what was on the slides. Teensy-weensy writing covering it. This is so frustrating.

HINT: limit yourself to 10 words per slide; use large letter typeface and font.

The five-minute comic
Do you know the one about the new comedian who was give a five-minute slot at the comedy club to try out some new material? Boy did she fall flat, it was so *embarrassing*!

HINT: try and inject some humour and entertainment into your presentation – remember you are going to get your point across if you engage their interest, BUT: don't try humour that is unnatural to you. If you can't tell jokes, try an anecdote or a visual cartoon, or illustrations but don't try to be something that you are not.

SUMMARY

This chapter has built on some of the communication skills identified in Chapter 5 in order to explore them in further detail with relation to presenting effectively. It has introduced you to the main techniques of giving written and verbal presentations. However, the only way you will really learn from this chapter is to practise. The key messages we focused on are moving your attention away from the writer/presenter and focusing on the needs of the audience and what the listener may be thinking or questioning. It has given you ideas on how to structure and organise your ideas in your presentation, so that the audience goes away with some key messages that were logically ordered and intelligible. Just as important, this chapter has suggested you pay attention to how you deliver the presentation and issues of body language, eye contact, voice projection and posture. Communicating assertively is an important part of giving verbal presentations, and the particular skills involved with assertiveness will be explored further in the next chapter.

REFERENCES AND FURTHER READING

BILLINGHAM, J. (2003) *Giving Presentations.* New York: Oxford University Press, One Step Ahead Series.

BLAMIRES, H. (2000) *The Penguin Guide to Plain English: Express yourself clearly and effectively.* London: Penguin.

BRADBURY, A. (2000) *Successful Presentation Skills.* 2nd ed. London: Kogan Page.

COMFORT, J. (1995) *Oxford Business English Skills: Effective Presentations: Students book.* Oxford: Oxford University Press (book and audio cassette).

CONRADI, M. and HALL, R. (2001) *That Presentation Sensation: Be good, be passionate, be memorable.* Harlow: FT/Prentice Hall.

GRIFFITHS, D. (1998) Presentation skills. Chapter 21 in CLEGG, C. LEGGE, K. and WALSH, S *The Experience of Managing: A skills guide.* Basingstoke, Hants: Macmillan Business. 193–203.

GRINT, K. (2000) Martin Luther King's 'Dream Speech': The Rhetoric of Social Leadership. *The Art of Leadership.* Oxford: Oxford University Press. Chapter 9.

HALL, G. (1998) *How To Write A Paper.* London: BMJ Books.

HERITAGE, K. (1998) *Report Writing.* London: Hodder and Stoughton.

HINDLE, T. (1998) *Essential Managers: Making presentations.* London: Dorling Kindersley.

LEIGH, A. and MAYNARD, M. (1999) *The Perfect Presentation.* London: Random House Business Books.

MINTO, B. (2002) *The Pyramid Principle.* London: FT/Prentice Hall, Pearson.

MURDOCK, A. and SCUTT, C. (1997) *Personal Effectiveness.* 2nd ed. Oxford: Butterworth Heinemann. Chapter 2, 54–76.

POWELL, D. (1990) *Presentation Techniques.* London: Little Brown.

POWELL, M. (1996) *Presenting in English: How to give successful presentations: Students book.* Hove: Language Teaching Publications (book and audio cassette 'The secret of successful presentations').

ROTONDO, J. and ROTONDO, M. *Presentation Skills for Managers.* London: McGraw Hill (E-book).

SIDDONS, S. (1999) *Presentation Skills.* London: CIPD.

WHETTON, D. and CAMERON, K. (2002) *Developing Management Skills.* 5th ed. New Jersey: Prentice Hall. Supplement A, 495–522.

Assertiveness

INTRODUCTION

When thinking about assertiveness, many people find it difficult to articulate exactly what it means: does it mean throwing your weight about, or standing firm whatever else happens, or acting bullishly? No, these behaviours could be counter-productive; developing your assertiveness should not be confused with aggressiveness. The chapter begins by helping you to tease out the difference between aggressiveness, assertiveness and submissiveness and come to a definition about what assertiveness is, and what it is not.

Assertiveness is not just about what you say. It is also about how you say it: your body language and voice, as well as your feelings and emotions. Assertiveness assumes that individuals have certain rights and we will explore these primarily within the work context. Most people can be assertive some of the time, it is just when faced with particularly challenging situations that they experience difficulties. Therefore, after defining your challenging situations, we focus on areas where you are likely to experience more difficulty, such as giving and receiving criticism, making and refusing requests. However, assertiveness is not a skill that can be learnt in the abstract, so we will utilise some real situations to identify what you would do, and what would be an assertive way of responding. It will help if you also seek out situations in which to practise assertiveness skills.

WHAT IS ASSERTIVENESS?

EXERCISE 7.1   THE DIFFERENCE BETWEEN AGGRESSIVENESS, SUBMISSIVENESS AND ASSERTIVENESS

In the table below brainstorm the words that come to mind when you think of the way a) aggressive people, b) submissive people and c) assertive people, speak.

Aggressiveness	Submissiveness	Assertiveness

It is likely that in doing Exercise 7.1 you found it quite easy to distinguish between assertiveness and submissiveness, but harder to differentiate assertiveness and aggressiveness. A common misconception is that assertiveness is to do with being aggressive. Table 7.1 identifies some of the words that you may have used to distinguish between the three ways of speaking.

Table 7.1   *Describing aggressive, submissive and assertive ways of speaking*

Aggressive	Submissive	Assertive

attacking and threatening
demanding
forcing
offensive
expressing opinions as
    facts
not listening
interrupting
blaming
crushing
humiliating
sarcastic
bullying
	weak and feeble
	impotent and powerless
	insubstantial
	saying 'I'm sorry' often
	saying 'I'm afraid' often
	saying 'I should/must/
	    ought' often
	not saying what I want/feel/
	    like
	indirect
	agreeing to things to keep
	    the peace
	backing down, giving in
	complaining behind the
	    scenes
	justifying opinion and self
	self-deprecating, putting
	    self down
		confident and self-assured
		decisive
		stating clearly what
		    want/need/feel
		standing up for self
		direct, getting to the point
		saying 'no' when want to
		giving praise/constructive
		    criticism when
		    necessary
		finding out the
		    wants/needs/feelings of
		    others
		acknowledging the other
		    person's standpoint
		speaking to people as wish
		    to be spoken to
		listening to others
		respectful – of self and
		    others

Assertiveness is being able to state your needs and wants and get these met.

Submissive people listen to and respond to the needs of others but ignore their own. Aggressive people state their own needs, but often in an inappropriately hostile way, and do not bother to listen to or respond to the needs and wants of others.

DEFINITION OF ASSERTIVENESS

Getting your needs met without ignoring the needs and rights of others.
Expressing your needs, wants, opinions, feelings and beliefs in a direct and honest way.

This requires you recognise in any situation:

- you have *needs* to be met and so do others
- you have *rights* and so do others
- the aim is to satisfy the needs and rights of *both* parties
- through *direct* and *honest* expression.

Communicating assertively means recognising you have one mouth *and* two ears: you express yourself, but also have the capacity to listen. In speech and other communication we may sometimes concentrate too much on what we say: communication is a two-way process, and being assertive is being skilled at speaking and listening.

Communicating assertively is not just about speech, it also involves ways of behaving and includes body language and non-verbal as well as verbal forms of communication. Table 7.2 provides some examples of these different ways of behaving. Chapter 5 also explains further these other forms of communication. Communication also involves thoughts and feelings, and one particularly important dimension is *locus of control.* A person's locus of control can be internal, that is, where they believe that things that happen to them are generated by their own efforts, or external, where they believe things that happen are due to luck or chance. A strong internal locus of control tends to lead to greater assertiveness and belief that one can control events rather than be controlled by them, and is empowering. More information on this can be found on the website. Beliefs such as this are also related to the cognitive processes such as self-efficacy mentioned in Chapter 1.

Table 7.2 *Status cues: ways of behaving, thinking and feeling*

	Aggressive	Submissive	Assertive
Thoughts	One-up position: superior or inferior but keen to hide it	One-down position: inferior, not as important as everyone else	Equal: having equal rights with everyone else. Respect for self and others
Feelings	Dominant emotion: anger. May feel tense, maybe scared deep down	Dominant emotion: fear. May feel frightened, nervous, anxious, guilty	Dominant emotion: well-being. May feel calm, confident, excited

Table 7.2 *continued*

	Aggressive	Submissive	Assertive
Stance and posture	Upright, expansive, leaning forward or coming too close, trying to be physically higher, eg standing when other person is sitting	Huddles up, round-shouldered, shrinking, chest hollow, turning away, half hiding, trying to be smaller, lower than others eg sitting when others are standing	Relaxed, but may appear energetic, well-balanced, facing the other person directly
Head	Head: in the air	Head: down or bobbing around, waggling. Fidgeting and touching head or face nervously	Head: keeps still, maybe slightly tilted when speaking
Legs and feet	When standing – feet firmly apart; when sitting – leaning forward, foot tapping or swinging; when moving – striding impatiently	When standing – shifting weight from one foot to the other, standing with weight on one foot, rolling one foot onto its side, stepping back, shuffling; when sitting – tied in knots, hidden	When standing – feet about shoulder width apart, weight equally distributed on both feet, standing still; when sitting – relaxed
Hands and arms	Hands or fists on hips; arms folded across chest; hand and arm raised; hands clenched tightly; fist thumping; finger pointing, or poking; hand crunching handshakes.	Hugging the body, wringing hands, covering mouth with hand, nervous fiddling, hands tightly clasped or fidgeting.	Open, expressive hand movements – arms comfortably by sides, or one hand in pocket, or arms folded loosely; relaxed gestures to emphasise points, when sitting, hands folded comfortably on lap, not fidgeting.
Eye contact	Looking down from a height, glaring, staring, hard gaze, narrowing of the eyes, unblinking, looking through or past a person. Holds eye contact for more than five seconds	Looking down, looking away, avoiding eye contact, quick furtive glances, and eyes darting from side to side when speaking. Holds eye contact for less than a second	Looking directly at other person at same level, agreeable and relaxed look, looking away every so often yet coming back to look person

Table 7.2 *continued*

	Aggressive	Submissive	Assertive
Expression	Jaw set teeth clenched; scowling, chin forward; turning red, blue or white with anger; eyebrows raised in disbelief; indignant or angry expression, sarcastic sneer	Worried, tense, apologetic look; biting lip or inside of cheek; pale or blushing, nervous smile; smiling when expressing anger or being criticised	Calm; facial muscles and jaw relaxed; firm and pleasant expression; smiles when appropriate
Voice and speech	Cold, loud, sharp, threatening, fast, abrupt, clipped	Hesitant, tentative, stumbling, mumbling, quiet, strained, wobbly, whining, dull or monotone, childlike. Or fast and breathless	Steady and firm, slow and deliberate. Reflects, takes time to think. Projects, low-pitched, medium volume, clear speech, warm tones.
Timing	Rushes other person	Rushes self	Takes own time
Use of space	Territorial, takes ownership of space, invades space of others	Hides in corner, kneeling, bowing, prostrating, avoids entering others' space	Relaxed use of space
Overall manner, way seen by others	Frightening	Powerless, helpless, fearful	Confident, authoritative, maybe quiet humility

STATUS WORK

Assertiveness involves underlying thought processes and beliefs about yourself, as well as how you position yourself in relation to others. Aggressive people tend to position themselves one (or more) up; submissive people position themselves one (or more) down, whereas assertive people take on more of an equal position.

The animal kingdom tends to arrange its groupings in terms of status differentials, the Alpha male of the deer for example being the strongest and most dominant stag, to which all others have to defer or remove themselves out of the way. Humans are not always as different as we might like to believe: how much jostling for status rivalry have you seen in the work context, or even in ritualistic games like football or rugby? Being assertive doesn't mean acting like the Alpha male attempting to make those around us our herd, it is more about removing oneself from the pecking order game, and having more versatility to behave in a more self-determined way, having more free will, and behaving without undue domination or grovelling. Often this means behaving more as equals, at least in terms of our rights as human beings, and the respect we pay ourselves and engender in others, even if our status denotes something different.

One way of understanding assertiveness is in terms of the status denoted in playing cards. Imagine taking a pack of cards and shuffling them, then picking out two cards. One card is the king of spades, the other the 2 of clubs. Now visualise a performance in which these cards are being played by actors as they pass each other in the street. The King would be likely to sweep past with his chin up, the 2 of clubs grovel and bow low. The actors may have taken on the mannerisms and behaviour of the aggressive or submissive person listed in Table 7.2. Of course the actors may play these parts more as equals, more like a 7 of hearts and 7 of diamonds, walking confidently, maybe nodding pleasantly to each other – but this would be unusual. What card do you habitually play when you are walking down the street? Do you stride imperiously like the queen of diamonds, sweeping everyone out of the way, or shuffle along timidly like the 2 of hearts? For fun you could play the card game when you are commuting, or out socially or shopping, taking out a card at random, and then playing out the status level given by the card. Very quickly you would find out your comfort level. You may also find out from the reactions of others what level they play. Not all kings and queens are as aggressive as the red queen in Alice in Wonderland, demanding 'Chop of her head' at will. Being assertive is more about taking on the versatility of the ace, assuming different positions as appropriate.

It is not always easy to shake up status positions, and in the theatre this is often used to dramatic effect, for example when the fool plays the king, or when princes and paupers change clothes and identities (see for example Johnstone 1981: 33–74). It is interesting that the status position we play may not always be appropriate or dictated by our role, and at work excessively dominant or submissive behaviour is rarely appropriate. The exciting opportunity for you in reading this chapter is that you may have more leeway than you think for changing the status roles that you play, becoming more assertive as a way of being heard, respected and also feeling more confident. If you now consider those situations in which you feel less confident and unassertive, you may find that this is partly because someone else is trying to play from a one-up position, or alternatively because you are not playing to your preferred level, in some way reducing or raising your position.

Exercise 7.2 will help you diagnose how assertive you are in different situations.

EXERCISE 7.2   REFLECTING ON YOUR OWN ASSERTIVENESS

The following questions will help you to consider how assertive you are. They may also indicate the areas in which becoming more assertive might help.

- Do particular people at work make you feel intimidated? In what situations? How do you normally react?
- What aspects of your job do you dislike the most? Tend to put off? Feel uncomfortable with?
- How self-critical are you? How do you react if you make mistakes? How do you react to being criticised?
- Does it matter to you what other people think/say about you? Do you hope that everyone likes you?

- Do you tend to accept the blame for things rather than make a fuss?
- Do you feel that other people's work is generally as good, better or worse than yours?
- Do you worry a lot about work? What aspects cause you the most concern/stress?
- Do you lose your temper at times? In what situations? Whose fault does this tend to be?
- Do you find yourself having to apologise often? Do you sometimes feel guilty about the way you have spoken to or treated someone? Do those around you have to tread carefully when you are in a particular mood?
- Are some people intimidated by you? How does this make you feel?
- How competitive are you? Is it important to you that you always win?
- What do you do when someone disagrees with you?
- How do you tend to react in a crisis?

The above checklist is designed to give you the opportunity to reflect on the way you behave and how you react to situations and people. Take time to reflect on each question carefully. You might find it useful to share your responses with others, such as trusted colleagues, family or friends. This can often give you valuable insight into the way your behaviour is perceived by others.

There are various reasons why we may find it so difficult to be assertive. Some of these are to do with the situation, and some to do with ourselves. Table 7.2 has revealed that we may have some fundamental beliefs about ourselves that lead us to behave in unassertive ways. In particular if we lack confidence in ourselves then it is harder to be assertive. People who want to 'please others' may find it difficult to stand up for themselves when faced with other people wanting them to do something different, and are more likely to relapse into submissive and unassertive behaviour. Chapter 9 will expand on the 'drivers' and 'injunctions', such as 'please others' that operate in our lives. Fear and anxiety can also send us in the opposite direction, where we become more aggressive to hide our insecurities. Ultimately assertive behaviour is more effective both for ourselves and for others around us, and so, despite these difficulties, it is worth training ourselves to become more assertive.

RIGHTS AT WORK

It was mentioned above that being assertive is about standing up for our needs, wants, and rights. To do this we need to know what we want, but we also need to know our rights, particularly in the workplace. Consider the list given in Table 7.3 and see how many of these you agree with.

Table 7.3   *Rights at work*

I have the right at work:
To express opinions/values and have them listened to
To express feelings and have them listened to
To express needs and have them listened to
To ask for what I want
To refuse an unreasonable request
To expect work of a certain standard from others
To constructively criticise other's performance where appropriate
To ask for information when needed
To make choices based on my needs
To have needs and wants that are different from those of others
To know what is expected of me
To receive honest, constructive and regular feedback on my work and performance
To be praised and thanked for doing a good job
To be informed and consulted about decisions that affect me
To take decisions that are within my area of work
Not to be pre-judged or treated unfairly
To be treated with respect
To make mistakes sometimes
To choose the time and the place to deal with an issue.
To choose not to be assertive

Aggressive people may assert these rights in themselves, but ignore them and trample over those of others. Submissive people overlook their own rights. Look through the list and ask yourself which of these rights you believe in and put into practice in your own behaviour with respect to yourself. Now examine these rights again and explore how many of them you actively put into practice with relation to others around you – for example do you praise and thank others who have done a good job for you? Ignoring our own or others' rights can lead to bad feeling and awkward working relationships.

The last one is particularly interesting: 'to choose not to be assertive'. Being assertive doesn't mean you have to fight every battle and put yourself on the line all the time. Instead there are times when you will want to let something go, or others when you may feel it is neither the time nor the place to take up an issue with a problem or person.

CHALLENGING SITUATIONS AND HOW TO RESPOND TO THEM

EXERCISE 7.3   TACKLING ASSERTIVENESS SCENARIOS

In the next few sections you will be presented with various scenarios to practise and check your assertiveness skills.

For each of these write down how you would respond to the scenario.

Is there a difference between what you would do and what you think you should do (which you could also note)? Why?

You could try to role play the scenarios, for example with a mentor or peer.

Making requests

> ### SCENARIO 7.1   MAKING REQUESTS
>
> You need some help with the design of a project (it could be a project for your course or for work) from the Project Director, Professor Plum who is very experienced in this area. You have tried e-mailing him over the last month to get an appointment to see him but he keeps putting you off as he is extremely busy. He is quite forbidding and abrupt at the best of times. You cannot proceed with your work until you have gained his advice. You have a review of your work coming up so it cannot wait, so you go to see him in his office, and pluck up courage to knock on his door. What do you say?

When making requests you need to avoid too much apologising 'I'm really sorry to bother you, and I realise this might be terribly difficult for you ...'. This becomes irritating and puts you in the submissive one-down position before you start, making it easier for the person to refuse. Also you want to avoid being long-winded and merely hinting at what you want: 'I'm sure you are very busy next week, and you have got lots of other things to do, and it is very tricky to fit in all the work you do ...' because we lose sight of the request and it is likely that your respondent will change the subject, go off onto another track, take issue with something you have said before you even get to the point, or even totally miss the request you are making. You also need to avoid being overly flattering and manipulative. Being assertive is about being direct and honest: 'I'd really appreciate it if you could give me an appointment today'.

When you are making requests it helps to state what you want to happen such as 'I would like one week's study leave at the beginning of next month'. As well as being clear and direct, you do need to let people know you are listening and appreciate their position, for example by saying 'I hear what you are saying ...' or 'I realise that ...'. However, you still need to be direct in stating what you think and feel, and what outcome you desire: 'I would like ...' 'Would it help to ...?'

Being fobbed off by busy people (as in Scenario 7.1) can be daunting. You may need to demonstrate how important your claim is, so a good response could be:

> Excuse me Professor Plum, I appreciate you are busy but I need to discuss something that is very important for the work. Without this discussion I cannot proceed and the whole project will be delayed.

It is sensible to come straight to the point and make your request clearly, being specific and firm. Do not attack or blame: 'You are never available, I don't ever seem to be able to get hold of you', as this can lead to whinging, recriminations and counter-recriminations, and also reinforces your failure. If you need to state the problems you have had, stick to the facts without attacking, for example: 'I've contacted you four times already, this is now urgent'. Giving a time limit for the meeting is helpful: 'This will just take five minutes of your time', but if he really cannot see you now you need to allow for alternatives: 'If you cannot see me now, then I need an appointment before the end of today'. Your statement needs to be supported by the appropriate body language – looking him in the eye, and also sitting down, or bringing out your diary to write down a time, all reinforce your expectation of success. The important thing is not to be fobbed off, so whatever his response you need to restate your request in a calm but assured way. You may also appeal to your common cause – the need to get the project going – so you could say: 'Any further delay will waste everybody's time, and could jeopardise the project'.

Refusing requests and saying 'No'

SCENARIO 7.2   REFUSING REQUESTS

You have always worked late when requested, but this time Mr Black, your Director, has asked you to attend a meeting on his behalf, which clashes with an important personal engagement. What do you say?

In refusing requests you again need to be direct, and maybe give a reason, but apologise only if you are sorry, and examine the possibilities and ways you may help solve their problem without giving in yourself.

Scenario 7.2 requires you to think about joint problem solving – how can you recognise and meet both your needs? You could say something like 'I'm afraid I can't, have you thought of approaching x or y?' Move quickly from a focus on the problem to a focus on alternative solutions, from reasserting your position, to looking for alternative ways to solve Mr. Black's problem. Don't emphasise your excuses otherwise Mr. Black may just start to unravel them: for example, if you mention that you are going to see a film he could say 'Can't you go another night?' or if you have childcare problems 'I'm sure you can get a babysitter'.

If you do find yourself caving in, such as in 'Well, I suppose I could give the tickets to someone else', think about trading, so instead you could say 'Well, you would need to reimburse the cost of the tickets', or 'If you pay for a slap up dinner for another night instead'. Or at the very least you could offer a concession: 'I will go but only for one hour to pick up the materials', or 'I can't go, but I can get hold of the papers for you'. However, this opens up another issue: *Don't make someone else's problem your problem.* Unassertive people allow others to dump all their difficulties on them. Therefore if you are providing help, check that you attach boundaries and don't end up taking responsibility, for example: 'I am sure you will find someone else in the department to go, and I will drop you a couple of suggestions by e-mail' is better than 'I will find someone else to go instead of me'.

Scratched vinyl/CD

This is a technique well known to parents and superbly executed by millions of children. Some of you may remember how LPs with a scratch used to repeat the same phrase over and over again. It is a technique which involves you in repeating yourself until eventually the other person is forced to take notice of what you are saying. It can be usefully employed when people are trying to manipulate or bully you into something you are not happy to do. It is sometimes easier to hold your ground if you just go on auto-pilot and keep repeating like a parrot. An example of this technique being used is given below. Alternatively you could repeat but rephrase the refusal, which may help you sound less like a parrot.

EXAMPLE 7.1   SCRATCHED VINYL OR CD

Colleague:	Come with me to the workshop this afternoon.
Busy manager:	I'm rather busy today. They are repeating it next week, I'll come to that one.
Colleague:	It only lasts for an hour, go on.
Manager:	I'd like to but I'm far too busy this week. I'll put next week's one in my diary though.
Colleague:	What about taking your sandwich to it and a coffee, you can eat your lunch while you are there. You look as thought you could do with a break. Is work getting you down as well?
Manager:	I'm dreadfully busy, which is why I must get on today. Shall I see you at next week's one?
Colleague:	Oh, all right then. We'll go to next week's one.

Being ignored, interrupted – being heard

SCENARIO 7.3   BEING IGNORED, INTERRUPTED – BEING HEARD

You are at a meeting with all those involved in a particular issue to discuss what actions should be taken. You put forward what you think is a good suggestion based on your experience in this area. Before you have finished speaking, Brian Mustard butts in to make a completely different point. What do you do?

In Scenario 7.3 Brian Mustard's interruption may not be a deliberately malicious act towards you, but derive from his focus on himself. It may just be that Brian has got carried away with his own idea, and hasn't even noticed his rudeness. A good response would be to acknowledge Brian's point, but firmly bring the topic back to the point under discussion, such as:

> That is a very interesting point Brian, can we come to that when we have finished discussing the previous issue

or

> If I may return and finish my point before we go on . . . .

Again, words are not enough, and body language needs to be used to draw attention to you so that you are not overlooked.

In the wild many animals have strong peripheral vision, so that if something is moving quickly their attention is drawn immediately to it. This is for self-protection against fast predators like a leopard or cheetah. Fascinatingly this also works with humans, so you could make a sudden hand movement or wave a pen forward to get everyone's eye contact. You could also lean forward to make your point. Use eye contact to engage people's attention and draw them to you. Remember the Bananarama song 'It ain't what you do/say but the way that you do/say it, that's what gets results'.

Making mistakes and dealing with criticism

SCENARIO 7.4 MAKING MISTAKES AND DEALING WITH CRITICISM

You are discussing an important piece of work with a member of your team when a senior colleague comes over to your desk and interrupts saying:

I am really unhappy with the way you dealt with the client yesterday.

Yesterday had been a very long day and you had snapped rather at the client.

What do you say?

Making mistakes can lead us to grovel and act submissively. We may become so wracked by guilt that this impedes effective communication with others and future work. There will be times when we do make mistakes, and in Chapter 1 we discussed the idea that everyone has the right to make occasional mistakes, we are only human. To be human is to be fallible. At times like these it is important to be seen to accept and handle the criticism well. The assertive way of dealing with justifiable criticism is to simply accept the comment and to respond in a simple and direct way. For example:

> You're right, I could have handled that better.

> I've forgotten to bring the report with me. That was careless of me. I think I'd better ring the office and get them to fax/e-mail it over . . ..

By reacting to your mistakes in a calm, detached manner, you are remaining assertive and not allowing the guilt you may be feeling to be used against you by others. It also helps to prevent you from acting submissively or becoming defensive and aggressive, and it may take the 'heat' out of others' emotions.

However, re-read Scenario 7.4, and remember the list of rights you had. Firstly you can choose the time and the place for some particularly sensitive discussions. You do not have to be chastised in front of someone else, or be caught unawares without having had time to collect your thoughts. In this case a better answer may have been:

> I'm with someone right now as you can see, can we discuss this later? . . ..

SCENARIO 7.5 DEALING WITH UNFAIR CRITICISM

You have been working with a particularly difficult client, and you have really had to struggle to keep your patience, but you are pleased to find that you kept your calm. Your manager Mr. Green walks in and the client turns to him in front of you and complains that you have been rude and haven't listened to her point of view. The manager says to you 'I expect my team to be courteous at all times, please apologise to the client for your rude behaviour'. You are fuming. What do you say?

Scenario 7.5 is particularly tricky and upsetting: you are being asked to apologise for something that you haven't done, and you feel unsupported by your manager. Of course there is always the possibility that you gave offence without even realising it, so you could provide an apology which doesn't require you to lose face entirely, such as:

> I am very sorry if I caused offence, I really had no intention of doing that . . . .

or

> I am sorry you feel upset . . . .

as this avoids taking the blame.

It is certainly worth taking a step back and questioning whether you could have been interpreted as being rude. You do need also to separate out the two separate issues of dealing with your client and dealing with the manager. You probably also want to diffuse the emotion and heat in the situation. Sometimes just recognising how someone feels can help calm a situation down. You could also focus on common ground:

> I'd really like to hear how you think we could sort out the situation/problem.

However, with relation to your manager it is clearly unfair that he has not bothered to get your perspective and has put you down in this way in front of your client. You would probably want to arrange a separate meeting with your manager to discuss your concern that you are not getting his support. You do have a right to voice your view and have it listened to.

Negative and positive enquiry, and probing

Sometimes we face continued criticism from people, or we may feel that the criticism is unfair. In this case it may not be assertive to apologise and take the criticism on the chin; you need to explore the situation further. Negative and positive enquiries are techniques to be used when you feel it is important to obtain more information about why the other person is either criticising or praising you. It involves you in actively seeking more feedback but in an unemotional and objective manner. You are in effect saying to the other person that you recognise something has happened and that you want to concentrate on establishing why, so that you can take any necessary future action. By reacting assertively to criticism in this way you are showing that you accept your mistakes but that you are not going to be made to feel guilty or to get upset about them.

Some examples of the questions you may ask include:

- 'What is it about my behaviour that has led you to think that?'

- 'What did I say to give you that impression?'
- 'What aspects do you feel I didn't perform well in?'

Probing helps you to stay detached from any criticism while seeking more information about exactly what it is the other person is saying. It involves moving the attention away from yourself and on to the other person by questioning them about what they have said. It will only be effective, however, if you appear unconcerned and unaffected by the criticism.

EXAMPLE 7.2   NEGATIVE AND POSITIVE ENQUIRY, PROBING

Boss:	I'm not at all happy with the way you're running the project and I want to see a vast improvement by the time we next meet.
Manager:	Could you tell me what is it about my project management that you're not happy with?
Boss:	The deadlines are slipping and this is simply not good enough.
Manager:	Yes, I know we are a week behind but the e-mail I sent to you explained the reasons for this – we are waiting for the parts from the suppliers. Your reply suggested you had accepted this was beyond my control. Do you now feel otherwise?
Boss:	No, I suppose this wasn't your fault but I still feel you could be running a tighter ship. We'll review things at our next meeting.
Manager:	I'm still concerned that you are not happy with my performance and I feel I need to know why in order to do something about it. Could you clarify what you mean by running a tighter ship?
Boss:	Umm …. Well ….

In this example the boss is clearly feeling put on the spot. He seems to have no justification for having been so critical and has little idea as to the changes, if any, he is looking for. The probing technique used by the manager reveals this information as well as helping her to remain calm and detached. The manager is also open about how she feels and shares this with her boss. While this may at first sight seem to be leaving her rather vulnerable, it can often add weight to what she is saying.

The best way to be assertive is to be straightforward and factual when responding to people. This helps to avoid appearing as either aggressive or submissive and will encourage the other person to react openly to what is being said.

In performance feedback you do have a right to have this discussed properly, and to be prepared yourself for that discussion. If your boss feels that there is a performance issue to be discussed, you may want to ask him or her for more information and arrange a meeting where you are in private and have access to all the information you need. As with many cases, don't be bamboozled and rushed into doing things immediately if it is not convenient to you. Usually it is only those who are assistants that have to respond immediately, most managers have freedom over how and when they deal with issues, as discussed in Chapter 2 on time management.

Fogging or 'water off a duck's back'

There are some situations where criticism is unwelcome and unjust, but is being used as a jibe to provoke you. In these cases there is a technique called 'fogging' which can be helpful to divert aggression or criticism and negativity.

It is based on the principle that if you try to argue against their criticism they will use this as further ammunition. You therefore make yourself into a small target by agreeing but by not making any kind of commitment. With this technique, the use of non-defensive or placating remarks is particularly effective as it leaves the other person unsure of how to respond.

An example of this technique is given below:

EXAMPLE 7.3   FOGGING OR 'WATER OFF A DUCK'S BACK'

Colleague:	Are you still here? Oh you are such a workaholic – sucking up to the boss again I see!
Manager:	Yes I'm here, yet again.
Colleague:	Determined to get that raise I see!
Manager:	I can see it might look that way.
Colleague:	You're obviously not satisfied with being promoted already this year then?
Manager:	Obviously not.
Colleague:	Why don't you get a life?
Manager:	Sad eh ….
Colleague	Right, well, ok, I'll leave you alone ….

As you can see, the manager may be appearing to go along with what is being said but is not conceding anything in reality. He is also making it very difficult for his colleague to continue with his attack.

When someone is being very critical, offering no resistance will make it very difficult for the other person to strike back. Most criticisms can be agreed to in principle and if you do this, as in the above example, you are telling the other person that you recognise what they have to say, that you accept that their point may be valid and, most importantly perhaps (for their eventual acquiescence), that they are entitled to think what they like. This can then enable them to accept your views.

Other fogging statements could include:

- 'You could be right.'
- 'That's a good point.'
- 'I can see why you might think that.'
- 'What you're saying makes good sense.'

Accepting and receiving praise

SCENARIO 7.6   ACCEPTING AND RECEIVING PRAISE

The leader of your department comes over to you and says 'That was a fantastic job you did on the special project, it was really impressive'.

What do you say and how do you behave?

It is not just criticism we may have difficulty dealing with, we may also find the reverse, finding it difficult to accept fair praise when we have done something well. It can be difficult to accept genuine compliments but being assertive is being able to say 'Thank you, I feel pleased with how it went', rather than shrugging it off with a red face and dismissive comment. After all most of our workplaces would be more motivating places to work if people spent as much time giving and accepting praise as they did giving and trading blame. Accepting praise is like accepting a gift, and should be done graciously.

Criticising others

SCENARIO 7.7   CRITICISING OTHERS

You are in a meeting and your colleague Kate Scarlett says she has a good idea of how to solve a problem, and then goes on to explain it. You sit astounded. That was the very idea you were suggesting to her the previous afternoon, and then she had brushed it off saying it would never work. Everyone congratulates Ms Scarlett, and you sit there smouldering. This is the last straw! What do you do and say?

How you deal with Scenario 7.7 depends in part on your relative status to Ms Scarlett. If you are high status, for example the director of the team of people at this meeting, and you are aware that this is an ongoing problem with Ms Scarlett, the team may expect you to take issue with her assertively and be pleased if you do this rather than let them fester behind the scenes. If you want to take the softly softly approach you may say:

> Kate, I did raise this solution with you yesterday, and I find it irritating that you are taking ownership of it now, especially as you dismissed it then. This is not the first time you have

> done this, I'd really appreciate it if you could act more as a team player. Now to develop the idea further . . ..

Or you could go in harder:

> Kate, I suggested this idea to you yesterday. I feel angry to hear you repeating this as your idea today. This has happened on several occasions. If it happens again, I will choose to stop sharing my ideas with you.

However, you may not be in a position of seniority over Kate, and moreover you may decide not to tackle the issue and divert the meeting. Giving criticism is difficult – you do need to choose the right time and place. Remember that we have already said that being assertive means having the right to chose not to be assertive at one particular time, or having the right to choose the appropriate time and place. It is unlikely that you want to give criticism in front of an audience. It is unlikely that a public row in front of those at the meeting will help your cause, particularly if Ms Scarlet is senior to you. A public attack can lead to the situation of attack/defend: what happens when a person is cornered? They come out fighting! You can therefore separate out what you would do there and then, and what you would do later. Your immediate response could be to put down a marker such as:

> I'm really pleased Kate you have come round to my point of view, I know when we discussed it last night you had reservations . . ..

This may be particularly effective if you then go on to elaborate further on the points which would demonstrate your familiarity with the issue. For some situations you may leave it at that. However, the scenario suggests that 'this is the last straw' and so you may want to tackle Kate privately at a later time about her behaviour towards you. Likewise you may want to think about allies – perhaps it happens to others and you could tackle it collectively. Sometimes avoidance is the best policy when people place you in situations where you can't win – just determine not to have much to do with them in future. Being assertive is about deciding which battles are worth fighting, taking clear action and moving on, not getting drawn into a game which you will inevitably lose, or being plagued by worries and anxieties about others' behaviour towards you.

When you have chosen the time and place to tackle her privately, you need to introduce the topic directly, state the problem and ask for a response. Then negotiate a solution and state and agree the solution. Criticising others is particularly hard when dealing with performance, such as in a performance appraisal. One approach is to take a 'merits and concerns' stance, where you point out the strengths of the other person and their behaviour (merits) and then focus on your 'concerns' about their behaviour. It is easier for someone to listen to concerns, than to criticisms. Approaches to 'giving feedback' are dealt with more directly in Chapter 5.

The positive and negative inquiry and probing techniques mentioned above can be used in potentially contentious situations where you are giving criticism, such as when you are having to point out to a staff member that they have not achieved an agreed task by the deadline. Pointing out the facts of the case, such as 'Paula, we agreed that you would have the accounts ready by lunchtime, it's now 3 o'clock, is there a problem?' is much better than showing annoyance before you have even established the reasons the work has not been done. This will simply lead to everyone becoming defensive and wasting even more time. Trying to get round someone by grovelling is also not an assertive way to behave – you are the manager and this was a task that was mutually agreed. You have a right to expect it to be completed on time. One approach here is to use the assertive script, which suggests four stages: describe, explain, specify and close. Begin by describing in a neutral way the concerns, then explain why they are important, then specify what you want from the person in terms of their behaviour in future, then close. For example:

> Paula I am concerned that the accounts are not ready yet, (describe), this is important because they are needed for the meeting tomorrow and you agreed to have them ready by 1 o-clock (explain). I need to know when they will be ready, and if I need to postpone the meeting tomorrow. Once the accounts are ready I would like us then to sit down to work out what went wrong and how you can stop this problem from arising in the future. It is vital that the time schedule that is agreed is kept to in future (specify), and I need you to assure me on that point. I look forward to the next assignment being delivered on time.

SCENARIO 7.8   WHOSE NAME GOES FIRST?

You are having a meeting with a senior colleague about the final draft of a paper you have written based on your research, for submitting to a highly reputable journal. As your colleague has given some useful comments and advice you have included his name on your paper: Professor White. His secretary has prepared the final draft for you and he hands you a copy and aghast you find that the paper now has his name first, before yours. The paper represents the culmination of three years of your own hard work. What do you do?

Scenario 7.8 is placed in the academic environment of journal article writing and concerns conventions for whose names should be first in writing papers. If you are in this environment, think about what conventions there could be. You will find it worrying that there are potentially so many different ones:

- the most senior person first, as they are eminent and will attract a readership
- the most senior person last, because they are important enough not to need to be first, and going last shows they have a 'stable' of new young talent who they are supporting
- alphabetically – this is great if you are 'Cox' or 'Brown' but is not so good for people like me called 'Winstanley'
- alternate – if you regularly write with someone else, take turns over whose name is first
- the person who did the first draft comes first
- the person who came up with the idea comes first
- the person who did the research comes first
- the person who is co-ordinating the article comes first.

Clearly there is a lot of room for argument and disagreement. The scenario also introduces a complication for giving criticism and being assertive: the person you are dealing with is higher status than you, and you are not sure whether what has happened is a mistake or not. It is important to think of your primary aim, which is probably not just letting rip at Professor White for pulling a fast one, but instead making sure your name is first on the paper. In this scenario you may need to find a back-out for Professor White – you could allow for it being a genuine mistake or typo: 'Excuse me I think there is a mistake here, the order of the authors has got mixed up, I'll put it right'. Also acting as if you assume you are right makes it harder for someone else to challenge you. However, sometimes academics can be unscrupulous. In this case you may need to protect yourself, for example with the support of other colleagues. The main way of protecting yourself from this situation is to avoid it happening in the first place: make sure the protocol for whose name comes first is clear and in writing before you engage in joint publications!

TRICKY FEELINGS AND EMOTIONS

In Chapter 1 on learning we learnt how our feelings and the way we think can get in the way, of learning: for example feelings of self-efficacy, or thinking errors. The same goes for assertiveness. We may want to be more assertive, but thoughts, feelings and emotions all get in the way.

Fear and anxiety

A particularly difficult emotion to deal with is fear and lack of confidence: 'I can't do it', 'I can't handle it'. Chapter 2 suggested that we often procrastinate because of anticipatory fear, but suggested that the anticipation is much worse than actually doing something. Jeffers goes further in *Feel the fear and do it anyway* (Jeffers 1991) and suggests that even assertive and confident people feel fear, but they don't let this stop them from doing what they want to do. Fear is like a fire whose flames are fanned by passivity and helplessness, the more you run away from something, the worse it gets. Taking action in spite of fearful feelings can lead to feelings of greater powerfulness which ultimately will help you continue to behave assertively, as well as feel assertive.

> ## EXAMPLE 7.4   FEAR OF PUBLIC SPEAKING
>
> My father was a doctor who was also a politician. He was approached on one occasion by a new Member of Parliament. The MP was particularly nervous about making his maiden speech, and asked my father if he could prescribe something for his nerves. My father refused and said:
>
> > If I prescribe something and you take it and your speech is fine, you will always feel you need to take the pill as a crutch. Fear is inevitable in this job, we all have fear on some occasions, sometimes at unexpected times. Much better to face up to the fear, get through the speech, and eventually you will get used to feeling fear and not being so affected by it.
>
> Funnily enough on my wedding day, my father got up to make his speech and I noticed he was shaking. He had made thousands of speeches by this time, but sometimes the fear pops up again. A new context can make even the bravest person fearful.

A good visualisation if you suffer from fear is to imagine being the cowardly lion in the Wizard of Oz and asking for courage at the end of the yellow brick road. It can feel better to say 'I seek courage' than 'I feel fearful'.

Another difficult emotion that can be paralysing is anxiety. Anxiety is future-orientated thinking that over-estimates danger and under-estimates the ability to cope (Neenan and Dryden 2002: 9–25). Avoidance and withdrawal escalate anxiety. The anxiety often takes the form 'What if . . . . I fail, I appear stupid, I make a fool of myself". Catastrophising can make things worse, but sometimes this can be turned around: 'What if . . .?' then becomes 'Well then what . . .'. Is it really so bad? Rational emotive therapy (RET) would encourage you to explore these worst-case scenarios and ask yourself 'Can I survive that, is it really so bad?' Alternatively a better question to ask and focus on may be 'What if . . . I can?' Take a few moments to think about how you would feel if you faced up to a situation assertively and succeeded – how would you feel then?

Negativity

Negativity and self-devaluation, depression and distorted thinking are also debilitating and can make it seem hard to be assertive. The lack of energy makes any attempt to be assertive feel like wading through a swamp. A negative view is a distorting view of the world, yourself, your future. In this situation it is important to realise that sometimes it is possible to change the behaviour first and let the better feelings follow later. To wait until you feel more positive or able to tackle a situation may not help. It is a fallacy to assume:

> *I MUST FEEL POSITIVE TO BE ASSERTIVE* (thought) → *THEN I WILL BEHAVE ASSERTIVELY* (behaviour) → *THEN I WILL FEEL BETTER* (emotion)

Instead you are more likely to be successful if you think:

> *I WILL BEHAVE ASSERTIVELY EVEN IF I DON'T FEEL LIKE IT* (thought)→ *ASSERTIVE BEHAVIOUR* (behaviour) → *I FEEL MORE POSITIVE* (emotion)

Negativity is not just about you, but who you have around you. There are two types of people who can hugely undermine your assertiveness: overly critical people and overly negative people. I advise you to keep out of their way, and seek out more positive people. Negativity is catching, and too much exposure to it can drag you down. Watch out for the effect that the people around you at work or on a course have on you. Are there some very negative people? How do you end up feeling after having spent some time in their company? Lethargic, lifeless, hopeless?

EXERCISE 7.4   'YES AND . . . .', 'NO, BUT . . .'

This exercise needs to be played out in a group, sitting in a circle, with a minimum of five people.

Hand out at random a slip of paper to each person, but every fifth slip (or less if there are more people) has a cross on it. Do not reveal whether you have a cross or not on your piece of paper.

Everyone who has a blank piece of paper starts their piece of the conversation when it is their turn with 'Yes, and . . .', and says something positive that builds on what the person before them said.

Everyone with a cross on their piece of paper starts their piece of conversation when it is their turn with 'No, but . . .', and says something negative.

You are going to have a conversation about what you are going to do today, going clockwise around the circle of people.

> The first person starts by saying something like:
>
> > 'Today I think we should go to Brighton ….' The next person may say:
> >
> > 'Yes and we can visit the lanes and go shopping, there are some great bargains to be had, and the clothes shops are fantastic ….' The next person may say:
> >
> > 'Yes, and we could buy some games and beach clothes and we could go on the beach and play rounders ….' The next person may say:
> >
> > 'Yes, and we could take a picnic and bathe in the sea ….' Then if the next person has a cross on the piece of paper, he or she may say:
> >
> > 'No but it is far too cold to go swimming, and we won't be able to park, the shops will be shut, and I don't like sandwiches with sand in them.'
>
> After going round for a couple of circles, stop and discuss how you felt when people were being positive, and what happened when the negative person spoke. It is likely your feeling of action and ability to achieve something dissipated.

Anger

Anger is another emotion that can get in the way when we want to be assertive, often leading us to be aggressive instead. We may lash out at the other person without thinking, purging ourselves of uncontrollable emotions. Anger often occurs when we feel that we have been thwarted or someone has somehow broken the rules or we have been treated unfairly. It is almost as if we revert back to a childlike state where we expect life, the world and everyone in it to act fairly. How angry a child may become when it perceives injury and injustice:

> No, it wasn't my fault – I didn't break the cup, Sebastian did it.

Unjust punishment, at school in particular, can smart, and as we grow older we may deal better with these situations superficially, but feel anger bursting out inside. It is important to realise that it is not other people that make you angry – you have a choice of response. You do not have to let someone wind you up until you explode, you don't have to rant and rave: you could choose to walk away, perhaps find some other way to deal with your anger, maybe face up to the situation when you have calmed down. Remember you can choose when and where to behave assertively, sometimes it is sensible to withdraw and rally your thoughts before diving straight in.

Guilt and shame

Unassertive people can be riddled with shame or guilt. Shame is the humiliating feeling of appearing unfavourably in another's eyes, being disgraced or bringing dishonour, not living up to a reputation or what is expected. Guilt derives from a feeling of wrongdoing and being found wanting. In both cases we approach ourselves in a one- (or more) down status position from our expectations: we are not 'good enough'. In typing this last statement I erroneously wrote 'God-enough' – and maybe that is right – perhaps we expect far too much of ourselves.

Neenan and Dryden (2002: 147) suggest that we need to separate out the 'BIG I' from the many 'little Is' that make up ourselves. The 'BIG I' is our whole identity, and the mass of behaviours, feelings and thoughts are our 'little Is'. Even if we feel ashamed of or bad about some of the 'little Is', that doesn't mean our whole self is bad. One way of seeing this is to separate out actions and behaviours from our selves: we are more than one action, one mistake we make, one thought or comment of which we feel ashamed.

Another way to deal with our shame or guilt is to be dangerous – engage in activities that invite ridicule, in order to desensitise ourselves to it. Sometimes changing our perspective allows us to 'right size' the problem. For example, if we have just moved house, changed job and gone through a relationship break-up, then one potentially difficult task, such as going into a shop to complain about a faulty product, is not going to seem so bad, whether or not we appear ridiculous or in the wrong. It is good to acquire some resilience, and to discover that nothing terrible happens when we stand up for our rights and ourselves.

EXERCISE 7.5   SHIFTING YOUR PERSPECTIVE – STAND UP FOR YOUR DAUGHTER!

Imagine there is something very difficult you are having to face up to. For example you are being bullied at work by a colleague. You may feel too frightened to address the problem. You may feel guilty – perhaps you have done something to invite this behaviour, perhaps it is your fault? You may feel ashamed of yourself that you are so pathetic that someone would pick on you.

Now shift your perspective. Imagine that you have a lovely daughter, and your daughter comes home in floods of tears feeling frightened, guilty and ashamed. You find she is being bullied at school. What would you do?

It is interesting that it is often difficult to stand up for ourselves and be assertive, but once we are in a position of looking after someone else, particularly if they are dear to us, then our courage expands to take the place of fear, and guilt and shame dissolve in the strength of feeling and purpose that ensues. It is much more likely you would be able to take up an assertive position for your daughter, for example by going to see the headteacher at the school to explore what can be done about the bullying, than to be assertive for yourself and deal with the bully. If you cannot be assertive for yourself in a situation, and you feel too guilty and ashamed to do anything, switch perspective and imagine it is your daughter in this position – the guilt and shame will soon dissolve, leaving you freer to be assertive.

CULTURAL DIFFERENCES

Before closing this chapter, I would like to sound a note of caution – there are cultural differences in expectations over appropriate assertive behaviour. This chapter has particularly focused on Anglo and American perspectives of assertiveness, but there are parts of the world where assumptions are very different, and even within countries in Europe there are different norms of behaviour. For example some Eastern and Asian cultures would not accept a lower status person looking a higher status person in the eye, and a junior person would be expected to act more submissively. An Italian student of mine said that it was quite usual for people from Mediterranean countries to talk over others, or all at once, with the conversation overlapping rather than being sequential. Argument, even to the extent of raised voices and shouting, was seen as normal, and a reflection on the energy of and engagement in the conversation. Yet she had been accused of being aggressive and disrespectful when she moved to England. A Portuguese PhD student said she would never be expected to challenge her supervisor and his authority, even if she was in the right. Therefore before putting these assertiveness tips into practice, think carefully about the cultural environment where you are working or studying. Cultural sensitivity is an important part of assertiveness and may require your behaviour to be modified in different contexts.

SUMMARY

As you can see, being assertive is not easy and it does require you to watch out for these tricky situations. However, by stepping back in a situation, by staying calm, and being direct and firm, it is likely you will feel much better about your work and working relationships in the long run. If you find this particularly hard, a good technique is to think of someone who, in your eyes, is a role model for assertive behaviour and ask yourself 'What would they say and do in this situation', and see if you can imitate them.

This chapter has defined assertiveness and explored ways in which you could build up your own repertoire of skills in this area. However, there are certain situations which are particularly difficult and require more attention, and in the next chapter we turn to negotiation situations and ways in which you can improve your negotiation skills.

REFERENCES AND FURTHER READING

BACK, K. and BACK, K. (1999) *Assertiveness at Work: A practical guide to handling awkward situations*. 3rd ed. Maidenhead: McGraw Hill.

BISHOP, S. (2000) *Develop your Assertiveness*. London: Kogan Page.

GILLEN, T. (1998) *Assertiveness*. London: CIPD.

JEFFERS, S. (1991) *Feel the Fear and Do it Anyway*. London: Arrow.

NEENAN, M. and DRYDEN, W. (2002) *Life Coaching: A Cognitive Behavioural Approach*. Hove: Brunner-Routledge.

REES, S and GRAHAM, R. (1991) *Assertion Training: How to be who you really are*. London: Routledge.

JOHNSTONE, K. (1981) *Impro*. London: Methuen.

Negotiation skills

AIMS AND LEARNING OUTCOMES

This chapter will improve your negotiation skills when facing others in situations where there are conflicting objectives. To achieve this aim, you will build on the assertiveness skills identified in Chapter 7 and be provided with some strategies and techniques for applying these in a negotiation. Once again, you are given the opportunity to try out the techniques learned in practice, and are encouraged to use these skills at work and home.

When you have completed this chapter you will be able to:

- **put into practice some key negotiation skills**

- **be able to appreciate whether a situation is a win-win one or win-lose and act accordingly**

- **overcome an impasse in negotiation**

- **achieve better outcomes in negotiation.**

INTRODUCTION

The thought of entering into conflict and negotiating a solution can make some people's blood run cold. Conflict, whether it is overt or covert, is uncomfortable, and as with assertiveness, it can take an act of will to enter the fray, express an opinion and seek a result. However, once the basic principles of negotiation are learnt, it can be tremendously exhilarating to emerge from a situation having negotiated a satisfactory outcome, whether it be to returning a faulty product to a shop to get a refund, obtaining a pay rise or change in job definition, or even negotiating the price of a house. Once you have mastered these skills, you will feel much more confident when faced with these situations.

WHAT IS NEGOTIATION?

The need for negotiation arises because two or more parties have different perspectives and conflicting objectives and priorities. The achievement of their objectives is inter-related and so co-operation and communication are necessary in order to address the differences and at the same time enable them to get what they want from the others. For example, think of the most common negotiation situations you are likely to face, and list these in Exercise 8.1.

EXERCISE 8.1   NEGOTIATION SITUATIONS

List here the main negotiation situations you have faced or are likely to face at work or at home. Try and think of at least three, with at least one that you have experienced in the past, and one that you may have a chance to practise over the next few weeks. These you will utilise throughout the chapter.

1.

2.

3.

Negotiation is a part of life, at work, home and in leisure. Even children's bedtimes and where to go for a holiday can become a negotiation exercise. Some common negotiation situations are:

Buying and selling

This may be in relation to a car, a house, or another consumer good where the crux of the matter is the price, with the buyer having an interest in getting the lowest price possible, and the seller having an interest in getting the highest price possible. Renting property also falls in the same bracket, and as with other goods, there is usually some leeway in negotiation, not just over the price itself, but also over what is and isn't included in it.

Salary, bonuses, terms and conditions

At work there may be different perspectives and interests with relation to salary, or terms and conditions of employment, or over the content of a person's role.

Who does what

A negotiation that is played over and over again in relationships and partnerships in the home is 'Who will do what?' This can concern undesirable jobs like housework, washing up, d-i-y, or more generally the division of labour within the home. This may also occur at work in relation to the division of work over a project or task. Once again there are different objectives and some leeway for trading.

Examine your list of negotiation situations and the list provided above and you will see that there are some common features:

- different objectives, goal incompatibility
- different perspectives
- inter-connectedness, interdependence and the need for co-operation to achieve objectives
- alternative outcomes
- possibilities for trading, room for manoeuvre.

Other factors may also suggest that, without negotiation, conflict could escalate, for example where there is:

- a lack of structure or procedures for resolving differences
- rivalry and competition over scarce resources
- the use of threats, and the resort to power and coercion.

These situations suggest there is a need to negotiate. But what is negotiation?

DEFINITION OF NEGOTIATION

Communication between parties with competing objectives to reach an agreement or joint decision.

Communication is at the heart of negotiation. Chapters 5, 6 and 7 have explored different forms of communication, but in this chapter you will be presented with a whole plethora of communication tactics and devices to keep communication open and dynamic between the parties with the purpose of moving towards a resolution rather than conflict. Getting to an impasse, getting bogged down and stuck is one of the main difficulties facing novice negotiators, and so we will explore a number of ways in which this communication can be kept going.

PRINCIPLES OF NEGOTIATION

The 'Principled negotiations' method, developed at the Harvard University Negotiation Project and explained by Fisher, Ury and Patton (1991), advises that effective negotiations should have four key features:

- separate the people from the problem
- focus on interests not positions
- insist on objective criteria
- invent options for mutual gain.

In separating the people from the problem you need to remember that as well as the substance under negotiation, the relationship between the negotiators is also important. In most negotiation situations keeping the relationship positive is helpful. For example, my mother runs an antique shop and regularly faces customers who want to barter over the price of a plate or other antique. If she focused entirely on driving the customer to the highest they are willing to pay, that customer may buy the plate, but never come back. Instead her antique shop depends on customers becoming regulars, enjoying the experience of browsing in the shop and bringing her goods to sell as well as coming to buy. She therefore has to maintain a positive relationship in the negotiation. Personal abuse does not enhance the relationship. Depersonalising a situation, focussing on the issue rather than attacking the person, makes it much more likely the negotiation can develop the constructive climate needed to progress.

Imagine taking a faulty good back to a shop. Saying:

> The vacuum cleaner broke within one week of my purchasing it

is going to carry more weight in negotiating a replacement with the shop assistant than

> You just want to make a quick sale and don't care if your goods are shoddy,

and:

> Let me explain that again . . ..

is much preferable to:

> Are you thick?

The principled negotiation method advises negotiators to be 'hard on the merits, soft on people' and to be objective and remove emotions. This is not always possible, and sometimes the emotional heat of a situation can require addressing in other ways – taking a break for example, or having a cool-down period. It can also help to allow the other person to let off steam, acknowledging their emotions as legitimate, even if you don't agree with them. Without using emotional intelligence to appreciate your own and the other's emotions you will have much less capability of progressing the negotiation.

Positions can become intractable and fixed, whereas attempting to understand the meaning, interests and perspectives that lead to the position can open more room for manoeuvre: one of the features identified above as being important. Gaining leeway, movement and some space is essential, it can create that light at the end of the tunnel. There may be alternative ways of meeting the other person's interests than the position they have taken. To find out people's interests, you may need to ask 'Why'?

EXAMPLE 8.1   INTERESTS NOT POSITIONS

Juliet states her position and demands:

> Sam, you must deliver that lecture on Thursday afternoon, because Sheila is off sick.

This gives Sam little space to trade, and they reach an impasse if Sam really cannot make that session, and just says:

> No, sorry, I can't Juliet.

However, Sam needs to look instead at Juliet's underlying interest, and ask why she wants the lecture delivered on Thursday. This may translate into:

> We must not let the students down and give them a poor service.

This opens up more options for his response, meeting both their interests. Such as:

> I can't deliver the lecture on Thursday afternoon Juliet, but I could give them a double lecture on Thursday morning instead, and that would mean I would then have time to run the business game. This would work well as long as we give them plenty of warning of the time and content change.

One way of seeking agreement is to identify objective criteria on which each side can judge the merits and strengths of their arguments. This could include notions of fairness and justice. *Procedural criteria* – the way in which the negotiation will take place – can help. For example, turn-taking, time taken, listening to the other's views, voting procedures, etc. This then it makes the discussion over substantive issues easier. Alternatively you could identify *outcome criteria* and those criteria that would ensure both parties had their objectives met.

Negotiation can be a creative pursuit, because when the impasse occurs, negotiators need to be able to invent *new options for mutual gain*, and ways around a seemingly intractable problem. It may be helpful to revisit Chapter 3 on creativity and ideas generation and explore ways in which you can generate new ideas and ways of looking at the situations you identified in Exercise 8.1. This requires a constructive outlook, and one that looks for options that meet the needs of both parties akin to the assertiveness position identified in Chapter 7.

Developing a constructive joint-problem-solving climate will increase the chances of your coming up with innovative solutions that can work.

NEGOTIATING APPROACHES

The principled negotiations method makes negotiating sound quite straightforward. However, it is not. For example attempt Exercise 8.2 and examine the complexity of negotiating approaches. The plethora of different negotiating styles and tactics, strategies and approaches can be bewildering. Another way to make sense of these is to move on from the principled negotiations method and explore instead what has become known as 'win-win' or 'win-lose' approaches to negotiations.

EXERCISE 8.2   ANIMALS

(with thanks to Sandra Jones)

1. Relook at the negotiating situation that you identified in Exercise 8.1. You were asked to identify at least one that you had experienced in the past. Alternatively contemplate a current situation for negotiation within your own workplace. What animals metaphorically represent the negotiating approach of the actors in the negotiation? Draw these animals in a notebook.

2. Now consider how the animal and their features represent what happens in negotiation.

For example: one person who considered a negotiation over the price of a car identified a *capricorn* and a *bull*. The car seller was the capricorn, not moving at all, whereas the buyer was the bull, aggressively charging and attacking on the price. The bull found he couldn't touch this immovable capricorn and gave up.

Another person identified a *butterfly* and a *spider* in a negotiation over a new telephone contract. The telephone company was like the spider trying to catch the customer in the net of the new contract, insurance and other terms, whereas the customer like a butterfly was trying to flit around and avoid being caught.

Another identified a *snake* and a *cat* in a negotiation over the contract for house purchase. A contract would seem to be agreed but the snake-like seller would keep slithering out of it, changing the price, for example, or saying that there were other offers, the market was changing. The cat-like purchaser would try and pin down the snake, pouncing on it to get a solution.

NEGOTIATION STRATEGY AND TACTICS: WIN-WIN OR WIN-LOSE

Ultimately there are two alternative strategies and positions that can be adopted: *win-win* or *win-lose*.

Win-win is where both parties enter the negotiation with an attitude of taking each other's views into account and come away from the negotiation believing they have succeeded. It takes the joint-problem-solving approach identified in the principled negotiation method and relies on trust, openness and communication. It allows for 'positive sum' thinking: that is, there isn't a finite sum of benefits available, where, if one person benefits, the other suffers. Instead it is possible for both to succeed. For example, an employee gets a week off but in return works with greater commitment and higher performance at other times for the employer. This assumes that for a negotiation to work, both parties must get something out of it. Openness is needed so the parties can find out about each other's interests and different ways of meeting their needs. Communication is required to explore all the possible alternatives, and trust is built up so that each can believe in the honesty and integrity of the other.

Win-lose, on the other hand, is an orientation where one party aims to win at all costs, irrespective of meeting the needs of the other. This relies on power, strength, manipulation and game-playing and results in 'zero-sum' thinking: that is, one party's gains mean the other party's loss. An example here would be an election, where a vote for one party is a vote lost by the other party. In negotiation terms it would be where a union goes on strike to achieve its ends, or where the employer imposes unilaterally a wage settlement. Clearly many win-lose situations are not truly negotiations and, as with a boxing match, there is no attempt at compromise.

Some situations invite one approach or the other, and where one party has much greater power, the temptation can be to take a win-lose approach. Some parties try and change their strategy within a negotiation, for example from win-lose to win-win, but this is notoriously difficult to do. For example if two countries are at war fighting win-lose battles, it can be increasingly difficult to get them to sit down at the negotiating table and jointly problem solve. The temptation is always to revert to win-lose behaviour. The difficulties of achieving negotiated settlements over Northern Ireland, or the Palestinian situation on the West Bank, are both testaments to that.

We can take the win-win win-lose alternatives and break them down further if we relate these to levels of self-interest and interest for others, and the adaptation of the Thomas-Kilmann

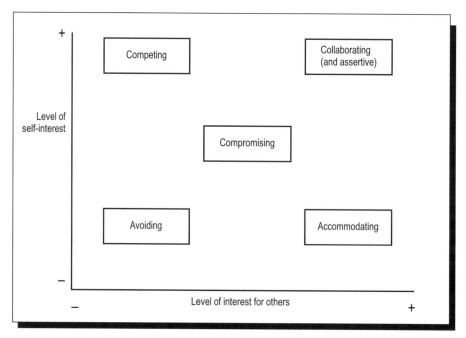

Figure 8.1 *An adaptation of the Thomas-Kilmann Conflict Mode Instrument*

Conflict Mode Instrument in Figure 8.1 below identifies five main positions an individual can take in conflict.

A win-lose approach would be typified by a competing approach where the individual pursues their own concerns at the other's expense, whereas a win-win approach would be to take the collaborating mode where individuals use empathy and joint-problem-solving to find creative solutions. However, some individuals do not even enter negotiation at all, generally avoiding the situation and the problem, putting their head in the sand and pretending the difficulty doesn't exist. Some individuals who are orientated to please others, as in the submissive attitude in Chapter 7, become far too accommodating and cave in early in negotiations, making all the concessions, allowing the other person to have their needs met, but not their own. Others occupy the middle ground of compromise. Overall, the win-win collaborating position is the one which is generally the most desirable, and the one which follows from the advice given in this chapter. However, a note of caution can be sounded here: if we explore negotiating positions in practice, the reality can be far from the ideal of the perfect 'win-win' scenario.

Win-lose tactics

In most situations your strategy and objective are likely to be win-win, although there are some business situations where win-lose approaches are appropriate, usually in situations of high competition. Many win-lose tactics are quite controversial. Some examples of win-lose tactics are:

Call my bluff and threat. For example: 'I'll get my solicitor onto this, see you in court' or 'I have other job offers'. If you are using threat can you be sure that your bluff won't be called? You can look really ridiculous if you then have to climb down, and you are left exposed and without a way out.

Shot gun. For example: 'The special offer ends today, unless I get your signature now, you will miss out on the 50 per cent discount'. This is the tactic utilised tirelessly by door-to-door salespeople, double-glazing companies, carpet warehouses. They know that putting you under time pressure shifts the balance of power and makes people make spontaneous decisions that they would be unlikely to make had they time to think. It is like the ABC – 'always be closing' mantra of sales training. The problem is in deploying this – do they or you mean it? What happens if it doesn't work? Surprise, surprise, there is a new sale on tomorrow, or you hear 'Well I can make a special exception and extend it just for you': the climb down.

Break off and shock tactics. For example: 'I'm going to walk out of that door and not come back'; 'If you don't do this I'll never see you again'. If you walk out those left behind can feel insecure, and you can damage the future relationship. What happens if they won't let you back in? When this is used repeatedly to get your own way the effect can lessen over time, the other person may just ignore you, or maybe there comes a time when they are weary of your constant brinkmanship and say 'OK, go'.

Tough person, nice person. We have all seen the episodes of police soap operas where the tough police officer and the nice police officer take it in turns to wear down the accused. The idea is that after the drumming of the tough one, the interviewee is so grateful for the kindness of the nice one that they spill the beans or admit to the crime. Take care the toughie isn't too tough and alienates the accused, undermining all the hard work of the softie!

Blackmail; who do you know? For example: 'If you don't do this for me, I'll have to tell the boss about how your expenses at that conference were spent'. Or 'Think of the adverse publicity if it should get out how little you pay your staff'. This uses the notion that you can't do that, demand that, agree to that, because of the adverse publicity or consequences. If this fairly sets out the likely impact of a decision, that is one thing, but if there is an underlying threat or abuse of privileged information and power involved, then that can become dangerous. Generating ill feeling can have negative consequences, and when you want a favour from the person you have treated in this way they are more likely to respond by dropping you in it than backing you up and supporting you.

Win-win tactics

Win-win approaches tend to promote positive constructive behaviour and communication. Some example behaviours you could try are:

- deal with points of agreement first: it is easier, and it encourages feelings of progress
- be positive: try to build on offers, say 'Yes, and ...' not 'Yes, but ... ', keep doors open. 'No' slams the door, it is better to say 'If we were to consider that ... what would you be offering?'
- listen and acknowledge the other person's viewpoint, it is often easier for them to hear you if they feel they have been heard themselves
- compare priorities and look for 'bridging factors': things that are important to them but may not be for you. Look for 'trade-offs'. Be conditional: 'I might consider that if you ...'
- be firm on generalities: 'I must have compensation'; flexible on specifics: 'I propose £100'.

Negotiating positions are clearly not simple, but having awareness of these tactics can help, even when finding a win-win position or strategy seems difficult. The win-lose approach places you in a position of being enemies, whereas the win-win approach places you in the position of being allies. Taking a two-dimensional approach to positions can, however, be limiting, as can seeing negotiation in terms of us and them, or just two sides. It can be helpful to look at the role of others outside of the conflict.

An alternative way to examine positions is to look instead at your own maximum and minimum position.

OBJECTIVES – MAXIMUM AND MINIMUM POSITIONS

Whatever your strategy you first need to be clear about your objectives. What do you want to achieve from the negotiation and what would be your best and worst outcome, your maximum and minimum position? The maximum position is the best outcome for you, and you achieve all your objectives. Your minimum position is the one lower than which you are not prepared to go. Because the parties often have different priorities, issues of great importance to one party will often be of less concern to the other. This opens the way for a settlement zone (see Figure 8.2) which is the space between their two minimums.

Bringing the two concepts from this and the previous section together – the notion of win-win or win-lose, and the maximum and minimum positions – enables us to see that if you end with lower than your minimum acceptable position and the other's maximum position this is 'lose-win'; your maximum acceptable position, and lower than the opponent's minimum one is 'win-lose'. However, somewhere in the middle between both your minimum and maximum positions is the settlement zone, which equates to a win-win position.

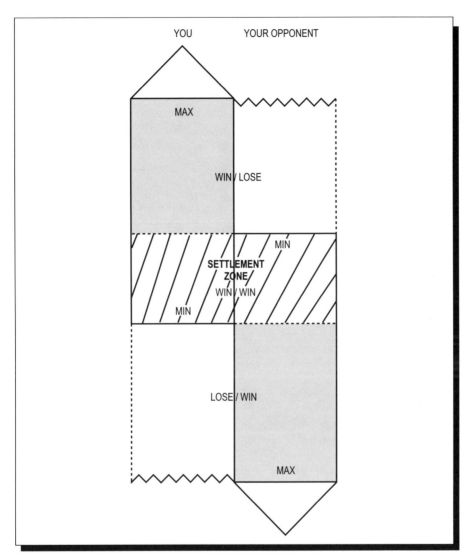

Figure 8.2 *The maximum and minimum position and the settlement zone*

Note:
Maximum position is the ideal outcome sought.
Minimum position is the lowest acceptable position
Anything in the white area below minimum is problematic

Some people enter a negotiation from a position of weakness, identifying their minimum position and losing any leeway for trade. But what you don't ask for you don't get, as in the following scenario.

EXAMPLE 8.2   MAXIMUM AND MINIMUM POSITIONS IN BUYING A CAR

Ted is buying a secondhand car, and the most he is willing to pay is £2,000. The car he wants has an asking price of £2,500, but the owner Ray seems willing to negotiate for a quick sale. If Ted at the outset states:

I'll give you £2,000 cash, today'

he is automatically negotiating about an amount between £2,500 and £2,000 and revealing his minimum position, and will quickly get stuck (because he cannot go beyond £2,000), when Ray responds:

No I want £2,500 mate. I tell you what I'll come down to £2,400 for cash.

No, I can only pay £2,000.

Instead, if Ted had started with:

I can give you £1,500 but you would need to fix the spare tyre and get an MOT for it'

he is much more likely to reach a deal within his budget and maybe with some extras thrown in:

'Phew, tricky, it's worth a lot more than that, say £2,250.

It needs a lot of work doing, and would need to be roadworthy for me to take it away, I can just stretch to £1,650 but that is pushing it.

Oh I really need over two grand.

I tell you what, if you will take £1,800 I'll get it for you today in cash, but I'd still need the tyre and MOT.

I'd like to sell it today but I can't get the MOT done till tomorrow.

OK I'll give you a deposit today, and then pick it up tomorrow when you've done the MOT – £1,800

Done.

In the example above, where Ted declares his minimum position at the outset, he already has lost a lot of ground. In general it is wiser to keep your 'bottom line' to yourself. Some negotiators deliberately take a position of offering their minimum position, as a form of loss leader. This is the concept of 'Sell cheap/get famous' and a classic example would be the teenager who so desperately wants that modelling or acting job they are willing to sign a contract that offers them very little, just to get their first step on the ladder. The job with low pay but 'prospects'! The free work is done up front but 'think what it will mean for future business', and so on. The danger is that these benefits are all in the future and all hypothetical.

At the other extreme you can aim too high. Being too unrealistic can just alienate the other party, and lose the chance of a solution at all. Be realistic, and maybe they will be too.

Once again we have returned to bargaining 'positions': something that we were warned against by the 'principled negotiations' method at the outset of this chapter. To revisit Example 8.2 from an 'interests not positions' perspectives, would be to acknowledge that Ted wants to buy a car at a reasonable price, but is also willing to pay for some enhancements that cost Ray very little to ensure that it is roadworthy, and Ray wants to sell it at a profit, and have a quick turnover of cars. Very quickly we can see there is a settlement zone that meets both their interests.

THE NEGOTIATION PROCESS

Kennedy et al (1984) have identified an eight-step approach to negotiation. Their model is based on many years' of experience in observing and managing negotiations and in training negotiators.

Stage 1: prepare

This is when you clarify your objectives, identifying things you must have, things you would like to have and things that are unimportant. You also need to clarify the strategic position which is appropriate: is it a win-lose situation or a win-win scenario? Having established your objectives and strategy, you need to gather all the information together so that you can clarify your minimum and maximum position, and plan your discussion. If you are in a team you will need to allocate roles and decide who is leading the negotiation, who is summarising or recording the information, who is providing expertise or observing.

Stage 2: discuss

When you open the discussion be business-like, brisk but co-operative. It is in the opening stages that negotiators form impressions of each other, and first impressions stick, so if you are fumbling and uncertain you will be sending the wrong messages to the other side. Then you will need to deploy your communication skills to the full, exploring the situation, starting to discuss objectives and exchange information with the other party. At this stage it is more important to listen and ask open questions, seeking and giving information, rather than interrupt, argue, attack or blame. By the end of this stage you should have established the essential needs, interests and priorities of both sides, as well as areas of common ground.

Stages 3 and 4: signal and propose

You will never achieve everything you want, but successful negotiators know when to stop rather than move on into deadlock. One you have all the information you need, move towards thinking in terms of 'a package'. The package will be different from what you or the other party want, but will build on the common ground and both your priorities. Signals are easy to miss as they are usually tentative movements towards a proposal, and it is important at this stage you pick up signals from the other party and respond positively as well as remember to reciprocate. Signals are often expressed as a qualification, and Kennedy et al (1984) say for example:

> a) It is not our policy to give discounts – and even if we did they would not be as large at 10 per cent

which signals

> Maybe we will give you 2 per cent discount.

> b) It is not our normal practice

may mean

> But we do make exceptions.

> c) We could not produce that quantity in that time

could mean

> We are prepared to negotiate on price, delivery, quality, quantity.

Once you have started signalling you are ready to start making proposals. Proposals should be tentative, not 'take it or leave it', and you should begin by aiming high, because 'what you don't ask for you don't get'. Make constructive noises to encourage the other party to make proposals and summarise as you go along. Be careful not to concede something without getting something in return, and trade what is cheap to you but valued by the other party, exploring high-value low-cost concessions.

Stages 5 and 6: packaging and bargaining

At this stage you should be thinking creatively about all the possible variables and value your concessions in the other party's terms. Link issues together in the package as a way to trade. Address your package to the interests and inhibitions of the other side but beware of making 'free' concessions, explore what is it worth, what will it cost, what will you ask for in exchange. Keep everything conditional: 'if . . . then . . .'.

Stages 7 and 8: closing, agree and record

There are different ways to expedite a closure. Some provide a small concession to secure agreement, and make the other party feel better about the deal, but better is to seize the opportunity when you seem to have identified some basis for agreement, and close by summarising the deal. The biggest dangers here are to close the discussion prematurely so the agreement comes unstuck, spend too long trying to get one final concession so the deal starts to unravel, or worse, forget to sort out and record the final details of what was agreed.

USING POWER CONSTRUCTIVELY

Emotional intelligence

Negotiation requires emotional intelligence and an ability to read a situation and think about the relative power of the two parties. Misjudging this power balance can lead to problems and further conflict or an impasse. Although you need to start with a realistic appraisal of the balance of power, there are ways in which you can tip this balance in your favour. Another aspect of emotional intelligence is good listening skills: these will enable you to increase the information you have about the other party's options and positions. Likewise the better you build a good working relationship the more powerful you will feel.

Bringing in others

Bringing in others, especially those more powerful than you, can help. For example, ask your boss to back you up in a tricky situation with a manager from another department. One principal behind trade unionism is that standing together can strengthen a position; there can be strength in numbers.

Who do you know? There may be fellow travellers that you can draw in who share your interests and can help reinforce your position, even if for other reasons. Alternatively there can be opponents who may not be on your side nor support your interests but that you trust to have some influence with relation to your adversary. For example, someone who may be a moderating hand, someone who may be listened to when you are unheard. Drawing in others constructively can head off problems where negotiation looks as if it is moving into conflict.

EXAMPLE 8.3   DRAWING IN OTHERS

Tara was at a meeting of members of her department. The meeting concerned the division of space within a new building into which the department were about to move. She felt strongly that the larger offices should be given on the basis of need and not hierarchical position. Her arguments were falling on deaf ears and the discussion had become heated, and the Head of Department, Steve, accused her of just being interested in expanding the size of her own office for her own selfish ends. Realising that she was losing her temper, she turned to Rachel a senior colleague and said:

> Rachel what do you think about this issue?

Rachel replied:

> Well, I can see that it would be important for Tara to have confidential discussions with clients, in fact all of us that see clients confidentially need this access so really it would be better if she had the office with the door rather than one of the open plan ones.

> And you Nigel, what do you think?

> Well I think there are others who have a greater need for those offices – so I don't think we can give Tara one, but maybe we could give her and Rachel priority use of one of the meeting rooms for confidential client discussions. What do you think Steve?

> Yes I can see that would be a point, and we do have meeting rooms available.

By bringing in others, a potential ally or fellow traveller like Rachel, and even opponents like Nigel, Tara was able to enable Steve to hear her argument in a way that had become difficult in the heated discussion that had taken place between him and Tara. She was able to open up a space for some compromise to enable at least her interest (having space for meeting clients confidentially), if not her position (having an office with a door), to be met.

Having alternatives

Before entering a negotiation, it is always worth considering what your options are should the negotiation fail. Take, for example, Jeremy and Jenny in the example below. If they hadn't stopped to consider their options they could easily have allowed themselves to be backed into a corner because they had no alternative. Having some options will give you confidence in your negotiations and enable you to feel and portray yourself as such.

> ## EXAMPLE 8.4   EXPLORING ALTERNATIVES
>
> Jeremy and Jenny were desperate to move house. They had two young but growing children and really felt their current house was just not big enough. Twice, buyers for their house had pulled out and the sale fallen through. Their recent buyers had got wind of their desperation and had reduced their offer by £10,000 on the pretext of work needing to be done on the house.
>
> Jeremy and Jenny were about to cave in, but when they assessed the implications of accepting the buyers' offer, realised they wouldn't have enough money to buy the larger house they wanted. They took a weekend off away from the fraught negotiation and visited the seaside. They both had always wanted to live by the sea, and they noticed there was a gorgeous new housing development going up on the quayside. For fun they looked round some of the flats. They then went into a café and reconsidered their options. Instead of pushing ahead with the current foundering negotiation, giving in to keep their buyers, they realised instead that they could choose to stay put, build into their attic space to give the children a loft-room, and with the rest of the money they would have used for buying a new house, buy a one-bedroom flat by the seaside.
>
> Returning to the negotiation they realised they had a lot more power, and wished they had thought through their options before. They were more confidently able to refuse the prospective buyers' latest offer. Ironically, although the buyers then did go on to offer the full amount, they were so taken with their new plan they took their house off the market, and bought the flat instead.

Start with the maximum not minimum stance and trade

Taking the maximum rather than minimum stance with relation to your objectives at the outset of the negotiation (as discussed above) clearly puts you in a more powerful position. Also reading the other party and finding out what is valuable to them can help, because then you can trade what is not important for you but may be vital to them, for something that is of value to you. If you are in the position of making a concession, make sure you always get something in return: a trade. 'I may be willing to consider extending my role, if you are able to offer me a salary rise'.

Quality of argument – prepare yourself

Rallying your arguments also puts you in a better position. Identifying as many good reasons why you should get what your want, and particularly reasons that the other party will accept have merit will advance your case.

Powerful body language

You can also use your own body language, and ways of speaking to give yourself more authority. Reread Table 7.2 in Chapter 7 on assertive behaviour and body language to identify ways to increase your presence in the negotiations.

Buy yourself time

There will also be times when you can feel your power dwindling, and maybe you feel yourself caving in and ready to back down. Maybe you are tired, or are rushed, or just feel confused or uncertain. At these times it is always worth buying yourself time: for example you could say:

> I will need to consider that more carefully, I'll get back to you tomorrow

or

> I don't have the authority to approve that right now, I'll check and talk to you when I have consulted.

However, there will still be times when you get stuck, when all your arguments seem to get you nowhere: you are at an impasse.

GETTING STUCK: MOVING BEYOND IMPASSE

One reason negotiations fall apart is that people run out of steam, get tired and irritable, and lose concentration. It can be worth setting a *time limit* for a negotiation. It is interesting to note that agreements often get reached close to time limits. You may have spent an hour discussing an issue, but three minutes before you have to pack up and go home, you might suddenly find you are both energised towards developing a solution.

Alternatively you can use breaks to give yourself space if you are getting stuck and going round and round in circles. Call for a break in which you can caucus or talk privately with other members of your team, or get some fresh air and a new perspective. Sometime negotiations get heated and without a break they just end up in pointless conflict. Once you have had a break, summarise where you left off before continuing.

Nature abhors a vacuum, and many novice negotiators do as well, and squirm when the talking stops. If you reach an impasse which moves into silence, sometimes the best tactic is to ride it out. If you sit tight, button up your mouth, it is amazing how much others may concede through their inability to cope with silence. If you get the opportunity to watch a skilled negotiator at work, you will quickly realise that their ability to *carry a silence* invariably leads to concessions from the other side. The negotiation skills CARP identified in the summary also help you to ride out an impasse without caving in.

ALTERNATIVES TO NEGOTIATION: BETWEEN THE DEVIL AND A HARD PLACE!

Negotiation can be tough, but it can be worth considering the alternatives to give you renewed determination. When in conflict, instead of negotiation you could consider:

- capitulation – but will you be happy about this later?
- avoidance – but will it go away?
- dictat – but what about tomorrow?
- arbitration – but you have less control over the outcome!

Negotiation is uncomfortable but if handled assertively it can be a real boost to confidence.

However, not all situations with competing objectives are open to negotiation! Take for example the humorous incident below.

EXAMPLE 8.5   NOT OPEN TO NEGOTIATION!

An alleged transcript of a radio conversation between a US naval ship and Canadian authorities off the coast of Newfoundland in October 1995. The conversation was released by the Chief of Naval Operations on 10 October 1995.

Americans: Please divert your course 15 degrees to the North to avoid a collision.

Canadians: Recommend you divert *your* course 15 degrees to the South to avoid a collision.

Americans: This is the Captain of a US Navy ship. I say again, divert *your* course.

Canadians: No. I say again, you divert *your* course.

Americans: THIS IS THE AIRCRAFT CARRIER USS LINCOLN, THE SECOND LARGEST SHIP IN THE UNITED STATES' ATLANTIC FLEET. WE ARE ACCOMPANIED BY THREE DESTROYERS, THREE CRUISERS AND NUMEROUS SUPPORT VESSELS. I DEMAND THAT YOU CHANGE YOUR COURSE 15 DEGREES NORTH, THAT'S ONE FIVE DEGREES NORTH, OR COUNTER-MEASURE WILL BE UNDERTAKEN TO ENSURE THE SAFETY OF THIS SHIP.

Canadians: This is a lighthouse. Your call.

SUMMARY

To recap some of the skills identified in this chapter, the word CARP is a useful device for remembering the key negotiation skills and style:

- **C**reativity: the capacity for lateral thinking is incredibly powerful in overcoming blocks in negotiation – the linear approach is not always best.
- **A**ssertiveness: standing up for your own needs and rights as well as respecting those of others.
- **R**esilience: remember it is 'always darkest before dawn' – poor negotiators often give up just before getting somewhere.
- **P**ositivity: being constructive and positive helps to create a climate of cooperation.

Reflect back over the negotiation situations you identified in Exercise 8.1. In those you have faced in the past, did you have an idea of your objectives, and your maximum and minimum position? Did you take a win-win approach to it or a win-lose, and use the appropriate tactics? Did you put into practice the principles identified in the principle model? Did you maximise your power situation and manage to overcome impasses? Ultimately did you get what you wanted from the negotiation, were you satisfied with the outcome?

Skills can be learnt, but need the opportunity to be put into practice. If you identified in Exercise 8.1 a negotiation situation you are likely to face over the next few weeks, use this chapter as a launch pad for practising your new skills.

Exercise 8.3 will also give you an opportunity to check what skills you have learnt and whether you feel able to put them into practice.

EXERCISE 8.3   COMMUNITY CHEST

Your local council Chagford Gate has decided to award a grant of £20,000 to be spent on local community projects that celebrate the special qualities of the local community and the wonderful features of its environment. They are hoping to use the award to promote *tourism* in the area, and also to support diversity and value all members of the community. The council is particularly committed to community participation. Therefore the mayor has short-listed four community organisations, all of whom have excellent ideas for community development, to come to a special meeting at 12.00 midday to decide on how to spend the money. At 1.00 pm the press will arrive for you to announce how the money is to be spent and this will be followed by a celebratory banquet to which various tourism organisations, the town twinning association and other local dignitaries have been invited.

You are a representative of one of the four community organisations short-listed to receive the money. However, each of the organisations have elaborate ideas on how the money should be spent, but the council has asked you collectively to come up with a plan that will achieve the best outcomes for the council, and the community, and that you all can support. You think your own organisation's ideas are particularly worthy of receiving the financial support.

Choose one of the organisations below to represent, and plan your approach to how you would tackle this negotiation. Alternatively you could join with others and each choose a different organisation, role play the negotiation itself, but for this you may want to bring in a facilitator.

Sport for All
Sport for All is a loose grouping of users of the local leisure centre, which is not in as good a state as previously. They want to buy some equipment to enable better disability access and use of the swimming pool (£10, 000), improve some of the equipment in the children's playground area (£10,000) and improve the facilities for the over-60s, including hosting a Sport for All day for older users (£5,000). They hope to help the leisure centre to be seen as a place in which all groups are welcome, and to continue to expand access arrangements.

The Chagford Gate School of Art
The staff at the local art college would like to get their best pupils to create a sculpture garden next to the council offices. This would act as a big incentive and encouragement for the pupils to perform to the highest standards. The pupils will be boosted by the display of their works of art. The garden itself would become a feature in the classical grounds of the large old Georgian manor in which the council is situated. The garden would be a tourist attraction and some of the sculptures would symbolise features and events from Chagford Gate's past. This scheme would cost at least £25,000, but the School of Art believes that £5,000 could be raised in fundraising.

The Nature Walk
Along one side of the council offices, next to where the proposed 'sculpture garden' would be sited, runs a large swathe of deciduous woodland which forms a habitat for many rare birds and creatures. The local wildlife preservation group would like money to

pay for equipment to help clear the local paths that run through the woodland and which have been clogged up by brambles and fallen trees. A nature trail would be cited along the walk with interesting trees and plants indicated by labels. They would build a small bird-watching cabin overlooking the lake, and inside the cabin would be exhibits and information, booklets and a children's quiz to accompany the trail. They would also like to cover the cost of volunteers staffing the cabin at weekends and pay for guides for local school trips. The trail would cost £3,000 to make, the cabin £15,000 to build and £5,000 to equip, and at least £2,000 would help to cover the expenses of volunteer staffing of the cabin, making £25,000 in total, but some of this could be raised in fundraising.

Youth Action

The local youth groups have banded together to develop proposals to support young musicians, enabling a young rock band, a folk band, a jazz band and an international ensemble to rehearse and perform. They want a sound system and equipment (£10,000), refurbishment of the youth centre where they could rehearse (£3,000) and money for their expenses in touring around the local area playing at local gigs (£2,000). They are organising a youth music festival to be held in the grounds of the council offices and this is likely to attract a lot of interest and bring many people in to perform or attend (£10,000 sought).

This chapter has taken you through the various approaches that can be taken to negotiation and provided you with a toolkit of skills to use in this area. It has advocated taking a win-win approach to negotiation and has shown that negotiation is a skilled activity and one which taxes our emotions, drawing on our attitudes and the mindset we enter as well as the behaviour we exhibit. As with many of the skills in this book, negotiation can only really be learnt by practice and so you are encouraged to seek out an opportunity soon to apply these skills. If you are nervous about doing that, start with a relatively unchallenging context before moving on to those which are more high risk.

REFERENCES AND FURTHER READING

COHEN, S. (2002) *Negotiation Skills for Managers.* Maidenhead: Briefcase Books, McGraw-Hill Education.

FISHER, R., URY, W. and PATTON, B. (1991) *Getting to Yes.* London: Random House Business Books.

FOSTER, D. (1992) *Bargaining Across Borders.* USA: McGraw Hill.

FOWLER, A. (1998) *Negotiating, Persuading and Influencing.* London: Management Shaper Series, CIPD.

GILLEN, T. (1999) *Agreed! Improve Your Powers of Influence.* London: CIPD.

HINDLE, T. (1998) *Negotiating Skills.* London: Dorling Kindersley.

KENNEDY, G. BENSEN, J. and MCMILLAN, J. (1984) *Managing Negotiations.* London: Hutchinson.

LABORDE, G. (1998) *Influencing with Integrity: Management skills for communication and negotiation.* Carmathen: Crown House Publishing.

LEWICKI, R. SAUNDERS, D., MINTON, J. and BARRY, B. (2002) *Negotiation.* 3rd ed. Maidenhead: McGraw-Hill Education.

Dealing with difficult people and difficult situations

AIMS AND LEARNING OUTCOMES

The overall aim of this chapter is for you to develop insight into why you may feel particularly ineffective in dealing with certain people in certain situations. With an understanding of why some people and situations seem particularly challenging to us, we will explore ways in which you can communicate effectively despite these difficulties.

When you have completed this chapter you will be able to:

■ **Understand why some transactions with people have an impact on us which appears out of proportion to the situation and lead us to feel incompetent or invite us to communicate in an ineffective way.**

■ **Identify some ways to communicate effectively despite this.**

■ **Spot some 'games' that get enacted at work and work out how to 'stay out of the game'.**

■ **Appreciate how 'learned helplessness' can develop and find ways to prevent our becoming 'a victim'.**

■ **Identify your own sources and symptoms of stress.**

■ **Put into action methods for reducing or coping with stress.**

■ **Deal with situations where bullying and harassment are experienced.**

INTRODUCTION

In previous chapters we have focused on communicating effectively (Chapter 5) and developing those skills that will enable us to be effective communicators, and also on how to behave assertively (Chapter 7) and deal with conflict through negotiation (Chapter 8). In this chapter we take the challenge one step further and seek to develop understanding of why some situations and people pose particular problems for us. Most of our everyday transactions and communications occur without any difficulty, but every now and then we crash up against a person or situation for which the problems of communication seem insurmountable. We may feel rising anxiety or panic, or alternatively a huge loss of self-confidence and esteem. We may find we start behaving uncharacteristically, becoming child-like or aggressive. Reflect back over the last few months of your working life and identify a situation in which this seemed to happen, and write this down as part of Exercise 9.1. This should not be too difficult for you, as it is likely that your emotions were magnified and you became preoccupied with thinking and worrying about it. Maybe even for a time you became quite obsessed with the person or situation, and it left a shadow over other areas of your life. Now step back and use this memory as you pass through this chapter to reflect on what was really going on in the situation.

In this chapter three angles will be taken to provide insight into these problems. Firstly we will examine 'transactional analysis' and explore how this theory can explain certain communications you have had and games that occur at work. Then we will explore our own sources of stress and the ways these impact us, identifying ways in which we can reduce or take action to alleviate the stress incurred from difficult situations. Finally we will take bullying situations as an area where severe stress can develop and impact us, and we will explore how we can remove ourselves from these debilitating situations so that we can continue to perform effectively and feel positive about our work.

EXERCISE 9.1   MY DIFFICULT SITUATIONS/DIFFICULT PERSON

Identify a person over the last few months with who you have had particular difficulty communicating. Identify the situations in which you commonly experience difficulty with this person. What typically happens? How do you feel in this situation? What do you say? How are you behaving? What is the other person saying, and how are they behaving? Who do they remind you of? What is the outcome of the situation?

A TRANSACTIONAL ANALYSIS APPROACH TO THE GAMES PEOPLE PLAY

An introduction to transactional analysis: the ego-states and transactions

Transactional analysis was developed in the 1950s by psychiatrist Dr Eric Berne as a theory to enable us to understand the 'transactions' that take place between people. Berne (1964) defines any act which implies recognition of another's presence as a *stroke*. He describes a stroke as the fundamental unit of social action, and when we exchange strokes we transact. Therefore a *transaction* takes place when one person offers some kind of communication, and another replies, such as 'Hi there', and 'Hi, how are you doing?' The opening of communication is the stimulus, and the reply is the response.

Berne suggests that each transaction comes from one of three ego states within ourselves: the Parent, the Adult and the Child.

- **P**arent: parental ways of thinking, feeling and behaving, copied from parents or authority figures, 'oughts', 'shoulds', the judgmental superego. This also encompasses positive parental behaviours such as encouragement, constructive criticism and love.
- **A**dult: adult ways of thinking, feeling and behaving, which are direct responses to the here-and-now, the reality-testing ego.
- **C**hild: child-like ways of thinking, feeling and behaving, replayed from childhood, uncensored instincts and drives of the id.

The parental ego state can be sub-divided into two: – the 'controlling parent' (CP) or 'critical parent' who is judgmental and directive about how we should behave or what we should do. The other is the nurturing parent (NP) who is caring, loving, positive and supportive, encouraging and developmental in attitude towards us. When our parental ego state is working positively it includes positive aspects of nurturing and controlling, but an inadequate parent ego state can occur by using these negatively, for example through trying to disempower others to dispel our own inadequacy, being indifferent, providing destructive criticism, being condescending and over-protective, sanctimonious and overly moralistic.

Likewise the child ego state can be sub-divided into two. First, the 'free child' (FC) comes from our spontaneous expression of emotions (happy, sad, angry, fearful) and tends to come from the free expression of our feelings in an open, emotionally responsive way. The free child can also be very playful. Secondly, the 'adapted child' (AC) ego state is one which responds in an adaptive way to the behaviours and responses of important others, and particularly parental figures. The adapted child state may be compliant, giving unquestioning reactions to demands, and may demonstrate apologetic, contrite, confident or hardworking behaviours. Alternatively the adapted child state may be rebellious, in revolt against the demands of others.

This may all sound very unfamiliar and complex, so how can knowledge of these ego states help us to deal with other people effectively and understand why some people have particularly problematic impacts on us? If Berne and many others are right, then it is likely that some of our difficult transactions have resulted in our being invited into games or transactions which generate a transaction from an ego state that is uncomfortable or inappropriate for us. Before we look at these transactions, let's first examine our own mode of behaviour: do we have preferred ego states that we inhabit?

The ego-gram

One reason why we may be frustrated or unhappy in our transactions with others may be to do with the balance of our time spent in different ego states. Exercise 9.2 invites you to estimate how much of your time you spend in the various ego states. It is possible that one way in which we end up in conflict with others is through having a very unbalanced ego-gram. For example, look at the time spent at work. If you are predominantly in 'critical parent' mode then it is quite likely that others will experience you as judgmental, critical and controlling, and may respond by avoiding you, being overly deferential to you, or even challenging you and drawing you into conflict. Even worse, if you are exhibiting inadequate parental behaviour in that state. Alternatively if you are spending much of your time in free child at work, others may get irritated with your constant messing about, antics and spontaneous outbursts of emotion and may feel drained and distracted by your play. Consider the balance of behaviour you exhibit in the ego gram, its effects on others and how you might like this to change.

Alternatively you might like to consider what the ego-gram of a person you find particularly difficult to deal with might look like. Maybe they are overly parental, controlling or child-like. Look back at Exercise 9.1 and consider the ego state you appeared to be in within the problem situation you have identified. Also consider the ego state the other person or persons were in within this situation. The explanation of the script matrix below may give you some more insight into what was happening at this time.

EXERCISE 9.2   TIME SPENT IN DIFFERENT EGO STATES

Consider the ego states listed below and consider the time you spend in these. Take a typical week at work, or just the last week overall, and use a bar chart to identify the approximate percentages of time you spend in the different ego states.

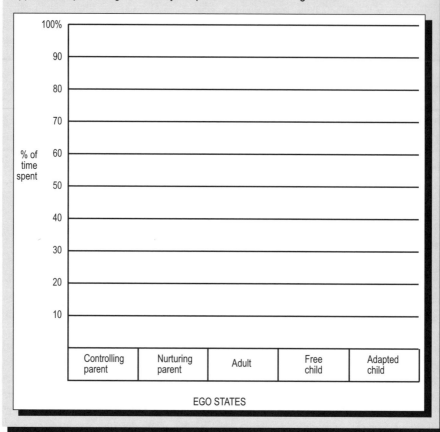

The script matrix

We can often analyse transactions according to the communication between different ego states. For example, assume you are waiting for a lecture to begin, but it is delayed by several students who are still in the cafeteria getting coffee. How might a transaction go between you and one of them? For example:

> **You** (P – C ie controlling parent to child): You should be upstairs, you are holding us all up.

> **Other** (C – P, ie rebellious adapted child to parent): Oh, I just wanted a coffee, don't give me a hard time.

Figure 9.1 represents this transaction as a script matrix.

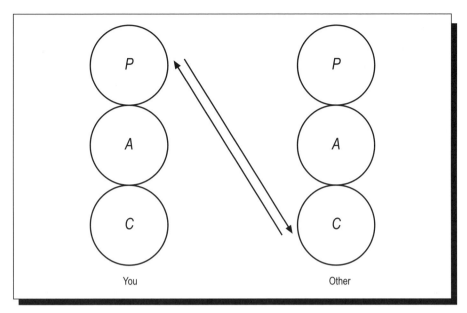

Figure 9.1 *A non-constructive complementary transaction*

The transactions can be complementary (parallel), as above, or crossed. Typically parent – child, and adult – adult transactions are complementary, but by responding to a parent – child transaction with an adult – adult one is one way of crossing the transaction. Using the example above, the response could be to cross the parent – child transaction with an adult – adult one thus:

You (P – C): Where the hell are you, we are all waiting?

Other (A – A): There was a very long queue, I didn't realise it would take this long. Please do start without me, I'm just waiting for my change.

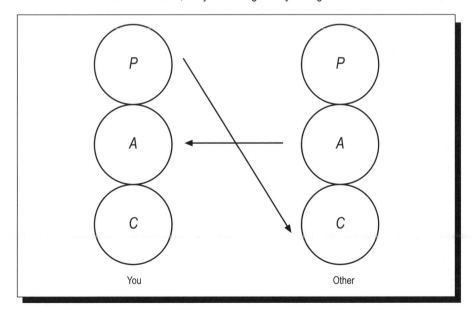

Figure 9.2 *A constructive crossed transaction*

This is shown in Figure 9.2.

A crossed transaction therefore occurs when the vectors cross, either when the responding ego state is different from the one addressed, or the addressed ego state responds back to an ego state that is different from the original stimulus ego state. Communication breaks down and one or both individuals will need to shift ego states to re-establish communication. So in the above example, where the transaction is crossed, you may then move from angry parent to an adult ego state and reply:

> **You** (A – A): OK, sorry to hassle you, I'm just keen to get on.

Many non-constructive exchanges at work occur when someone has invited us into a parent – child exchange, and to maintain complementarity we respond from our child rather than our adult state. So an explanation as to why communication might go so wrong is that someone is approaching us from an ego state which we perceive as being inappropriate for the situation, or it is a non complementary ego state, or alternatively because the transaction is crossed. The exchange presented in Figure 9.2 could have developed into a full blown argument had it not been crossed. Below is another example of crossing a transaction constructively in a work situation:

EXAMPLE 9.1 A CROSSED TRANSACTION AT WORK

David (P – C): How come you're always raising difficult issues at the end of the meeting? [David says this with great exasperation, making an inadequate parent comment intended for Christine's adapted child]

Christine's instinctive response is to come from rebellious adapted child:

Christine (C – P): Oh I see! We're only supposed to agree with you rather than have ideas of our own.

However, instead Christine allowed herself time to think and instead switched to adult:

Christine (A – A) [thoughtfully]:Look, if there's not enough time for this issue now perhaps we could add it to the early part of the agenda for next week.

David (now switches to adult): Yes that would be helpful, that will give us time to prepare for this important issue.

This crossed transaction, from Christine's adult, will encourage David to shift his ego state to adult and for the communication to continue. Crossing the transaction offers different possibilities, and more room for manoeuvre in awkward situations. Some people successfully use a 'free child' playfulness to divert a potential conflict. So in the situation above, Christine's response could have moved away from adapted child to playful child by joking or saying:

> Because I'm just so difficult and awkward!

Complementary and crossed transactions are examples of overt communication at the social level. However, there is a third type of transaction, called ulterior, in which two messages are conveyed at the same time. One is the overt social message, while the other occurs beneath the social level communication at the psychological level. The social level content is often adult – adult, with the psychological level content between parent and child (or less often parent – parent or child – child).

For example:

> **Iain**: How long will you be on the photocopier, you have been here an hour already? [expressed in a tone of controlled anger]
>
> **Diane**: I just want to complete this work, I'll be finished by 5 o' clock [said apologetically)]

At the social level this is an adult – adult complementary transaction (see for example figure 9.3). However, the psychological level messages might be:

> **Iain** (inadequate parent – adapted child): Why are you always in my way, I can never get on because of your incompetence.
>
> **Diane** (adapted child – inadequate parent): I know you are right, I'm useless. I'll rush to finish this job and then do better next time.

Ulterior transactions may be a reason why some people make us feel really uncomfortable or bad about ourselves but without our really being able to put our finger on what it is they have done to upset or enrage us. Superficially we or others may appear to be being adult and friendly, but underneath there may be a war going on. By developing awareness of these hidden messages we can grasp more clearly what is going on and at least comprehend our feelings and maybe even stay out of the game altogether. Usually our emotions warn us of what the ulterior communication may be below the surface.

Now return again to Exercise 9.1 and examine what ego states were being used in the transaction that was taking place between you. Were these appropriate to the situation, was

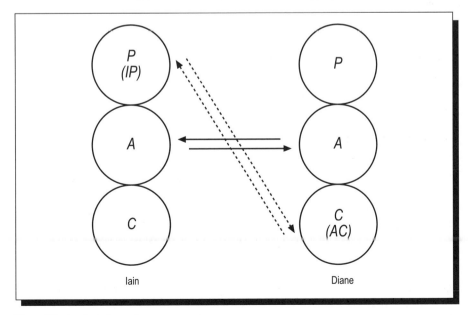

Figure 9.3 *An ulterior transaction*

the transaction crossed, or was there an ulterior transaction going on, or alternatively were you being invited into an ego state that you did not wish to inhabit, such as adaptive child?

The script matrix can therefore help us understand the nature of our exchanges. Some exchanges follow a pattern or sequence that develops into a full-blown game, and in the next section we examine how games may make us find dealing with some people particularly difficult.

Games

Games are interactions between people that can seem very familiar, and generally end up with the participants feeling bad (see Berne 1964). They are repetitive, often played outside our awareness, and end up with players having 'racket' feelings, entailing ulterior transactions, and sometimes containing the moment of surprise or confusion. Racket feelings are familiar emotions, learned in childhood, experienced in stress situations, and become maladaptive in our adult life: for example we may feel incompetent, useless, helpless, angry or defeated.

Table 9.1 contains some examples of common games which are played out at work. See if you can spot any in which you have engaged, and maybe one of them epitomises what happened with regard to your difficult situation/person in Exercise 9.1.

Table 9.1 *Games people play in organisations*

1. **Why Don't You ...? Yes But .... (WDYYB)**	When a colleague is helpless we may be drawn into making suggestions to assist, but these can constantly be rebutted with 'Yes but ...'. The effect of this game is either to make us feel helpless and frustrated, and the 'victim' to reinforce their position of 'there is nothing that can be done'. For example: **A**: I can't do these plans for scheduling the project. **B**: Why don't you get Ted to help you? **A**: Yes but, Ted is too busy at the moment. **B**: Why not ask Sarah then? **A**: Yes but she is off on holiday tomorrow. **B**: Why don't you let me have a look at the plans? **A**: Yes but you don't know all the background and problems. **B**: Well why don't you explain them to me? **A**: Yes but, I haven't got time, I've got to go in 10 minutes. **B**: Oh I give up! Another version is with a boss responding with 'Yes but .. .' to every good suggestion made by the staff. By doing this the boss can maintain a superior position and keep the staff in their place.

Table 9.1 *continued*

2. Ain't it Awful! (AIA)	The aim of this game is indemnification, as well as sympathy and the satisfaction that can be wrought from the situation. It is commonly used at a time of organisational change, and acts to undermine the change and render anyone who is trying to make the change work, powerless. For example:
	A: Ain't it awful about the new merger.
	B: It's terrible, no one knows what they are supposed to be doing.
	C: It's awful, the old system used to work so well, but this is a shambles.
	D: This is so typical of this firm – they don't care about the staff, the managers just make changes and expect us to manage.
	E: Oh it's awful, if only I could I'd leave, I'm so stressed out.
	A variant of this is 'Look what they are doing to us now!' This game enables people to evade taking any responsibility, and to place all the blame for problems on 'the organisation' or 'the management', and can lead to widespread demoralisation and a feeling of helplessness.
3. Why does it Always Happen to Me? and Poor Me	In this game the person is in the depressive position, with a monopoly on misfortune. Here the locus of control is seen as external, or even out of human control totally, with luck and fate playing a strong role. In this game the person is complaining and bitter about their misfortune, which they use to negate their own power and abnegate responsibility in a situation. A good example in relation to your studies is around the handing in of assignments:
	A: I need an extension, because I'm so unlucky, the printer ran out, and my bag was taken with my notes in and I've had such bad migraines this week. Typical! Why does this always happen to me?
	A variant of this is 'poor me', where the person presents himself to the boss or colleagues as so helpless that others truly feel sorry for the individual who then successfully evades chastisement or criticism for inadequate performance, and may even manipulate others into doing their work for them.

Table 9.1 *continued*

4. Look how Hard I've Tried	This occurs where a person can demonstrate how hard they have worked, even though they may have done a lousy job. This is common amongst staff who appear to work long hours, but with very little result.
5. Harried	Harried occurs when someone takes on many roles, maybe because they are unassertive and can't say no, or are desperate to 'please others', but the effect is that they then collapse at the crucial moment, leading to a mass of self-reproach and problems for others working with them. These people rush around looking harried and busy, but can cause havoc through their stress and anxiety. A person playing harried may subconsciously choose a boss or partner who he or she won't be able to please, in order to reinforce the game.
6. If it weren't for you ….	Another game that evades personal responsibility is where a colleague blames someone else: their peer or boss for their problems. This is more commonly the case in marriages and partnerships, for example a husband/wife says: 'If it wasn't for looking after you I could have gone out to work, travelled round the world, done interesting things'. It is interesting to find out what they really would have done had they not had the excuse of the other person stopping them.
7. Blemish	This can occur when someone appears to be objective in evaluating you and your performance, but is actually seeking out the one little error you have made, in order to magnify it and infer that the whole project/task/report is inadequate. This may satisfy your own deep feelings of being unworthy, and their own superiority.
8. Now I've Got You (NIGY)	In this game someone appears to have a good working relationship with you, but underneath they have somehow rigged the situation so that you can only fail. When you do fail the person pounces on you and publicly embarrasses you. For example your boss may have appeared to be very supportive, giving you a new challenging assignment, but then you discover you haven't been given the time or resources to do it, and your failure is inevitable.
9. Hero	As with 'Now I've got you' you may have been set up to fail, but in this situation the boss or colleague miraculously steps in at the last minute to help you, enabling them to appear glorious and indispensable and steal the limelight, and at the same time making you appear pathetic and in need of their help.

Table 9.1 *continued*

10. King of the Hill	This can occur when a competitive situation is set up in which the other person will inevitably win and demonstrate their competence and superiority. Never mind the crucial fact that they were privy to more information in writing their proposal, they are still crowned champion.
11. Cops and Robbers	Alternatively 'cat and mouse', like the cartoon Tom and Jerry. This is where one person, maybe the boss, is constantly trying to catch you out, and you spend all your time planning how to evade him/her, stay one step ahead and outwit them. This can be very wasteful of energy and resources in a work environment.
12. Prosecutor	You may find that there is someone in the organisation who knows all the rules – backwards. They may dare you and tempt you to step out of line, for example by enticing you to lose your temper and shout at them, and then wham! They have got you. They hurl the whole rule book at you. This is often the case with difficult employees who deserve to have been sacked years ago, but always manage to keep their position through this game, maybe even obtaining compensation for the unfair treatment you have given them.
13. Uproar	This occurs when you find yourself in an argument with a colleague, and gradually you both stop listening to each other's point of view and get wrapped up in making your own position heard, but neither of you are willing to listen. Eventually the exchange becomes louder and louder and ends with one of you shouting, slamming a door or walking out, leaving you both feel injured and upset. This is also a game commonly played by parents with teenage children.
14. Kick Me	A good example of 'Kick me' is where you are attending a lecture by an eminent person, and when it comes to questions you get carried away and show off your skills by clever criticism. What you haven't realised is that you are unwittingly persecuting the lecturer, and when you finish he demolishes your critique with one carefully chosen sentence, at which everyone in the audience laughs. You now feel rejected and useless, and being down, you enable everyone else to aim a well-chosen kick in your direction.
	This is often played out at academic conferences.

(Drawn from and extending some original games identified by Eric Berne 1964.)

In the table above one row is left open to enable you to add in your own game – there are so many games played in the workplace it is quite likely you have experienced one that is not mentioned here.

It is one thing to recognise a game but another to know what to do about it (see Stewart and Joines 1987, Chapter 25 for more information). One approach is to spot the opening gambit ('the con'). If you can catch the game right at the beginning, you can forestall it altogether. You have a number of options here. You can bring the game into the open: it is much harder for someone to play 'Ain't it awful' for example if you have already aired the ideas behind it. Other options are to remove yourself from the game: refuse the invitation into the familiar 'locked in' response. You do this by crossing the transaction or changing the ego state, or even just refusing to play the game and walking away from it. For example if the game has invited you to come in as the nurturing parent, as in 'harried' or 'poor me' and rescue and protect the person, you can instead switch to adult, so rather than saying 'Poor you, how can I help?' you could say 'Unfortunately the rules say your assignment has to be in by 12.00, I'm afraid we don't alter them under any circumstances'. You could try to disown the negative pay off, which is the bad feeling that the game can leave behind, refuse to take the blame, or feel useless, drawing on your adult to think 'Interesting, I've just been set up in the game of "kick me"' for example. Alternatively you could go straight to the positive pay-off, or recognise the underlying reason. So for example in 'Ain't it awful' you could recognise the fear that may push people into playing this, or the fun they get from not having to take responsibility. With relation to yourself playing this, you could recognise the need to be supported and find more appropriate ways to satisfy this need.

The drama triangle

A common pattern which can occur in various games is 'the drama triangle' depicted in Figure 9.4. This usually occurs when someone is playing the role of 'victim' as in WDYYB. The helpless victim invites someone to come in and rescue them, but all attempts to provide advice are rejected in WDYYB. After a time playing this game the rescuer may get fed up with the victim's helpless responses, turn into a persecutor and maybe say 'Oh, sort it out yourself'. Alternatively the victim may start to get fed up with the person giving advice and perceive them as a persecutor rather than a rescuer – 'Why don't you just leave me alone'. At some point the victim may turn the tables and switch into a persecutor and say 'Stop telling

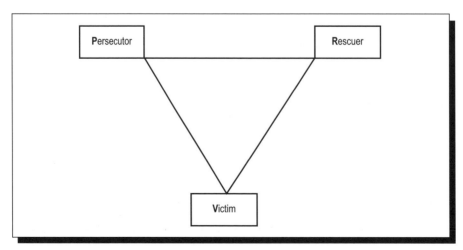

Figure 9.4 *The drama triangle*

me what to do' or 'See, you are useless, you can't help me'. One way out of this triangle is for the rescuer to refuse the invite to sort out the victim's troubles and instead stay detached, let the responsibility stay with the victim and say 'What do you think the best thing for you to do is?', or 'What are your options?' This is a form of helping without getting drawn into taking responsibility and any subsequent criticism.

As with all games you need to ask yourself various questions to understand what is going on. Exercise 9.3 aims to help you do just that.

EXERCISE 9.3   GAMES I PLAY

What games do you think you get hooked into? Ask yourself:

1.   What keeps happening to me over and over again?
2.   How does it start?
3.   What happens next?
4.   (Mystery question – come back to this at the end)*
5.   And then?
6.   (Mystery question – come back to this at the end)**
7.   How does it end?
8.   How do I feel?
9.   How do I think the other person feels?

Once you have answered these questions you can look at the mystery questions below:

*   What is my secret message to the other person?
**   What is the other person's secret message to me?

Games generally occur outside our awareness and reinforce a decision made in childhood. By examining the series of transactions and becoming aware of ulterior messages, you may be able to engage your 'adult' and explore the options. The mystery questions in Exercise 9.3 are intended to help surface some of these unconscious messages. To go into further depth you could examine contracts for change and approaches to 'redecision'. If you want to delve further into this area, read Stewart and Joines 1987, Part 7.

STRESS

There are some situations which can result in an overwhelming loss of personal effectiveness, such as situations of severe stress at work. In this section we will examine the symptoms, causes and effects of stress and identify strategies to maintain your effectiveness and at the same time deal with these situations. To illustrate this further the example of bullying is taken as a situation which can lead to severe stress and loss of effectiveness.

DEFINITION OF STRESS

Stress exists where the perceived demands made on a person and pressure they are under exceed their capacity to cope and respond effectively.

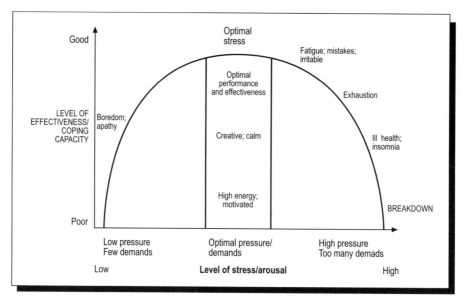

Figure 9.5 *Stress and effectiveness*

For most people a certain amount of pressure is a good thing. Having a total lack of pressure can lead to apathy. Some stress or pressure can be energising and promote good performance. However, where this is excessive an individual can lose energy and performance and effectiveness deteriorate, as shown in Figure 9.5.

Sources of stress: work-based

In 1967 Holmes and Rahe identified a Social Readjustment Rating Scale to measure the impact of major sources of stress in life events (see Holmes and Rahe 1967, and website material). They found the most major sources of stress were death of a partner or close family member, divorce or separation, personal illness and injury, moving house, and financial loss, as well as retirement and redundancy. There have been a proliferation of tools and indicators of stress since then, confirming these. If we focus primarily on the work context, and drawing on a number of studies including the work of Sutherland and Cooper (1990: 7, 26, sourcing a number of earlier studies by Cary Cooper) and Newton (1995) we can identify the following major sources of stress:

- **Personal competency.** Competences needed in the job; personal lack of competence at working with budgets, people, computers.
- **Intrinsic to job.** Issues such as work overload, too much responsibility, fear of mistakes.
- **Job environment**. Poor physical working conditions, interruptions.
- **Role in organisation.** Role ambiguity and conflict, boundary conflicts, image of occupation.
- **Relationships at work**. Poor relations with boss, subordinates or colleagues, problems with delegation, ineffective team working and dysfunctional group dynamics, lack of trust. Dealing with others' poor performance: reviewing performance, disciplining, firing.
- **Organisational structure and climate** Lack of participation or consultation,

surveillance, excessive evaluation, unachievable performance targets, management control methods, organisational politics.

- **Organisational change**. Constant and unproductive organisational change.
- **Career development**. Over or under promotion, job insecurity.
- **Work life balance.** Juggling careers and families, time pressures.

Sources of stress: person-based

Not all sources of stress come from our work or external events, but are our own self-generated mindsets which we carry around. For example, we may have a personality that is high on anxiety and neuroticism. We may demonstrate type A personality and behaviour (drive, achievement, ambition- orientated). Alternatively we may have low tolerance for stress and score low on tests of resilience (for further exercises to assess whether you are more of a type A or type B person see the website material).

The influential person centred therapist Carl Rogers wrote widely on the problems people face from a term he called *conditions of worth* (for example see Rogers 1967). We may have high conditions of worth for ourselves, where we cannot feel relaxed unless we have achieved certain conditions. Conditions of worth can be very powerful, they are essentially ways in which we make our self-esteem conditional on achievement, rather than it being a basic human entitlement. Many of these conditions are externally based, where we have an external *locus of evaluation,* dependent upon validating ourselves to others, and meeting others' demands upon us.

A good example of how conditions of worth can impact us is the 'driver' theory. Transactional analysis identifies a number of drivers for our mindset and behaviour. A driver is a belief we have learnt and developed in earlier life in response to the positive strokes we receive from significant others, such as parents. Learnt early, they become deeply-held, implicit values, which drive our behaviours in later life. They can be enormous strengths, and often account for a great deal of the success we have in our working lives, but can also become a source of stress for us or our colleagues and loved ones. Each of these lead to different forms of stress: see Table 9.2.

Table 9.2 *Understanding our drivers*

Hurry up

Myth: Everything must be done as quickly as possible. Gets rewarded (and feels OK) for finishing things quickly.

Symptoms: Rushing everywhere, driving fast, over-filled diary, speaking quickly, interrupting others, fidgeting, writing fast, hating queuing.

Productive behaviours: Efficiency, gets a lot done, quick thinking.

Unproductive behaviours: Mistakes, carelessness.

Stressors: Never having enough time to think or plan, or space with nothing to do

Antidote: Plan sufficient time, plan work in stages, learn listening skills, learn to relax and be alone.

Be perfect

Myth: Everything must be right first time, every time. Gets rewarded (and feel OK) for getting it done right.

Symptoms: Deliberate speech, jargon, immaculate clothes, stiff, everything 'just so' before can start, getting into detail.

Productive behaviours: Completer-finisher with an eye for detail, logical, accurate.

Unproductive behaviours: May be slow, not meet deadlines, overly critical of self and others, too much detail and over complexity, over-questioning.

Stressors: Gets wound up when self or others are careless, worries about things, struggles in times of high ambiguity or change.

Antidote: Goal clarity, prioritisation, use mistakes as a source of learning not punishment, take a risk, identify 'fit for purpose' or 'good enough' appropriate quality levels at outset.

Please people

Myth: Must please others, even if not asked. Has to get it right for others, by doing the right thing – which may have to be guessed.

Symptoms: Lots of smiling, good eye contact, nodding, listening. Anxious when there is conflict and anger, presents views as questions, concerned about other's opinion.

Productive behaviours: Flexible, adaptable, concern for others, intuitive and empathetic listeners, good team workers.

Unproductive behaviours: Difficulty in confronting others, over-sensitive to criticism.

Stressors: Fear won't be liked when disagree, feel misunderstood when offers of help rejected, feeling responsible for others emotional states. Being ignored, criticised or blamed.

Antidote: Learn to confront constructively, learn to say 'no', learn to accept constructive feedback, give others responsibility for their feelings.

Try hard

Myth: It is the effort that counts. Must try hard (not necessarily to get a result). 'See how hard I have tried!'

Symptoms: 'I'll try and do that …', 'that's interesting …' volunteering, interested, enthusiastic, lots of questions. But goes off at a tangent, with a trail of unfinished jobs.

Productive behaviours: Hard worker, sets high goals, enthusiastic, innovative, creative.

Unproductive behaviours: Unfocused, doesn't finish jobs, abdicates, gets bored easily, constantly changing priorities.

Stressors: Not getting pleasure of completion, hates being criticised for not caring, fear of failure, lack of success but also overwork.

Antidote: Clarify goals and direction, learn to finish and recognise and celebrate successes. Stop volunteering. Instead of 'trying' – do it!

Be strong

Myth: Must cope, by self, 'I have to do it all'. Showing any form of weakness means doesn't feel OK.

Symptoms: Distant, aloof, unemotional, detached, calm. 'The facts are here ...', 'Pull yourself together ...'. Doesn't smile much, is a loner, doesn't ask for help.

Productive behaviours: Calm under pressure, firm but fair, strong sense of duty, works at unpleasant tasks, gives honest feedback, can work well alone.

Unproductive behaviours: Delegation is a sign of weakness, working long hours, unemotional when situation demands emotional contact, lacks empathy, highly self-critical and task-focused.

Stressors: Feels stressed when forced to expose feelings, or to be vulnerable, or close to others. Doesn't seek support when needs it.

Antidote: It is OK to ask for help. Check work-life balance – are the work levels realistic? Recognise the importance of the feelings of others. With new task check the resources are sufficient and the targets realistic.

It is a good idea to check your own sources of stress, and also signs to indicate whether these are acceptable or demonstrating an 'excessive' level of stress.

EXERCISE 9.4 RECOGNISING THE SOURCES AND SIGNS OF STRESS

1. **Sources of stress** Write down your main sources of stress:

2. **Signs of stress** Write down below if you have noticed any changes in yourself from your usual state utilising the following categories.

Cognitive /thoughts	Affective / feelings
Pysical	Behavioural

3. Now appraise the information you have provided and identify if you think you are suffering from an excessive amount of stress.

4. After you have completed this section return to identify an action plan of what you will do to reduce your own stress levels

Common cognitive changes when experiencing stress relate to difficulties concentrating, making decisions, and remembering things, confusion and difficulty 'turning off'. In terms of emotions, moods and feelings people can experience anger, bitterness, unease, panic, guilt, self-condemnation, sadness and even depression. In terms of physical changes these can encompass sleeplessness, headaches, nausea, chest pains, breathing problems, repeated infections and slow recovery from them. Behavioural changes experienced by someone suffering from stress may include taking longer to do things, making more mistakes, absenteeism, and even smoking, drinking or eating disorders. If these symptoms are persisting it is better to take action rather ignoring them.

Dealing with stress

Muddling through is not usually the most sensible coping strategy, and if you feel you are suffering from undue stress, whatever the cause, it is important to consider your options. You can:

- do nothing (not usually the wisest alternative)
- change the situation, by acting on it
- change your reaction to the situation, by building personal health and fitness, emotional resilience.

To change the situation it is helpful to have identified the source of the problem, and the previous section and Exercise 9.4 should have helped you to get to the causes of the problem. Consider the following:

- develop your personal competency: identify key skills that you lack or are under-developed and initiate some training or coaching in these. Put time aside each week to develop your competency
- better time management (addressed in Chapter 2)
- who has ownership of the problem? Discuss the situation with those involved, or alternatively a coach or mentor. The discussion could be focused on identifying:
  - a clarification of personal and professional goals
  - conflicting roles – what are the priorities, can time be ring fenced for certain activities, what are the boundaries of your role, what is achievable?
  - approaches to sharing work or delegation
  - action plans for dealing with poor working conditions – ask for better resources, change your working pattern
  - problems with professional relationships – can these be discussed? Focus on constructive feedback (relook at Chapter 7 on communication skills). Sometimes colleagues do not know when they are causing us stress
  - stress related to organisational change – see Chapter 10
  - realistic boundaries for work and home. It can help to ensure balance in your life: see the quadrants below and identify if there is something in each quadrant you want to do, and objectives for the year. Are any of the quadrants overcrowded? Can you withdraw from certain activities or get more help and pass them on to others?

EXERCISE 9.5 BALANCE OF LIFE QUADRANTS

Work	Home
Finance	Leisure
Personal development	

Alternatively you can change your reaction to a situation and focus more on building up your capacity to cope with it and your own resilience. Personal fitness, with regular exercise, a healthy diet, enough sleep and enough time for leisure and relaxation has been mentioned throughout the book as the baseline for being able to be resilient and personally effective.

There are also some short-term coping strategies that can help deal with excessive stress. Some people use relaxation techniques, or yoga and meditation. One method is progressive relaxation using the clench-relax technique, or alternatively use creative visualisation or 'right-sizing' to help calm down in a stressful situation. These and other relaxation techniques to adjust your mindset to deal with short-term problems are in the examples below.

EXAMPLE 9.2   RELAXATION AND CHANGING THE MINDSET TECHNIQUES

Progressive relaxation: Jacobsen's clench-relax technique

Find 10 minutes in your day before you start work, in your lunch hour or in the evening when you can lie down and relax. Lie on your back, and make sure you are warm and comfortable. Beginning with the tip of your toes clench them as you breathe in deeply, then relax them as you breathe out. Then move up to your ankles, then calves, thighs, etc, working through the whole body clenching the muscle group then relaxing it. After working your face: jaw and around the mouth, eyes, and finally your forehead, you should end at the top of your head. It is believed that muscle groups achieve a greater state of relaxation when they are put under pressure and then relaxed, than if you just concentrate on relaxing them. Although you should achieve a state of relaxation in doing this exercise, you may also find that there is a certain part of the body where you hold a lot of your tension, and you might not have realised this before now. Common areas, for example, are the hips, and the jaw area. To allow these to relax, breathe deeply as you work, imagining you are releasing the tension as you exhale and release your breath.

Creative visualisation

Once again find somewhere peaceful where you can lie down or at least sit comfortably. Shut your eyes and concentrate on slowly and gently breathing in through the nose and out through the mouth from deep in your abdomen. As you do so, clear your mind of thoughts. Then gradually imagine a happy memory of a peaceful place: it may be a beach on holiday, a walk up a mountain or a view from a window. Imagine yourself in that place, taking in the sights, the sounds, the smells. Conjure up the feeling of peace and contentment you experienced there. Take five minutes to absorb the atmosphere and feel part of the environment. Then gradually bring your awareness back to your breathing and return to your body, taking a few moments to recognise where you are. Try and keep the feeling of the peaceful place with you as you go about your daily activities.

Right-sizing

Find yourself a comfortable place to sit or lie and relax. Begin by seeing yourself as you are, then gradually move your consciousness away from inside to looking at yourself from the outside, gradually draw further and further back so you are looking at yourself from a distance, then maybe an aeroplane, then from a star in a distant galaxy. You are now one little dot in an infinite space. In the big scheme of things your life is a fleeting thing, your problems tiny compared to what you can see happening in the world.

When you return your consciousness to yourself, remember this feeling of infinity and how insignificant your problems are in the whole universe.

Perspective

As a last resort, I heard one facilitator say in exasperation at someone who was bound up with their feelings of failure –

Look Lou, failure is relative – to a dead person, you're a success!

It is interesting that many people at the pinnacle of their profession have been crushed by senses of failure. Take the life story of the Nobel Prize winning mathematician John Nash, as captured in the film 'A Beautiful Mind'.

Rarely is our sense of failure in direct relation to our performance.

Anchoring

If you are really struggling with a particular problem that is getting you stressed, for example learning computer competence, then 'anchoring' is a technique which invites you to transfer confidence from one situation to another. Stop the stressful activity for a few moments and visualise a situation in which you felt very confident and managed to master a new skill. Remember the feeling of confidence you experienced in the previous situation, and the techniques you used to achieve success. When you then return to the stressful situation, remind yourself of your 'anchored' position, your islands of competence, and how you will feel when you have mastered this new stressful situation. Instead of thinking how poor you are at this task, remind yourself how wonderful it feels when you have mastered a new proficiency, and remember the strategies you previously adopted to develop a skill. Can any of these be used in the stressful situation?

Are you going about it in the right way? Are you too problem focused rather than solution focused?

For example, Mark was struggling revise for a finance exam, and was getting nowhere and feeling very frustrated. He stopped to think about how he had mastered playing the violin, a difficult and arduous process. He remembered he did short bursts of practice, and then would share his skill with others (at that time his long-suffering mother). He also found an uncle with who he could play some fun duets. He remembered feeling really pleased when he passed his grade 4 exam and his family had taken him out for a meal to celebrate. In returning to his finance exam revision, he put short one-hour slots in his schedule for revision, and rang up a friend on the course to arrange to discuss the practice papers together the following lunchtime. He tried to keep the feeling of pleasure of success in his head, and arranged with a group of friends to go out for dinner once the exam was over. This helped him get through the difficult experience – effectively he was transferring the learning from one situation to another.

Re-frame the problem

Instead of seeing the problem as something negative, if you can see the problem as an opportunity for improvement, where you can ask for feedback (rather than criticism) from others then you can move yourself out of the 'victim', helpless state of mind (where you indoctrinate yourself with negative, destructive thoughts and feelings) into the active frame of mind. To help you do this attack your destructive self-talk (techniques for this were mentioned in Chapter 1), and in particular question:

- is the thought true, what other ways are there of seeing the situation?
- is the thought helpful, does it help you to move on to better ways of thinking, feeling and behaving, or does the thought paralyse you into inaction, cynicism, and apathy?

Presence in the here and now

Some people get stressed because they spend too much time in the past, regretting previous events, or in the future, anticipating the worst that can happen. A friend told me how she survived a difficult time was to think of the saying:

> The past is history, the future is a mystery, now is a gift – that is why it is called the present!

If you live in the present, you will realise that unless you are standing in the middle of a road with a double-decker bus bearing down on you, then life is not immediately dangerous!

Being centred in the present, focusing on what you are doing one thing at a time, getting pleasure from each activity as it arises, is important to building up resilience. Panic is future-orientated thinking that focuses on all that might go wrong. What if it goes right? More importantly, focusing on the present and what you are doing right now is helpful. It is likely that if you are getting stressed you are allowing your thoughts to wander away from the present to a future scare or past shock.

Laughter

We can get very negative when going through a stressful experience. Sometimes we need to use the equivalent of 'jump-start' leads on our brain to force it out of a negative, way of thinking in order to see things in a different way. Laughter can be a great way of inducing a feeling of well-being and happiness. When you have fun, who makes you laugh? Can you arrange to see a funny movie or friend to get you to lighten up and re-engage with the happier side of your nature?

Resources

There are many books and tapes with exercises and relaxation music to help people calm down. If you find it difficult to relax on your own try and purchase one of these and use it regularly. Some people also establish a bedtime ritual which involves a warm bath, candles or good bedtime reading to help them switch off and relax.

Relaxation techniques and short-term emotional self-management may not be enough, you may also need to build up longer-term resilience.

Not everybody can do this alone. It may help to identify supportive relationships, nurturing people (such as partners and friends), to help you find perspective on the source of your stress, and ways of tackling it. Build attachments with others such as mentors, coaches, advisers – and if you haven't got one of these then find one! Also, if necessary, seek further support from a counsellor.

Helping others to manage their stress

If you are in a managerial position you can raise the effectiveness of those around you by helping them to manage their own stress. Here are some actions you could consider taking:

1. Get to know your staff, and if possible, how to recognise when they are under stress.
2. Make time to listen and provide appropriate support.

3. Use active listening skills to help your staff identify the causes of their stress.

4. Help staff find the way forward which is right for them.

5. Point out negative thinking as appropriate, but with sensitivity.

6. Help people articulate any fears and concerns, even if there are no immediate solutions.

7. Ensure your staff take proper breaks and do not work excessive hours.

8. Ask yourself whether you give staff consistent messages by what you say and what you do.

9. Check to what extent your management contributes to the stress.

10. Take action to reduce any staff stress caused by your management.

11. Encourage staff to look for choices rather than use only one type of behaviour.

Increasingly taking no action to address excessive stress is no longer an option for employers. A key legal case in the UK illustrates this fact.

EXAMPLE 9.3 A LANDMARK CASE

Walker versus Northumberland County Council (1995) concerned a social worker, John Walker, who suffered two nervous breakdowns caused by work stress. He had frequently asked his superiors for more staff and for management guidance, but received no help. John Walker's mental health deteriorated to such an extent that he was unable to return to his 20-year-long career. The claimant must be able to prove a breach of the employer's duty of care: injury; causation; and foreseeablity. In the *Walker* case the type of injury sustained was reasonably foreseeable since *Walker* had already suffered one breakdown. The second breakdown was foreseeable in the absence of any action taken to alleviate the pressures he was clearly under. The judge pronounced that the employer's duty of care extended to protection against psychiatric harm.

BULLYING AND TOXIC WORK ENVIRONMENTS

Bullying

In a survey of 5,300 respondents, in both the private and public sectors, it was found that 24.4 per cent of people were bullied within five years, 10.5 per cent within a six-month period (Hoel et al 2000). Clearly this is something that affects a number of people, and the problems caused by this affects not just the bully and the victim: there is the impact on others around them (Rayner 1997).

Bullying is a form of aggressive and destructive behaviour that inflicts misery on its victims. The many strategies for causing harm may be consciously pursued or out of awareness. Bullying in the workplace is typified by emotional abuse, such as constant criticism, and words and actions that are designed to undermine the confidence and the competence of the victim, making it very difficult for them to perform effectively. Although the victim may feel that they are being treated unfairly, it is likely that the bully has identified the victim's weak spots, giving more credence to their attacks, and making it more difficult for the victim to retaliate and repudiate. The bully may play to the victim's own fears and so it is likely that the indignation of the victim is tinged by uncertainty and the victim's armoury of defences become eroded by doubt.

It is difficult to identify specific examples of bullying behaviour, because these need to be seen within the context of an overall pattern of abuse. Typically some of the behaviours of a bullying boss are:

- withholding information
- not giving the person the tools, skills or support to get a good job done
- unrealistic performance criteria, setting the person up for failure
- contradictory messages and behaviour
- public humiliation of the victim, putting them down and ridiculing them in front of others
- constant criticism, negative feedback, highlighting failure
- personal abuse
- threatening behaviour.

The example below illustrates an interplay of critical and undermining behaviour that leads to a victim feeling persecuted and debilitated.

EXAMPLE 9.4   BULLYING BEHAVIOUR

Jane had once loved her job, enjoying the challenge of public relations, its variety and creativity. Since the new boss had taken over six months ago, she has dreaded going in to work, feeling sick in her stomach as she woke each morning to face up to the day. The new boss Nick had begun his tenure by making a very macho speech to the staff on the need for the organisation to change drastically, he had said 'the work here has been slack, you will all need to shape up. Anyone who doesn't feel they can keep up – should get out of here!' This had been followed by a series of sweeping changes to their working practices, to the effect that the culture had changed from one of high trust, high support and hard work to constant monitoring and surveillance. Almost every week Jane received on her e-mail details of new performance monitoring systems, work quotas, absenteeism reporting systems, productivity objectives.

For the first few months Nick had totally ignored Jane when he walked past her in the corridor or met her in reception: he acted as though she were invisible. He had a series of on- to-one meetings with all the staff, one-third of whom he had made redundant at these 'inquisitions'. At her own meeting she had worked up the courage to ask him about her position and he had said 'Well we are not getting rid of you now. What happens in future will all depend on your quality of work, and I will be watching you very closely'. Although he asked for feedback and ideas from her to improve the organisation at the meeting, he had failed to listen to anything she said, and when she had started to make some constructive suggestions he had interrupted and talked over her, giving his views on the organisation.

Although Jane knew everyone felt threatened by his behaviour – she was not alone in this – he had left her feeling unappreciated and scared. Over the next few months he had e-mailed her erratically and unpredictably, asking for performance data and action, or to give her critical feedback. He would send her a critical e-mail for every small slip-up she made: once when she hadn't locked the door of her office when she had popped out for lunch, leaving some equipment open to security threat, once when she had been

10 minutes late for a meeting (having been stuck in traffic after an accident had closed a road). He was a micro manager par excellence.

In the last two months he had taken to giving her unrealistic ultimatums: 'You must have your client information placed on the IT system by next week'. For example, when the IT support person was away on holiday and she had no way of getting access to the system or training on it. She hadn't got to grips with the new administrative system either, but since he had sacked the administrator involved with her campaigns her workload had doubled and she felt totally unable to meet the demands of the job, and as a result she felt de-skilled and incompetent. Nick rarely let anyone know what was going on, and so she was often in a position of saying one thing to a client, only to be contradicted by Nick who had changed the policy without telling her. For example, on one occasion in front of a client he had said 'Don't be ridiculous Jane, we changed that feature of the publicity campaign last night. We are not now doing phone-ins, instead we are running a conference – do keep up'.

At meetings he would make sarcastic comments about her 'If everyone was as slow as Jane, we would never get anything done'. Or 'In the new recruitment drive we will attract better people than you Jane'. Once he said she had the work speed of a 'snail' and she had tried to tackle him saying 'That is really unfair and uncalled for' but he had sneered at her 'Oh don't be such a wimp, can't you take a joke!' leading her feeling even more inadequate. She knew that she did take time over her work, but had always been congratulated before for being meticulous and thorough. She knew that he was critical with all the staff, but felt she was being targeted for special treatment.

She dreaded being made redundant or being dismissed, and her fears of inadequacy were now so paralysing that when she received a new e-mail from Nick asking for information or for her to do something she would get into a confused panic. She had not been sleeping well and her exhaustion was making it hard to concentrate.

Toxic cultures and workplaces

Bullying can occur interpersonally, where a bully targets a victim, and picks them out for this demoralising attention. Alternatively it can seep into an organisational culture, where the negative feedback, dominating and intimidating atmosphere and behaviour cause problems for a wider range of individuals who get caught up in destructive working patterns and management practices. A culture of bullying can lead to group behaviour where others join in to attack an individual, a practice called 'mobbing'.

There are a number of workplace situations and practices that can promote the possibility of bullying: downsizing, restructuring, computer monitoring, performance pressure, negative role models and leadership, for example. These can act as a catalyst for bullying and make a culture of fear and paranoia a more likely prospect.

Whether the bullying is individual or across a workplace culture its effects can be devastating.

Table 9.3 identifies some of the symptoms experienced by victims of bullying and ways these can be spotted or experienced in individuals' states of mind, physical health and behaviour. Some of these symptoms are remarkably similar to those experienced by people with post-traumatic stress disorder.

Table 9.3 *Symptoms experienced by victims of bullying*

State of mind
    confusion, an inability to think clearly, loss of memory, cognitive dysfunction
    feelings of loss of competence, incapability.
    paralysis by fear and anxiety.
    obsessiveness, constant worry about the situation, within and away from it.
    feelings of helplessness and powerlessness.
    emotional mood swings (lability), heightened emotional arousal or apathy
    excessive introspection
    loss of sense of self, identity and self-worth.
    suicidal thoughts.

State of physical health
    sleeplessness, unable to get to sleep, waking up prematurely, chronic tiredness.
    erratic eating patterns, loss of appetite, or binge and comfort eating.
    shaking limbs, sweating
    racing heart, chest pains, raised blood pressure.
    headaches or nausea.

Behaviour
    ineffective working, deteriorating performance.
    absenteeism through stress and sickness.
    distracted interpersonal behaviour, inability to focus or listen in conversations.

The theatre of the mind

Within a bullying relationship or culture, emotions and perceptions can be heightened, magnified and distorted to such an extent that anyone outside the situation will find it difficult to understand the sheer terror and pain being experienced. Small incidents and comments that in normal working life would be shrugged off as unimportant, become played and replayed endlessly in the mind of the victim, creating a theatre of torture, which the victim can neither turn off nor ignore. The scenes becoming imbued with meanings and projections that become terrorising spectres. The individual feels powerless to alter the script, yet subconsciously they are adding their own frightening fantasies to it. The victim gets caught along with the bully in a process of escalation.

The emotional drain of dealing with the bully in real life as well as again and again in fantasy, can lead to exhaustion and despair. It becomes almost impossible to escape, as the mind cannot disconnect from the experience. Rather than the mind dwelling on realistic appraisals of the situation or positive ways in which the individual can remove themselves from it, it is more likely that the victim's mind conspires with the bully to confirm their own helplessness and inability to effect any change in the situation at all.

EXERCISE 9.6   IDENTIFYING BULLYING – CAUSES AND SOLUTIONS

Look back over Example 9.4 and identify:

1. Ways in which Nick's behaviour constitutes bullying.
2. Ways in which there may be a bullying culture developing.
3. Symptoms of bullying being experienced by Jane.
4. Actions Jane could take to deal with this situation.

Countering bullying

Taking action on bullying is not simple, as by the time it has been recognised the victim may be in such a poor mental state that almost any problem appears insurmountable and any action unachievable.

Removal from the situation

In severe cases the only sensible solution is for the individual to remove themselves from the situation. This may be a temporary action, such as getting a doctor to sign the person off as sick, or taking holiday leave. Removing oneself from the situation can be essential for the feelings of panic and fear to reduce, and enable the individual to regain sufficient sense of balance and emotional health in order to think through the situation and decide what to do next. Alternatively for some, permanent removal – such as moving jobs – may be the answer, especially if other jobs and roles are available and the individual feels well enough to apply for them.

Support

It is essential that the individual seek out as many sources of support as possible, to provide emotional support, advice and a realistic appraisal of options. It may be through peers at work, friends and relatives, or professionals such as counsellors, coaches, therapists and doctors. Sometimes people outside of the situation are in a better position to identify courses of action than the person who has become paralysed and invaded by feelings of helplessness.

Emotional reappraisal – building a barrier

It requires great strength of character and courage for the individual to positively re-examine their feelings and emotions. To right size magnified emotions, to locate the causes of the problems and to get angry rather than fearful. The individual may need psychologically to put on a flack jacket of emotional resilience, and erect barriers between themselves and the bully, such as by working at home, refusing to enter emotional game-playing situations and questioning who has the problem; maybe to put the bully's behaviour under scrutiny rather than the victim's own. Do they appear to be overly anxious and paranoid? Sometimes the feelings of the victim are projections of the bully who has such a level of discomfort in their own feelings they have somehow managed to shift them into the mind of the victim.

Taking action

There are a whole host of actions that can be taken, and the difficulty for the victim, or in fact anyone helping the victim, is to move out of an 'infantilised state' where the person feels helpless, and instead move into action. It can help to try and re-orientate fearful and guilty feelings into ones of anger directed at the bully. Anger can be a catalyst for action whereas fear tends to lead to paralysis. Many workplaces have a bullying and harassment policy that can be activated, and some support may be obtainable from a trade union or other people in the workplace. More importantly it is not legal for an individual to be bullied or to feel such stress in their work that they become unwell. Moreover, an employer has a duty to safeguard the health and well-being of an employee, and can be found to be culpable if an individual experiences severe symptoms of stress, such as a nervous breakdown. Not surprisingly many organisations are now taking more preventative action with policies, line-manager training, and also wellness audits and counselling services.

The *Radcliffe* case (1998) builds on the success of the *Walker* case mentioned above. Radcliffe, a primary school deputy head, won a £100,000 out-of-court settlement after suffering two nervous breakdowns allegedly caused by bullying at his workplace.

Employers must be aware and actively manage issues of bullying or harassment of a member of staff by other employees.

Of course there is another angle to this: it is not just the victim that may lose their own personal effectiveness –the bully and those around them also may need help.

SUMMARY

This chapter has focused on three particular areas to help you understand and cope with the difficulties you may have with certain people and situations: transactional analysis, as an approach to understanding underlying reasons for interpersonal difficulties; sources of and approaches to dealing with stress; and bullying, as an example of a severely stressful situation and major trigger of emotional stress and loss of effectiveness.

It is likely that in engaging with this chapter you have brought to the surface many uncomfortable feelings, and this may have been a very unsettling experience. In everyday life we have a number of defences to protect ourselves from these uncomfortable feelings, and some of these you may be experiencing now – you may feel angry, dismissive or confused. Chapter 1 on learning encouraged you to be a 'reflective practitioner', and this is a major theme of this book. Developing personal effectiveness does require that we open ourselves up to probing self-inquiry. You may want to share some of your thoughts about this chapter, your own behaviour and that of others with someone else – maybe friends, trusted colleagues, a mentor or coach, or even a counsellor. Although the chapter is putting you under the spotlight, remember this information is within your control, it is up to you how you use it to your own benefit. Learning more about ourselves can be exciting and information can be 'power', providing us with options for changing situations in which we have become stuck.

REFERENCES AND FURTHER READING

BERNE, E. (1964) *Games People Play*. Harmondsworth: Penguin.

HOEL, H., RAYNER, C. and COOPER, C (1999) Workplace Bullying. *International Review of Industrial and Organizational Psychology*. 14, 189–230.

HOLMES, T. and RAHE, R. (1967) The Social Readjustment Rating Scale. *Journal of Psychosomatic Research*. 11, 213–218.

HONEY, P. (1992) *Problem People: and how to manage them*. London: CIPD.

NEWTON, T. (1995) *Managing Stress: Emotion and power at work*. London: Sage.

RANDALL, P. (2001) *Bullying in Adulthood*. East Sussex: Brunner-Routledge.

RAYNER, C. (1997) Incidence of workplace bullying. *Journal of Community and Applied Social Psychology*. 7, 199–208.

ROGERS, C. (1967) *On Becoming a Person: A therapist's view of psychotherapy*. London: Constable.

STEWART, I. and JOINES, V. (1987) *TA Today: A new introduction to Transaction Analysis*. Nottingham: Lifespace Publishing.

SUTHERLAND, V. and COOPER, C. (1990) *Understanding Stress*. London: Chapman and Hall.

WINSTANLEY, D. (2000) Conditions of worth and the performance management paradox. *Ethical issues in Contemporary HRM*. Hants: Palgrave/Macmillan. 189–207.

Managing personal and organisational change

AIMS AND OBJECTIVES

The aim of this chapter is to enable you to engage in change and understand some of the barriers you may come up against when you do so. The focus of this chapter is on personal change, but this will be set within the broader context of organisational change. As a result of reading this chapter you should be able to:

■ be aware of the opportunities and threats faced by the individual engaging in change

■ in particular to appreciate many of the difficult feelings around change, and find ways of dealing with these in yourself and others

■ identify likely blocks to change and ways to remove them

■ capitalise on the drivers for change and positive feelings which will enable change to happen

■ be familiar with some of the key models of the change process, as they apply to individuals and to the organisation

■ identify some tools to enable you to make a transition or change.

INTRODUCTION

Most of this book has been about making changes: for example changes to improve your time management, your assertiveness, your creativity, and your team skills. In this chapter we focus more closely on the process of change itself, and ways in which intention becomes action.

Change is never easy. As Andre Gide, the French Nobel prize winning author said in his oft-used quote:

> One doesn't discover new lands without consenting to lose sight of the shore for a very long time. Andre Gide

One interpretation of a Chinese character for change is that it is part opportunity, part threat and danger. Both these aspects are very important, the danger is in giving up something that you have done or somewhere you have been before, and the uncertainty of knowing what this change will bring to you in the future. The opportunity is the excitement of something new, something different. It is therefore not surprising that people often have ambivalence and mixed emotions when faced with change.

Change is all around us and part of our lives. Even things that appear to stay the same, do so by changing. As Giuseppe di Lampedusa said: 'If we want things to stay as they are, things will have to change'. Every day we wake up we are changed in some way, we are a day older, our past has been changed, and each day is different. An interesting analogy here is of the river.

EXAMPLE 10.1   THE ANALOGY OF THE RIVER

Over two and a half thousand years ago Heraclitus of Ephesus remarked that we cannot step in the same river twice.

If we were to stand paddling barefoot at the edge of a river, that river appears to be the same river today as it was yesterday and will be tomorrow, but as every instant passes, the water that gushes past our feet and through our toes is different. Each moment we are also changing, but we also in some ways remain the same.

The river is not just defined by the water that runs through it, its identity is created by the course it takes. As a young stream it cannot dictate its direction, it follows the terrain and the lie of the land. Likewise we are not responsible for our origins, but as we become older and mature, choices become more available to us. Not only are we constantly renewed like the water of the river, but we can start to take responsibility for the direction we take, making changes as we go. Like the river we may have a course mapped out for us, and it may become difficult to change that course because the environment around us steers us in a particular direction, but with effort we can use the fluidity and energy of the water to change our shape and direction.

Paradoxically the notion of change includes the idea of something staying the same. To experience a change there must be a continuous identity that is changed, otherwise the two states are merely different. Change is about making choices. To prepare yourself for this chapter attempt Exercise 10.1.

EXERCISE 10.1   LIFE COURSE

1. What course is mapped out for your life, what direction is the environment pulling you in?

2. In what ways have you changed the course of your life? Think of yourself five years ago and reflect on the ways you are different now to how you were then, in lifestyle, interests, role, feelings, states of mind, identity.

3. What factors have enabled you to make changes in your life? Draw a lifeline on a large sheet of paper. Start at the left at the beginning of your life, and from this lifeline write above it major changes that have occurred. Below each change write in a different colour underneath the lifeline the factors that impacted the change, and also your feelings about the change. Draw it up to the present. You could use colour or pictures to illustrate your lifeline. The shape it takes, whether it goes up or down, can reflect your positive and negative feelings about the lifeline.

4. Continue this life course into the future. What changes would you like to see reflected in this lifeline and its direction?

This chapter starts from the perspective of the individual: the continuous identity that is engaging in change. This is partly pragmatic, because ultimately you are the only person you have any right to change, and, moreover, you are the only person you really have a hope of changing! However, not all changes are initiated within the individual, so the chapter also raises issues of organisational change. At the organisational level there are tools to help us analyse the need for change and also to appreciate the drivers for and resisters of change, and ways in which the change process can be smoothed.

There are a number of models that we can draw on to help our understanding of the change process, but it is important to recognise that they are aids only, and do not have predictive power for all situations.

IDENTIFYING THE NEED FOR CHANGE AND GETTING STUCK!

The change equation

With relation to conscious and personally initiated change, there usually is a catalyst, a reason for the change to happen. One approach is to utilise the change equation below, which has been produced in a number of different variants (for example see Gleicher in Beckhard and Harris 1987). To engage willingly in change and move from thought to action requires there to be enough discomfort with the present situation combined with a knowledge of what change is needed and how to make that change, including a knowledge of the first steps in making the change, *and* these need to be greater than the present comfort and fear of change.

EXAMPLE 10.2 THE CHANGE EQUATION

$$(F + C) < (P + V + S)$$

F = fear of change, resistance to change

C = present comfort

P = pain in and dissatisfaction with the present situation

V = vision of the future desired state

S = knowledge of the first steps

If P, V and S are greater than F and C then change is likely.

If P, V, and S are smaller than F and C then change is unlikely to be initiated.

One example might be a person, Sue, wanting to change her job. She is currently a secretary. Her current level of dissatisfaction with her current job is running very high: she feels overworked, under-valued and is not earning as much as she needs to get a mortgage, and moreover she is bored with the work. She is young and highly mobile and quite welcomes the opportunity to move to a new area and take up a new challenge, having neither family nor ties to keep her in her current location. She has identified an alternative career — being a teacher — and has already made inquiries about PGCE training courses to give her the qualifications alongside her degree in mathematics which she completed two years ago. The training would enable her to become a secondary-school mathematics teacher. She knows her first steps will be to fill in application forms and to apply for possible grants and loans to pay for her time training. In Sue's case the change equation would suggest she is highly likely to make the change.

Another example is Michael. He also wants to change career, being very fed up as a financial adviser. However, he does earn good money working in this area and has a heavy mortgage and two children. His wife is a part-time nurse but doesn't earn enough to pay for him to take a career break. He is also not sure of what job to aim for, and currently doesn't have a degree or many formal qualifications to enable him to take up other high-paying roles, although he is interested in working with computers and information technology. Instead of making the change, Michael's current dissatisfaction is not high enough to overcome all the potential problems in making the change and moreover he hasn't yet formulated a direction in which to move. Instead of making a change Michael currently engages in avoidance behaviour by putting up with his lack of motivation at work and by channelling his creative energies into doing up his new house, and playing computer games.

Five things in particular are important for change to be initiated: intention, solution-focused thinking, motivation, task and ability. To change, an individual needs to have the intention to change, be motivated to change, as well as having identified an appropriate change to make and have the ability to carry out this change. Review the changes you made in Chapter 2 in relation to issues of time management. It is likely that for you to be successful, you had the intention and motivation, the appropriate task and the ability to make the change with a knowledge of the first steps, and as the change equation implies, enough discomfort in the present to make the effort worthwhile.

Intentionality

If you are really willing a change and getting stuck, finding it difficult to put the intention into practice, let alone identifying the first steps, then there is a technique that you can use to help the change move along, particularly where the change seems too big or difficult: 'the intention check'. This is not a promise to yourself to make the change, as a promise can be too binding and abstract and the chances are you are setting yourself up for failure. First you need to identify what your intention is, and in the case of the example above Michael could say 'My intention is to develop my IT skills and identify possible careers in this area in order to change jobs'. Then, every time there is a decision to be made, Michael would need to think 'Which course of action will make my intention more likely to be achieved?' So, for example, Michael finds he has an alternative for his free evenings in the week between:

a) taking on more overtime at work to pay for a more luxurious holiday, or

b) taking the time to engage in further IT and computer training to formalise his skills in this area.

Alternatively he may also have some spare time on a Saturday afternoon and has the choice between:

a) doing some more d-i-y

b) looking up job vacancy sites on the computer which are IT related to identify the kinds of jobs available and the skills needed in this area.

In both of these decisions, B is more likely to lead him towards his intention. Over time, these small steps can make a big difference in achieving the main intention. You could also try this in Exercise 10.2.

EXERCISE 10.2   THE INTENTION CHECK

Re-examine your lifeline in Exercise 10.1 and see what types of changes you had identified you wanted to happen in future. Now rephrase one of these changes as an intention:

My intention is ...

Now for the next month notice when you have decisions to make, and stop and ask yourself:

Which course of action will make my intention more likely to be achieved?

Solution-focused thinking: using fantasy as enabler or block?

Fantasy can be a great enabler, but also a block, for change. A fantasy can be one way in which we begin to identify a solution to a problematic situation and identify a direction for change. When someone feels a great deal of dissatisfaction in the present but finds they are just getting bogged down moaning about it, they become too problem focused. People can get stuck in a tangle of their problems and not see a way to make a change. Allowing a problem to occupy one's thoughts in an unproductive way can become draining and depressing, and lead to helplessness and despair. Focussing on these problems can be debilitating – and it may be worth asking of a thought 'Is this true' and even if it does appear to be the case, it is also worth asking 'Is this helpful?' Thinking of problems is not the same as dealing with them, and sometimes in order to effect a change, thinking has to shift to more productive waters.

Solution-focused brief therapy steers people to become 'solution-focused'. Solution-focused brief therapy was developed in the US at the Brief Family Therapy Centre principally by therapists Steve de Shazer and Insoo Kim Berg (for example see O'Connell 1998). It is brief in that it not only aims to enable change to happen quickly but enables the achievement of short-term change through small steps which can then lead to major change. It is also solution-focused in that it moves people away from discussing problems, to focusing on solutions. One way of doing this is to ask the miracle question which is given in Exercise 10.3.

EXERCISE 10.3 THE MIRACLE QUESTION: SOLUTION- NOT PROBLEM-FOCUSED

Imagine you were to go to bed tonight and sleep. When you wake up tomorrow morning a miracle had happened, your problems are solved, you have made the change you desire. When you wake up tomorrow morning, what will you notice, what will give you the clues that a miracle has happened? Visualise what would be different, describe how you would get up, what you would be feeling and thinking. Take us through this fantasy morning.

Once you have fully explored your miracle morning, and have really entered into the experience of what it would be like, return to the present, and start identifying those small steps that would lead to the miracle solution and situation.

The miracle question steers the person to focus on solutions by identifying the desired fantasy state. The intention is to enable the person to experience positive feelings that might lead to changes in behaviour. The person is encouraged to focus on the experience of being problem-free rather than permanently restricted or caught in the web of their problems. Once the future can be visualised as problem free, even if this is a fantasy, then the steps can be identified which trace from the present to that desirable future.

However, fantasy can also sometimes be a 'racket' (see Chapter 9) (an avoidance of reality by the creation of an unrealistic world) which prevents someone making the changes to improve their current situation because none of these changes meet the fantasy criteria. Sometimes people get stuck because there doesn't seem to be an ideal option or course of action. They get stuck because their fantasy of themselves doesn't match up with the reality. In this case realism is required, change doesn't happen without effort, and it may be that the options a person is faced with do not seem appealing: none of them represent the ideal option, the fantasy solution, and all entail problems. For example, in Michael's case he may think the first option (b above): 'to engage in further information technology and computer training to formalise his skills' is difficult – it may cost money, and he will have less time to spend with his family. However, in these situations it is sometimes worth thinking 'Which is the least bad option?' Realism over options, ability to change and also the ability to know when change is not possible is also important. The prayer attributed to St. Francis of Assisi is relevant here.

EXAMPLE 10.3 PRAYER ATTRIBUTED TO ST. FRANCIS OF ASSISI

God, grant me the serenity to accept

The things I cannot change;

The courage to change the things I can,

And the wisdom to know the difference.

Making change is therefore about using fantasy creatively to enable yourself to be solution-focused rather than problem-focused, but not using the fantasy as a barrier or block to avoid taking any action at all to help the situation and create small changes. It is also about being realistic and not setting unachievable targets that will almost certainly lead to failure. It is about identifying those things that can be changed, and also accepting the things that can't. There is no point in Michael applying for jobs that require a degree in computing without a computing degree, and then becoming annoyed because he doesn't get an interview and ringing to create an argument with the recruiters.

Motivation, task and ability – self-efficacy

Self-efficacy was discussed in Chapter 1 on learning. Self-efficacy was defined by Bandura as being concerned with people's beliefs in their capabilities to mobilise their motivation and their cognitive resources as well as courses of action to make something, in this case change, happen (see Bandura 1977, 1986). Having self-efficacy beliefs is associated with an individual's readiness for change (Cunningham et al 2002).

Self-efficacy can be developed by performance accomplishment, realistic goals, opportunities to develop and acquire new skills, role-modelling, verbal persuasion, and having positive psychological and emotional states (see Chapter 1). Use Exercise 10.4 to assess your own self-efficacy with relation to a change you are trying to make.

EXERCISE 10.4   SELF EFFICACY

With relation to one difficult task or change you are trying to make, examine your own self-efficacy with relation to this change using the following questions. With relation to this difficult task or change do you tend towards the a) or b) aspects of each question:

1. a) do you believe you can muster sufficient motivation to keep at it until you succeed or

   b) do you feel so disheartened that you are likely to give up prematurely?

2. a) do you believe you can rally your thoughts and concentration to enable you to work out a way through this change using your knowledge and thinking capacities? or

   b) does your mind switch off and feel so confused that you can't think straight?

3. a) do you believe you can rise to the challenge, or

   b) do you feel you are likely to crumple under the challenge?

4. a) do you believe you are able to take practical steps to deal with the task, or

   b) do you feel incapable of taking any action?

5. a) do you believe that by making a huge effort of will, use of brainpower and action that you can deal with this task, or

   b) do you believe that the effort will be fruitless and a waste of time?

6. a) do you feel you have resilience when you hit hurdles in this task to keep going, or

b) do you feel you are not strong and capable enough to keep going when the task is very difficult?

If you are erring more to a)s in answer to the questions you have a more developed sense of self-efficacy, whereas if you are erring more to the b)s in your answers then your self-efficacy is low.

You can try and build up your self-efficacy by finding small steps that you can accomplish to give you a feeling of achievement. You need to set yourself realistic goals that you think you can achieve, and find ways to develop your skills to meet the challenge. Finding role models who have also found the change difficult but have managed to make it will help, as will finding out how they went about the change. Getting others to encourage and persuade you will reinforce your sense of determination. Keeping healthy will help, as well as managing your anxiety and difficult emotions that get in the way. Try and avoid panicking, instead focus on the task in a calm way.

THE REACTION TO CHANGE CURVE AND RESISTANCE TO CHANGE

It must be considered that there is nothing more difficult to carry out, nor more doubtful of success, nor more dangerous to handle than to initiate a new order of things; for the reformer has enemies in all those who profit from the old order.

N. Machiavelli *The Prince*

So far in this chapter we have focused on self-directed change. However, for some people the change is presented to them as a *fait accompli* – something they are expected by others to engage in and accept. A common reaction to enforced change is denial, anger and resistance.

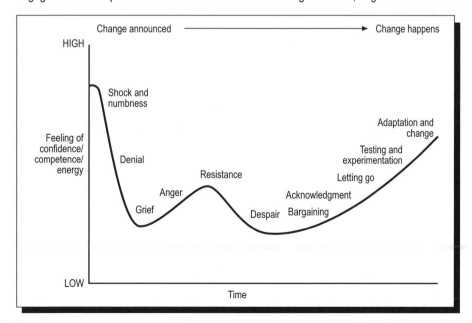

Figure 10.1 *The reaction to change curve*

The reaction to change curve is particularly useful in the context of enforced change on the individual.

Early research suggested that people go through a series of stages in response to a major change. The original research which prompted the reaction to change curve was conducted in the 1960s by Elizabeth Kübler-Ross (Kübler Ross 1969). This was based on a study concerning people being told they were terminally ill and did not have long to live, and focused around stages of shock and denial, anger, bargaining, depression, acceptance and hope. Another popular model of transitions was popularised by William Bridges in two books on managing transitions (Bridges 1980, 2003) which focused more specifically on work organisations and the wider context of life change. Bridges takes us through three stages: endings, which need to be recognised as opportunities as well as losses and require letting go, a neutral zone (time-out where we may feel disconnected and fearful), and then the new beginning. These works have spurned a number of variants in the organisational and management area (for example Jaffe and Scott 2004 focus on denial, resistance, commitment and exploration). My version is provided in Figure 10.1.

In Figure 10.1 an individual faced with the announcement of a change may begin by feeling shock and numbness, and this is followed by denial: 'It can't be happening'. Once realisation sets in, anger grows at what is happening, and the potential for resistance, which can be energising. But as reality takes hold and resistance is seen as futile, feelings can turn to loss, grief and despair and feelings of confidence, competence and energy dive. Over time people begin to face up to the reality of the situation, maybe even bargaining to make it more beneficial to them. This leads to greater acknowledgment, both that the change is happening but also maybe the need for change. As this happens individuals begin to let go of the past and move to testing and experimentation with new ways of working, ultimately leading to adaptation and change, and once again growing in competence, confidence and energy.

EXAMPLE 10.4   USING THE REACTION TO CHANGE CURVE: BT'S DOWNSIZING PROGRAMMES

When BT went through major downsizing and redundancy programmes in the early 1990s a number of staff were in a state of shock. In 1990 Project Sovereign aimed to reduce 12 layers of management to 6 by shedding around 12 per cent of the workforce through an early release programme, which was followed by a series of annual release and rebalancing programmes. On 31 July 1992 20,000 people left on the same day, with 45,000 taking voluntary redundancy between 1990 and 1992!

Initially many of the workforce disbelieved that so many redundancies could be made. For a while some were in denial, assuming it would go away, which it didn't. Each year brought in new redundancy and release programmes. Even staff who stayed with the organisation were affected, experiencing symptoms of 'survivor syndrome', suffering problems with stress, insecurity, a reduction in motivation and loyalty as well as facing lack of clarity in work roles. They were upset by the loss of friends and colleagues who had gone, and felt guilt that they still held a job, as well as anxiety and stress in dealing with high work volume to compensate for the holes in the organisation caused by the departures.

Some staff were extremely angry, feeling that the traditional culture that had been built up over the years was being eroded, and many staff who had worked hard for the organisation felt they were being seen as expendable, as were their skills.

However, over time the redundancies were achieved by voluntary means. Many staff began wondering whether perhaps it may be an opportunity and engaged in discussions with managers to see how much their redundancy package would be worth, and began to find that there were a number of possible benefits. The packages were generous and included outplacement advice, opportunities for reskilling and also the chance to carry on working as a consultant. The workforce began to accept the changes and the redundancies were carried out. The remaining staff proceeded to examine how to move the organisation in the new directions identified and how to develop the new skills needed for this new competitive business environment.

However, these 'conventional wisdom' models enshrined in many texts and training packs on change, and used to coach people through the change process, are flawed. Although it can be useful to be aware of the likely reactions the change may have and plan for these, some of the fundamental assumptions underlying these models need to be treated with caution. Not all changes are the same, nor do they replicate responses to loss and dying. To assume that reactions to this situation would be typical of all change situations is clearly ludicrous. The models often focus on the likely negative feelings and reactions to change and anxiety around it, but pay less attention to some of the potential positive reactions to change that can be engendered. It may be as productive to focus on wherein lies the energy for change and empower the change to happen, rather than focus on the problems. This approach focuses on 'accelerators', supporting and providing resources to those areas where there is a will to change which can be capitalised on and used as role models for other parts of an organisation. It also seems unlikely that everybody goes through the change process in exactly the same way: these models are an aid to our understanding, but only that.

Taking these cautionary warnings into account, the reaction to change curve and other change models can still be helpful in supporting an individual through a change process. One reason is that it can be extremely beneficial to have someone aware of and acknowledge the negative feelings and anxiety associated with change, which can be a precursor to moving on. The change process models also teach change agents to appreciate that it may take time for people to make the 'mindset change' required, and so too early an evaluation of change could be counter productive.

Another approach highlighting the change process and problems with forcing through change is drawn from Gestalt psychology and focuses on energy under pressure as a force for resistance.

THE CONTRIBUTION OF GESTALT PSYCHOLOGY
The paradoxical theory of change

DEFINITION OF THE PARADOXICAL THEORY OF CHANGE

People change not by trying to make themselves into something, or someone which they are not, but by becoming more fully themselves. *Change occurs when one becomes what one is, not when one tries to become what one is not* (Beisser, 1970, 77).

The 'Paradoxical Theory of Change' focuses on resistance at the individual level. It is taken from Gestalt psychology and suggests that if we collude with 'the tyranny of the "shoulds"', by cajoling or persuading ourselves (or others) into obedience to change, pushing hard for change, then we activate the counter-force which seeks to maintain the status quo. The 'tyranny of the "shoulds"' is essentially the conflict between our will power – the top dog as Fritz Perls would have called it – and the 'underdog' part of ourselves. This process can be intra-psychic or interpersonal. Change driven by willpower, coercion or persuasion is likely to be short-lived, and characterised by a split in energy, with underlying passive aggression or rebellion to sabotage the change.

Machiavelli may have believed that change succeeds more through fear than love when he asked is it:

Better to be loved than feared or feared than loved? . . . it is much safer to be feared than loved . . . .

Because this is to be asserted in general of men, that they are ungrateful, fickle, false, cowardly, covetous, and as long as you succeed they are yours entirely. [However they] have less scruple in offending one who is beloved than one who is feared, for love is preserved by the link of obligation which, owing to the baseness of men, is broken at every opportunity for their advantage; but fear preserves you by a dread of punishment which never fails.

N. Machiavelli, 1513 *The Prince*

However, in modern society too much fear and anxiety in the change process, force and pressure, can simply result in longer-term problems, whether this force and fear is internally generated or created by an external change agent. There may be times when force becomes inevitable, such as when an organisation has made a decision to change and its senior managers may have to put to the workforce the question 'Come with us, be a part of this, but if you can't then maybe you should look elsewhere'. However, where there is choice over how to change and when to change, other approaches are more likely to be successful.

Instead of forcing through change, as a change agent Gestalt psychology suggests we should take the role of investigating all the factors in the field, becoming an active research partner finding out about all the forces for and against, working together with others to conduct the change, more like 'collaborative' or 'co-operative' enquiry (Reason and Rowan 1981).

The paradox of change is only one of Gestalt psychology's tools for understanding change. Gestalt is a German word for which there is no direct translation. It means a complete pattern

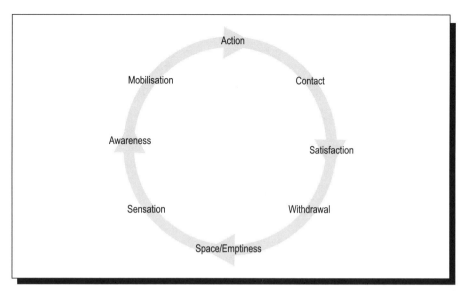

Figure 10.2 *The Gestalt cycle of change*

or configuration, a meaningful whole which is different from, and more than, the sum of its parts. There is a Gestalt cycle of change which is a complete configuration of a change process that is particularly relevant here. There are many versions of this, one good example is provided in Clarkson 1997: 19. The one provided above in Figure 10.2 adds an extra part to the classic cycle of 'space/emptiness' as this can be a particularly difficult area for individuals to find themselves in – the space or vacuum between two cycles.

The cycle describes the essential nature of the interaction between an organism and its environment. Let us take the example of eating a meal. I may begin with the sensation of hunger, perhaps my stomach starts rumbling and mouth feels dry, and gradually this sensation enters my awareness as 'being hungry'. Maybe I am finishing a report on the computer so decide to delay eating for 15 minutes until lunchtime. Then I decide to mobilise energy to meet my need – I decide to turn off the computer and go down to the canteen to get a sandwich. I then take this action and buy a sandwich and maybe then go and eat it in the park. At the moment of contact I become engrossed in eating the sandwich, until I have satisfied the original need. After a time I have finished the sandwich, maybe have eaten a biscuit and packet of crisps and start to feel full. Having then satisfied the original need I withdraw from the activity, throwing the wrappers in the bin, start walking through the park and my mind moves on to something else, and the lunch then moves out of the foreground of my thoughts to the background, from figure to ground. I then enter a space, a vacuum in which new gestalts can arise, thinking about the next piece of work or a party to plan for example.

In becoming aware of what the sensation is telling us, we give it meaning. In knowing what we want, we mobilise energy towards the external object. In clarifying the nature of the interaction, we know what to do to bring about contact and final satisfaction. Many of these gestalts happen outside our awareness, but at other times we may find that the gestalt cycle is dealing with a change where we get stuck. We can get stuck at any stage of this cycle.

For example, if space is not allowed to enable a person to rest and replenish, it is difficult for new change cycles to develop. This typically happens in an organisation where change after change after change is introduced and people become 'change weary'. Some people find the vacuum between two cycles difficult, especially if trying to make a difficult change, and can as a result fall back into an old state or cycle rather than move on to a new one. It is not surprising that at this stage some people revert back to old ways when making a change, and return to the comfort of familiarity.

Other people interrupt themselves before the sensation stage – they get stuck because they are scared to feel, become withdrawn and solitary. They may be rigid and fearful of change, but instead experience emptiness. Others get stuck before the awareness stage – being very emotionally excitable and carried away with sensations without stopping to analyse what these are. Others interrupt themselves before mobilisation of energy for action, they are aware of a change they want to make but can't quite make the transition into mobilisation for action – they don't actually do anything to make the change happen. Instead they become frustrated and angry, both at themselves for not being able to make a decision, and also at their stagnant situation, maybe even blaming others for their lack of action.

It is not just individuals that get stuck at stages of the cycle, but organisations also. For example, an organisation may constantly mobilise itself for action but interrupt itself before the action takes place. These organisations may appear very busy, with masses of plans for organisational change, interventions and programmes, but none of these ever seem to get off the ground, as the organisation lurches from one plan for change to another. A task organisation takes a great deal of action, but somehow doesn't improve its performance, there is no full contact that leads to satisfaction. On a personal level some people take action as a deflection from their true need, for example they may feel lonely, but instead of taking action to make more friends, they indulge in eating, which may comfort them but does not actually provide the satisfaction they seek.

EXERCISE 10.5   INTERRUPTIONS IN YOUR CHANGE CYCLE

Return to the changes you identified you wanted to make in your life course in Exercise 10.1, and also previous changes you have tried to make.

Mentally take yourself through the Gestalt cycle of change and question yourself where are you most likely to get stuck: do you find it difficult deciding which changes to make in the first place, or mobilising yourself to change, or moving from thought and planning into action? Do you find it difficult to persevere with a change until it has been made? Do you abandon the attempt prematurely? Do you allow yourself space to just be, space to reflect and replenish rather than always being active?

If you think you have a regular interruption of your change cycle, is there someone you could discuss this with, or could you set yourself an 'intention to get over this hurdle' as in Exercise 10.2?

Kurt Lewin and the force field model

Kurt Lewin is an organisational theorist who drew extensively from Gestalt psychology. He identified a useful force field model to help understand the dynamics of organisational change, identified in Figure 10.3. The underlying theory of this approach is that there is a quasi-stationary equilibrium in a change situation which occurs between the driving forces for change on the one hand, and the restraining forces for the status quo on the other.

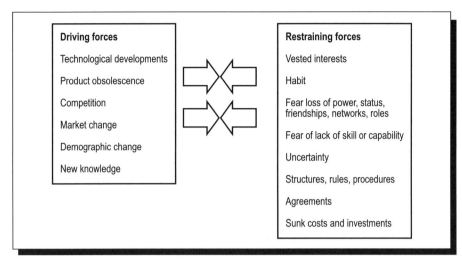

Figure 10.3 *Lewin's force field model*

EXERCISE 10.6   APPLYING THE FORCE FIELD MODEL

1. Take one organisational change you have come across in your organisation and analyse the driving and resisting forces for change.

Driving forces	Resisting forces

2. Do you see any patterns in the driving and resisting forces?
3. How would you move the equilibrium to enable change to happen: work on the driving forces or the restraining forces?

If you examine the force field model more closely you will realise that on the whole, the driving forces for change are often external to an organisation, and arise out of its environment, whereas the restraining and resisting forces are more usually internal to the organisation or internal to individuals within it.

But what happens if you try to disturb the equilibrium to push change through? Lewins argues that if you increase the driving forces all that happens is that you create more resistance. A simple example of this is in an argument. You may be getting more and more heated with your partner over wanting to move house for example, yet the more you argue for moving, the more she or he seems to refuse to budge. 'We really must move, this house is far too small, it is a bad location, etc, etc'. 'No, I don't want to move'. Yet once you take the pressure off, the partner may start to open themselves up to the idea 'Yes, you may be right, it would be good to have a room for a study . . .'. It is almost as if there is a line of equilibrium, where if you go too far to one side of the line, the other person goes far in the other direction, yet as you come closer to the line, so they do.

Another example is of pouring water into a funnel: if you pour it too fast the water just bubbles up and spills over, whereas if you pour it slowly, all of the water can be absorbed. So what does this mean for Lewin's model? Essentially, to break the equilibrium you need to focus on unfreezing the restraining forces, deal with their causes, before you can move towards to the new position. Therefore if fear of lack of skills is the restraining force in accepting an organisational change to introduce new technology, the answer is to weaken this fear by providing education, training and coaching in the technology.

Lewins therefore argues for a process of:

Unfreeze the current situation $\rightarrow$ move to new situation $\rightarrow$ refreeze the new

Reconsider your example: how would you go about addressing the restraining forces, to unfreeze the current situation? Have seminars to discuss with people how the change will affect their jobs, organise retraining to enable them to develop the skills to meet the change, redesign procedures and so on? Do you think this would work?

SPEED AND SCALE OF CHANGE

Before we move more into looking at managing organisational change and transitions, it is worth stopping to query how quickly change occurs. Some changes happen very slowly and imperceptibly. Others occur in gradual steps where one change happens after another. Others happen chaotically.

It is comparable to the different approaches taken to swimming in the sea. There are those who feel the very cold water in the sea and inch their way in bit by bit, whereas others plunge in. There is no clear best approach to change: in some cases it may be best to plunge in and make the change quickly to prevent a gradual build up of resistance taking shape and forming a critical mass. Others would suggest that it is better to give yourself and others time to make the change, particularly those who propose the stages of change models reviewed above. This is an issue that should perhaps be dealt with on a case-by-case basis.

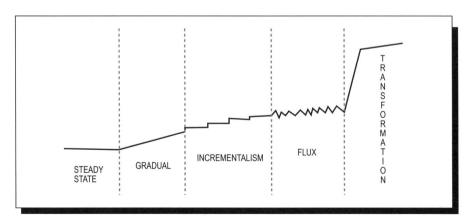

Figure 10.4 *Speed and scale of different types of change*

Some changes are made by small steps but others are huge organisational transformations. Transformational change is particularly difficult to manage. Kotter 1996 identifies eight reasons why change may fail:

- not establishing a great sense of urgency
- not creating a powerful enough guiding coalition
- lacking a vision
- under communication of the vision by a factor of 10
- not removing obstacles to the vision
- not systematically planning for and creating short-term wins
- declaring victory too soon
- not anchoring changes in the corporation's culture.

It is not possible in this book to look at all the areas of organisational transformation, but if you examine these closely, many relate to working with people in the change process, creating a vision for them, and finding ways in which they can achieve that vision. In the next section we examine how to manage others in the change process.

MANAGING OTHERS IN THE CHANGE PROCESS

This leads us to the issue of dealing with others in the change management process. If you are leading a change Lewin's model (above) is useful for identifying the driving and restraining forces and how to help a move to a new condition. However, we can go further into exploring the different stakeholder positions in change, and identifying their reasons for supporting or resisting the change. We also need to be able to identify our allies (those who support the change), and our opponents (those who may actively work against the change). Table 10.1 identifies the reasons why people might resist or support change.

Table 10.1 *Reasons for supporting or resisting change*

Reasons /beliefs for resisting change	Reasons / beliefs for supporting change
Fear, frightened of change	Excitement, excited by change
See change as unnecessary	See change as necessary
Change could make the situation worse	Change could improve the situation
Change may mean personal loss; or loss of status or position	Change may mean personal gain; an increase in status or position
Not being consulted, and no personal input into the change	Involvement in the change; time to consider it carefully
Not confident it will succeed	Confident it will succeed
Not the right time to change	The right time to change
May not be able to cope with the change; they have not the skills to manage after the change, the change will make their skills obsolete	Have the skills to change and the confidence they will be able to manage successfully after the change
Like the status quo	Feel dissatisfaction with the status quo
Believe previous changes have not worked	Believe previous changes have been successful
Lack faith in their leaders	Respect and feel confident in those that are leading the change

223

It is therefore important to identify those stakeholders who will be feeling apprehensive about the change and those who are actively seeking it out. We can also examine their behaviour in response to the change.

One form of negative reaction is avoidance, like the animal that sticks its head in the sand. This may be conscious or unconscious. There are some people who just do not recognise that change is happening, sometimes until too late. This is like being a frog in a basin of water that is gradually being heated up, the water gets hotter and hotter and hotter, but because the change is gradual the frog does not notice it is being boiled alive until it is too late. Others are more conscious in their avoidance, and decide not to engage in change.

Another form of negative reaction is resistance. Resistance can take two forms, active or passive. Active resistance occurs overtly where there is a conflict of interests and people may publicly speak out against the change. More difficult to deal with is passive resistance, which could take the form of disinterest, or even covert sabotage.

We can go even go further and identify the different stakeholders in relation to their readiness for change and their likely reaction to it.

The readiness matrix

The readiness matrix in Figure 10.4 identifies different stages of readiness to change. This has drawn on the work of a variety of authors (for example Block 1996, who discusses cynics, victims and bystanders and Clarkson 1995a, 1995b, who discusses bystanders, and in particular some unpublished work by David Mathews of Change-fx).

The matrix looks at change along two axes: the recognition of the need for change, and the willingness to change behaviour. It suggests that when involved with managing a change process, there are different types of people at different stages of readiness, and each group needs to be dealt with differently.

Cynics are often change-weary people who have low willingness to change and low recognition of the need to change. They may have lived through countless abortive change programmes, and would say something like:

> The organisation has been through this before, it always fails.

> We may support this, but other parts of the organisation don't, and you won't get top management to agree, how long do you think we would last if we went ahead with this?

> I am against change – count me out.

You could ask them how they see the change and try to reframe the change for them until they can see the benefits, or even try to persuade them to change. However, one problem is that according to Block (1996: 222–223) there is always a grain of truth in what they say, and moreover they express everybody's doubts. They want assurance and a level of safety you cannot deliver. Block suggests you need to acknowledge their position but continue to state that there is a choice for faith and commitment in the face of shared reservations. Cynics are unlikely to take up the choice, however. Your danger is that by involving them in the change they become enemies and demoralise others. It may be easier to marginalise and ignore them.

Complainants may recognise the need for change but are unwilling to change themselves: 'something must change – but it definitely isn't me!' One type of complainant is the person who sees themselves as a victim. They may even blame others or look for others to make the changes rather than themselves. They seek security and do not like to take responsibility, preferring a strong leader to take it for them. They may say things like:

We don't have the power to make the change.

I haven't the responsibility, someone else must do it.

Something must change – but it definitely isn't me!

Another type of complainant is the 'bystander'. As with the victim they avoid responsibility, and also lack commitment. They prefer to stay on the fence and exercise caution, only committing themselves once something is totally safe (Block 1996, 226–227). Clarkson (1995a: 122–124) suggests that the kind of statements bystanders make are:

It's none of my business.

This situation is more complex than it seems.

I do not have all the information, I am not qualified to deal with this.

I don't want to get burned again.

I want to remain neutral.

I'm just following orders.

I don't want to rock the boat.

You could try to explore their resistance and explain to them the consequences of no-change. Alternatively you could help expand their comfort zone, finding ways to support them through the change, as well as stressing the need for solutions, not blame. Being strong and full of conviction can encourage some victims and bystanders to follow your lead. However, if they continue with their victim-like behaviour the other option is to force them to face up to the situation and even treat them with the 'FUGL' approach: 'You are either for us or get lost!' This is more likely to be put euphemistically as 'This change is really exciting, we would love you to be a part of it and to come with us on this, but if you won't, we will find someone who will'.

Collaborators are those who are willing to change but may not actually see the point: 'I don't see the point but I will change if you want me to'. They are overly amenable, helpful but probably quite directionless themselves and can be moulded to make the change. Given their willingness you may want to explain more fully the rationale for change, but beware the fact that they are also bandwagon jumpers and so if another regime and group seem to be more powerful, they may switch allegiances very quickly!

Champions are those who recognise the change and are willing to make it: 'Something must change and I must change'. These are people who are put in positions of responsibility to enable a change to happen: the 'accelerators' mentioned above, and you need to build visibly on their commitment.

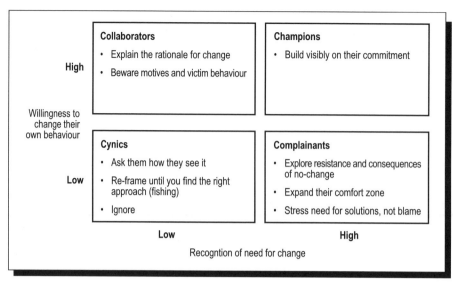

Figure 10.5 *The readiness matrix*

(*Source:* drawn from David Mathews, Change-fx unpublished material. Used with permission.)

Stakeholder analysis

Both Lewin's Force Field Model, and the 'Change Readiness Matrix' suggest that if you are instigating change, you need to know who the different stakeholders are, and what their likely position will be on the change: will they be for it or against it, and why? To do this you could draw a stakeholder map with the change identified in the middle and all the stakeholders around in a circle, placing those that are more in favour of the change on the left, and those who are against it on the right, and then explore the reasons for their position. This may give you good information on how to deal with those stakeholders in the change. You could then identify these stakeholders in a list (as in Exercise 10.7) and identify what their current position is (from hostile, let, help, to make happen) through to what their necessary position needs to be to enable the change to happen.

To show you how to use stakeholder mapping take the example of one GP surgery moving towards electronic healthcare records (refer to Exercise 10.7). A change champion emerged in the guise of a GP who had undergone a number of management training courses, including an MBA. This is GP A in the example stakeholder map below. He wanted everything to be paperless: all test results, patients' notes, every single record kept on a patient. GP C had worked as a doctor for 35 years and really didn't see the need to change now, whereas GP B was neutral, she had recently graduated as a GP and was keen to take on new innovations in healthcare but at the same time was anxious to become more competent – there was a lot to learn as a new GP and that may just be one too many new developments. The receptionists were dubious, they were worried that this could increase their workload and also that they would not have the skills to cope with the change. One in particular was quite fearful of all new technology and frequently grumbled with GP C about all these new-fangled ways which just obstructed good communication with the patient. The practice manager was uncertain, this would look to be a good development, making them a modern surgery, but she was unclear about the benefits. On the other hand the practice nurse was in favour, it would make her life much easier, and she could see that it would really speed up the administration in her area and give her easier access to records and information. The Primary Care Trust, the purchaser of the healthcare, was in favour because research- and evidenced-based healthcare suggested this was a worthwhile step to take. The patients on the whole were not well informed about the development, but GP A had seen it in practice at another surgery where patients were enthusiastic because it meant that the speed of receipt of their results was enhanced. The stakeholder map is drawn in Exercise 10.7.

The change champion, GP A, realised that he had to get the support of his colleagues to make it work, and, following on from a recent seminar on managing change, he sketched out both the stakeholder map and then the current and needed position of each of the stakeholders to make it happen. He realised he needed the practice nurse's support to make it happen as she had a lot of influence with the practice manager and the receptionists. Given her positive attitude he took her aside and got her agreement to work with the practice manager to persuade her of its benefits. This was supplemented by a seminar to which he invited a Primary Health Care Trust member and also a GP at another practice who had adopted the system and could extol its speed and enhancements for productivity. The practice nurse's influence was vital to get the practice manager on board, who, once she had grasped the benefits, helped to organise the training and support, and also made it clear to all the administrative workers that non compliance was no longer an option. She helped the IT company supplying the software to adapt it to the needs of the practice, and organised some mentoring and one-to-one coaching for the other GPs and the receptionists in how to work the new system. Her husband was an IT enthusiast and he volunteered to spend an afternoon with all the staff, coaching them on the system. Initially there was a lot of anxiety and complaints as the new system experienced teething problems, but because the practice nurse also brought in an IT student on placement (a friend of her son) to help deal with these, they were successfully overcome. Patients began to provide positive feedback on the speed with which their test results were being returned, and this moved both GP B and C to feel more positive about the system. GP C had initially found it difficult to make the transition, as had one of the receptionists, but the support and coaching that were provided meant that instead of giving up they gradually acquired the skills to make it work. GP A also gave very positive feedback to GP B on her quick ability to fit into the practice, and all the work she was doing. The fact that she seemed to be finding it easier to use the new electronic system than GP C improved her self-esteem enormously. Over time the improved communication, access to up-to-date records and speed benefits started coming to the fore. For example the practice found that the electronic health records were extremely useful for their own internal audit processes. After several months all the staff wondered how they had ever managed without it, and the receptionist who had initially been the most negative pioneered the effort to load all the old records onto the system.

EXERCISE 10.7   ANALYSING STAKEHOLDER POSITIONS

Return to the organisational change issue you identified in Exercise 10.6. Draw a stakeholder map with the change placed in the centre and the stakeholders arranged around in a circle, with broadly those for the change to the left and those against it to the right. Write under each what their reasons are for or against the change.

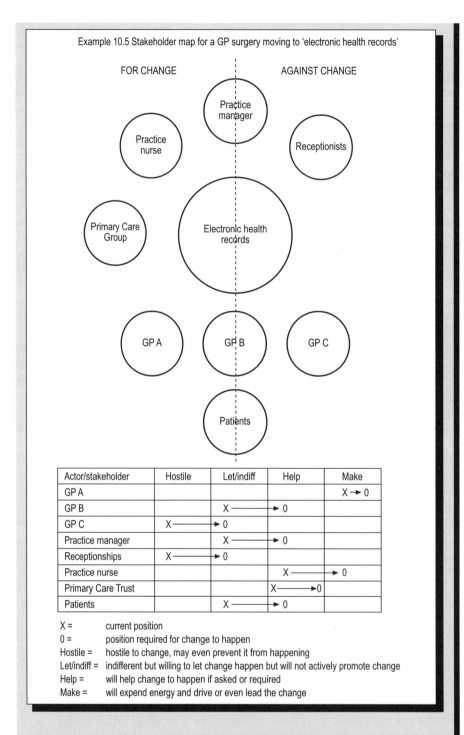

Example 10.5 Stakeholder map for a GP surgery moving to 'electronic health records'

FOR CHANGE   AGAINST CHANGE

Actor/stakeholder	Hostile	Let/indiff	Help	Make
GP A				X ➞ 0
GP B		X ――――➞ 0		
GP C	X ――➞ 0			
Practice manager		X ――――➞ 0		
Receptionships	X ――➞ 0			
Practice nurse			X ――――➞ 0	
Primary Care Trust			X――――➞0	
Patients		X ――➞ 0		

X =   current position
0 =   position required for change to happen
Hostile =   hostile to change, may even prevent it from happening
Let/indiff =   indifferent but willing to let change happen but will not actively promote change
Help =   will help change to happen if asked or required
Make =   will expend energy and drive or even lead the change

Then list the main stakeholders below and identify what their position is with relation to the change and what position you need to move them to: do they need to make the change happen, help it happen, let it happen, or does it not really matter if they are hostile. These two activities will help you identify the barriers to change but also where you need to put energy in overcoming those barriers.

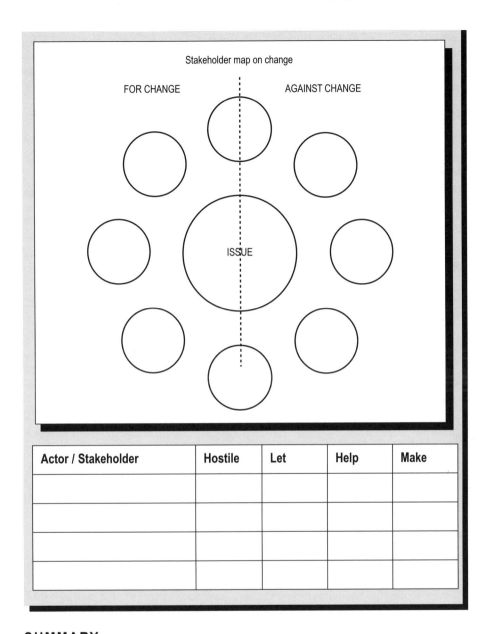

Stakeholder map on change

FOR CHANGE   AGAINST CHANGE

ISSUE

Actor / Stakeholder	Hostile	Let	Help	Make

SUMMARY

In this chapter we have followed two themes: one is that change is all around us and is something we have to engage in whether we like it or not; the other is that change inevitably raises resistance of various forms, both at the individual and organisational level. This chapter has focused on identifying the need for change and also the sources of resistance and providing information to enable resistance to be overcome, if appropriate, and also to enable change to happen. However, as we suggested at the outset, the only person that can change you is you, and this requires an act of intention your behalf.

This book in general has been about personal mastery, and about moving from thought into action. The intention has been to give you ideas that don't just appeal to you intellectually, but that in some way makes a change happen for you. I hope you have enjoyed reading this and have been stimulated to make some changes in your working practices. I have spent many years coaching and counselling people through the change process, and my last words to you are: don't be too hard on yourself, change doesn't come easily, and you need to, as the saying goes, 'cut yourself some slack'. Don't expect everything to happen at once.

Note: More examples and information on how to make change happen can be found on the website.

REFERENCES AND FURTHER READING

BANDURA, A. (1977) Self Efficacy: Toward a unifying theory of behavioural change. *Psychological Review.* 84(2), 191–215.

BANDURA, A. (1986) *Social Foundations of Thought and Action: A Social Cognitive Theory.* Englewood Cliffs, New Jersey: Prentice Hall.

BECKHARD, R. AND HARRIS, R. (1987) *Organizational Transitions: managing complex change.* 2nd ed. Wokingham: Addison-Wesley.

BEISSER, A. (1970) The Paradoxical Theory of Change in FAGAN, J. and SHEPHERD, I (eds) *Gestalt Theory Now.* CA: Science and Behaviour Books, Palo Alt. 77.

BLOCK, P. (1996) *Stewardship.* San Francisco: Berrett-Koehler Pubs.

BRIDGES, W. (2004) *Transitions.* Virginia: Da Capo Press. Perseus Pub.

BRIDGES, W. (2003) *Managing Transitions: Making the most of change.* 2nd ed. London: Nicholas Brearley.

CLARKSON, P. (1995a) *Change in Organisations.* London: Whurr Pubs.

CLARKSON, P. (1995b) *The Bystander.* London: Whurr Pubs.

CUNNINGHAM, C., WOODWARD, C. SHANNON, H., MACINTOSH, J., LENDRUM, B., ROSENBLOOM, D. and BROWN, J. (2002) Readiness for Organizational Change: A longitudinal study of workplace, psychological and behavioural correlates. *Journal of Occupational and Organizational Psychology.* 75(4), 377–392.

JAFFE, D. and SCOTT, C. (2004) *Mastering the Change Curve.* 2nd ed. HRDQ.

KOTTER, J. (1996) *Leading Change.* Boston, Massachusetts: Harvard Business School Press.

KÜBLER-ROSS, E. (1969) *On Death and Dying.* New York: Macmillan, also published 1970 by Tavistock, 1973 by Routledge, London and reprinted many times since.

LEWIN, K. (1951) *Field Theory in Social Science.* London: Harper and Row.

MACKEWN, J. (1997) *Developing Gestalt Counselling.* London: Sage.

O'CONNELL, B. (1998) *Solution Focussed Therapy*. London: Sage.

PERLS, F. HEFFERLINE, R. and GOODMAN, P. (1994) *Gestalt Therapy, Excitement and Growth in Human Personality*. New York: Gestalt Journal Press.

REASON, P. AND ROWAN, J. (1981) *Human Enquiry, A sourcebook of new paradigm research.* Chichester: Wiley.

Index